A HISTORY OF JEWISH LITERATURE
VOLUME VIII

Israel Zinberg's *History of Jewish Literature*

Israel Zinberg

A HISTORY OF
JEWISH
LITERATURE

TRANSLATED AND EDITED BY BERNARD MARTIN

The Berlin Haskalah

HEBREW UNION COLLEGE PRESS
CINCINNATI, OHIO
KTAV PUBLISHING HOUSE, INC.
NEW YORK, NEW YORK
1976

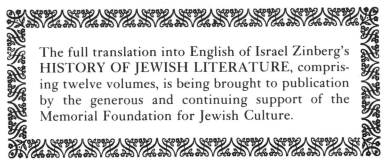

The full translation into English of Israel Zinberg's
HISTORY OF JEWISH LITERATURE, compris-
ing twelve volumes, is being brought to publication
by the generous and continuing support of the
Memorial Foundation for Jewish Culture.

Library of Congress Cataloging in Publication Data

Zinberg, Israel, 1873–1938.
    The Berlin Haskalah.

    (His A history of Jewish literature; v. 8)
    Translation of Berliner Haskalah, pt. 9 of Di ge-
shikhte fun der literatur bay Yidn.
    Bibliography: p.
    Includes index.
    1. Hebrew literature, Modern—Germany—His-
tory and criticism. 2. Haskalah—History. I. Title.
PJ5008.Z5313 vol. 8 [PJ5018] 809'.889'24 75–37794
ISBN 0–87068–477–9 (v. 8)

Contents

PART IX: THE BERLIN HASKALAH

Chapter One: THE JEWS OF BERLIN AND MOSES MENDELSSOHN   /   3

Frederick II and the Jews in Prussia—The Jewish community in Berlin—Its economic growth and lack of civic rights—The social contradictions—The influence of the French "enlighteners"—Doctor Aaron Gumperz—Moses Mendelssohn; his role and significance—Mendelssohn as a personality—Mendelssohn and Lessing—Mendelssohn's *Phaedon*—His treatment of the question of the immortality of the soul.

Chapter Two: MENDELSSOHN'S TRANSLATION OF THE TORAH AND HIS *JERUSALEM*   /   25

The extraordinary success of Mendelssohn's *Phaedon*—Mendelssohn's controversy with Lavater—Mendelssohn's reply—His attitude towards Christianity and Judaism—His journal *Kohelet Musar*—His commentary to *Ecclesiastes*—Mordecai Schnaber against Mendelssohn—Schnaber as a physician—His

Contents

Contents

A Note on Israel Zinberg

Dr. ISRAEL ZINBERG is widely regarded as one of the foremost historians of Jewish literature. Born in Russia in 1873 and educated at various universities in Germany and Switzerland, he devoted more than twenty years to the writing, in Yiddish, of his monumental *Di Geshikhte fun der Literatur bay Yidn* (History of Jewish Literature). This work, published in eight volumes in Vilna, 1929–1937, is a comprehensive and authoritative study of Jewish literary creativity in Europe from its beginnings in tenth-century Spain to the end of the Haskalah period in nineteenth-century Russia. Based on a meticulous study of all the relevant primary source material and provided with full documentation, Zinberg's history is a notable exemplar of the tradition of modern Jewish scholarship known as *die Wissenschaft des Judentums* (the Science of Judaism).

In addition to his *magnum opus*, Zinberg, who earned his living as a chemical engineer, wrote numerous other valuable monographs and articles on Jewish history and literature in Russian, Hebrew, and Yiddish. In 1938, during the Stalinist purges, he was arrested by the Soviet police and sentenced to exile in Siberia. He died in a concentration camp hospital in Vladivostok in that same year.

The reader who wishes a fuller introduction is invited to consult the Translator's Introduction to Volume I of Zinberg's *History of Jewish Literature*.

Foreword

In 1972 the Case Western Reserve University Press began publishing an English translation of Israel Zinberg's *History of Jewish Literature*. Zinberg, an engineer by profession, was a scholar by choice and inclination. In thiry years of intensive study in the great Jewish libraries of St. Petersburg (later Leningrad), he produced eight volumes in Yiddish portraying the course of literary creativity among the Jews beginning with the Golden Age of Spanish Jewry and continuing to the end of the last century. It was not until many years after Zinberg's death that a Hebrew translation was prepared and published in the State of Israel.

There has been no work of similar scope and magnitude in the English language, despite the fact that the Jewish reading public in Britain, South Africa, Canada, and the United States constitutes about half of the Jews in the world. Now, however, the Zinberg volumes have been beautifully translated into English by Dr. Bernard Martin, Abba Hillel Silver Professor of Jewish Studies and Chairman of the Department of Religion at Case Western Reserve University in Cleveland, Ohio. All the English-speaking lands are indebted to Professor Martin for his endeavor to make accessible a literary history such as Zinberg's, a history which depicts the intellectual strivings of the Jews, their aspirations, yearnings, and spiritual search in the medieval and modern worlds, in both of which they have played a not undistinguished role.

Special gratitude is due to the Press of Case Western Reserve University which inaugurated the challenging task of publishing this handsome and very important series of books. Each volume is an aesthetic as well as intellectual delight. The Case Western Reserve Press was aided in publication by a generous grant from the Memorial Foundation for Jewish Culture. The grant is, indeed, a memorial to the martyred Zinberg, who was arrested by the Soviet police in 1938 and deported to Siberia, where he died. We, for our part, are pleased with this opportunity to express our gratitude to the Memorial Foundation for the support which made possible the publication of the first three volumes.

Unfortunately, the economic difficulties from which many universities are now suffering has led to the dissolution of the Case Western Reserve Press and made it impossible for it to continue with the remaining nine volumes. That is why the Hebrew Union College—Jewish Institute of Religion, realizing the importance and cultural implications of this work, is cooperating with the Ktav Publishing House, Incorporated, in the publication of the remaining volumes.

The completion of this series will make available to the English-speaking world a magnificent account of the literary and cultural treasures created by the Jewish people during their millennial history.

Hebrew Union College—   Alfred Gottschalk
Jewish Institute of Religion   President
Cincinnati, Ohio
January 1976

Acknowledgments

The generous support of the Memorial Foundation for Jewish Culture, New York City, of the Morris and Bertha Treuhaft Memorial Fund, the Leonard, Faye, and Albert B. Ratner Philanthropic Fund, and Mr. and Mrs. John K. Powers, all of Cleveland, is gratefully acknowledged by publisher and translator alike. Without this generosity it would not have been possible for Israel Zinberg's monumental work to reach the new audience that it is hoped a translation into English will afford. The editor and translator wishes to express his appreciation to his friend Dr. Arthur J. Lelyveld, Rabbi of the Fairmount Temple of Cleveland and President (1966–1972) of the American Jewish Congress, for his aid in securing a grant from the Memorial Foundation for Jewish Culture for the publication of this work.

The translator also wishes to express his deep appreciation to Dr. Nathan Susskind, formerly Professor of German at the College of the City of New York and Visiting Professor of Yiddish at Yeshiva University, for his invaluable help in clarifying the meaning of many terms and concepts in Zinberg's Yiddish and Hebrew text. Responsibility for any errors of translation is, of course, the translator's.

It should be noted that Yiddish books with Hebrew titles are usually rendered according to the modern Sephardic pronunciation of Hebrew.

A gift to my loyal friend
and life-companion—my wife.

Israel Zinberg

Transliteration of Hebrew Terms

א is not transliterated   ו = v (where not a vowel)   ל = l   פ = f

ב = b   ז = z   מ = m   צ = tz

ב = v   ח = ḥ   נ = n   ק = k

ג‚ ג = g   ט = t   ס = s   ר = r

ד‚ ד = d   י = y   ע is not transliterated   שׁ = sh

ה = h   כ = k   פ = p   שׂ = s

כ = ch   ת‚ ת = t

⸜ = a   ⸝ = e

⸗ = a   ⸯ = i

⸳‚ ו = o   ⸗ = ei

⸽‚ ו = u   ⸗ = e

short ⸜ = o   ⸗ = o

י ⸗ = ei   ⸗ = a

vocal *sheva* = e

silent *sheva* is not transliterated

Transliteration of Yiddish Terms

א	not transliterated		יי	ey
אַ	a		ײַ	ay
אָ	o		כּ	k
ב	b		כ,ך	kh
בֿ	v		ל	l
ג	g		מ,ם	m
ד	d		נ,ן	n
ה	h		ס	s
ו,וּ	u		ע	e
וו	v		פּ	p
וי	oy		פֿ,ף	f
ז	z		צ,ץ	ts
זש	zh		ק	k
ח	kh		ר	r
ט	t		שׁ	sh
טש	tsh. ch		שׂ	s
י	(consonant) y		תּ	t
י	(vowel) i		ת	s

Abbreviations

JQR	*Jewish Quarterly Review*
JQR, n.s.	*Jewish Quarterly Review*, new series
MGWJ	*Monatsschrift für die Geschichte und Wissenschaft des Judentums*
PAAJR	*Proceedings of the American Academy for Jewish Research*
REJ	*Revue des Études Juives*
ZHB	*Zeitschrift für hebräische Bibliographie*

This volume is dedicated
to
Sadie Klau
a lovely person, generous, kind, gentle,
a true woman of valor

A Note from the Author

With this volume we begin the second half of our *History of Jewish Literature*—a portrayal of the new era, from the efflorescence of Haskalah and the Hasidism of the Baal Shem Tov up to the World War.

Hence, the present volume is constructed in a fashion different from the previous ones. First of all, there the "Judeo-German" literature was generally treated in isolation from Hebrew literature. With regard to the literary legacy left by Jewish thinkers and poets in other languages, those works which found a home among the people through translation into Hebrew and thus exercised an influence on the development of Jewish culture were mainly discussed.

The Enlightenment era, a consequence of complicated social and ideological factors, however, evoked great changes in Jewish intellectual life. Literature cast off its religious vestment and assumed more secular, modern forms. With the capitalist-bourgeois order of society, the isolation of the ghetto wall was broken through, and the requirements of Jewish life and awakened thought already find their expression in the European languages as well. Also in the "languages of the fatherland," during the nineteenth century a memorial dedicated to *Hochmat Yisrael* or *Wissenschaft des Judentums*, dealing with the historical past of the Jewish community, was constructed. In the introduction to our work we already noted that we set ourselves the task of providing the fullest possible portrait of all of Jewish intellectual and cultural creativity in the course of the period in question, and that the development of poetic forms will be explored on the basis of the entire Jewish cultural environment, with its intellectual and social tendencies.

In accord therewith, in the second half of our *History*, we shall treat not merely "Hebraica" but also "Judaica," insofar as the latter actually affected the development of Jewish national culture and reflected in their pages the ideological tendencies of certain strata of the Jewish intellegentsia. Hence, in the present volume Mendelssohn, for example, is portrayed not only as the founder of *Kohelet Musar* and the creator of *Or La-Netivah*, but also as the author of *Jerusalem* in German. Solomon Maimon is pictured not only as the writer of *Givat Ha-Moreh* but also as author of his *Lebensgeschichte* (Autobiography). Along with Isaac Euchel and Aaron Wolfsohn-Halle, who were active in the realm of Hebrew and Yiddish literature, David Friedlander with his German writings will be discussed. This will occur even more prominently in the subsequent volumes. From this volume on, moreover, literature in Yiddish will be treated not in isolation from, but together with, neo-Hebrew writings.

Finally, we consider it useful once again to mention what we have already indicated in the introduction to the first volume: that we do not, in general, intend to provide a kind of encyclopedic compendium from which no Jewish author will be missing. Our task is to acquaint the reader only with the major and significant phenomena in the realm of Jewish cultural creativity. Hence, we shall dwell only on those Jewish writers and thinkers who actually had, at least for their generation, some influence on the development of Jewish culture and Jewish thought.

—ISRAEL ZINBERG

Leningrad, November 20, 1935

THE BERLIN HASKALAH

CHAPTER ONE

The Jews of Berlin
and Moses Mendelssohn

[Frederick II and the Jews in Prussia—The Jewish community in Berlin—Its economic growth and lack of civic rights—The social contradictions—The influence of the French "enlighteners"—Doctor Aaron Gumperz—Moses Mendelssohn; his role and significance—Mendelssohn as a personality—Mendelssohn and Lessing—Mendelssohn's *Phaedon*—His treatment of the question of the immortality of the soul.]

 N THE post-Haskalah period, after the ideals of enlightenment so sadly forfeited their erstwhile radiance and many of the former battlers for them became penitents, a hostile attitude toward the Berlin Haskalah and its standard-bearers came to clear expression in Hebrew literature. It suffices to mention the struggle Peretz Smolenskin carried on against Moses Mendelssohn's enlightening activity, or Ze'ev Wolf Jawitz's *Migdal Ha-Me'ah*, in which the creators and representatives of the enlightenment movement among the Russian Jews are spoken of so bitterly. Several decades, a whole era of enormous social and intellectual revolutions, separate us from these penitential moods which the unanticipated collapse of the ideals of Haskalah evoked. Hence, we now have the possibility of presenting a more objective and historically more accurate estimate of the fighters for Haskalah in Berlin at the end of the eighteenth century.

First of all, one must take into account the unusually difficult and contradictory circumstances under which the Jewish en-

lighteners of that era, when the "philosopher and freethinker"
Frederick II sat on the throne of Prussia, had to live and struggle. Frederick did, indeed, declare proudly that in his realm
everyone could hold to his own faith freely and without hindrance. This, however, did not in any way prevent him from
regarding the Jews with the most venomous hatred. In his
hostile attitude toward the Jews, remarks the historian of culture Ludwig Geiger,[1] Frederick II surpassed his predecessors
to a certain degree. Like all the backward German provincials
of that time, this crowned "thinker" was firmly convinced that
the Jews, being an extremely noxious element, must be restricted as much as possible in their civic rights, and that the
only benefit to be derived from them was to extract as much
government taxation as possible from their purses. The civic
condition of the Prussian Jews under his regime became, therefore, in certain respects, even more difficult than it had been
under that of his predecessors.

According to the edict that Frederick William I had issued
in 1714, every *Schutzjude* ("protected Jew") had the right to
transmit his "privileges" to his three oldest children. However,
Frederick II found this excessive and, according to the "General Privileges" of the year 1750, the *Schutzjude* was permitted
to bestow his rights of residence and trade only upon his eldest
son. The reason for this had been explained by Frederick himself a year earlier, when he noted that if every *Schutzjude* were
allowed to transmit his rights not to one but to two of his heirs,
then the specific purpose which the Prussian law sets for itself,
namely, to reduce the number of Jewish residents as much as
possible, would not be attained. As a result of this goal, the
privileged Jew's younger children, who could not enjoy their
father's *Schutzrecht*, were not granted the right to marry. The
so-called *ausserordentliche Schutzjuden* ("extraordinary protected
Jews") also did not have the right to carry on a family life in
Frederick II's capital city. Aside from *ausserordentliche Schutzjuden*, the General Privileges also distinguished so-called *gedul-
dede Juden* ("tolerated Jews")—all this with one definite goal: to
limit the rights of the Jews to the greatest possible extent.

Frederick II, however, was shrewder and more practical
than the Russian czarina Elizabeth Petrovna (1709–1762) who, in
her hatred for Jews, went so far as to declare that she "would
not enjoy any benefit from the enemies of Christ." The Prussian monarch regarded his Jews precisely as cows to be milked,
and endeavored to have the maximum "benefit" from them.

1. See his *Geschichte der Juden in Berlin*, I, 69.

Hence, during the time the "philosopher" Frederick ruled Prussia, the number of special Jewish taxes increased tremendously. To the old levies many new ones were added. So, for example, from 1766 on the Prussian Jews had to provide annually for the royal treasury, as raw material for the minting of coins, all of twelve thousand bars of silver according to a firmly fixed price—twelve thalers per bar. The actual price, however, was considerably higher—from thirteen thalers and twenty-two silver *groschen* to fourteen thalers. Thus, in this transaction the Jews each year lost some twenty-four thousand thalers.[2]

It was to the "philosopher on the throne" that the Prussian Jews also owed the well-known "porcelain tax." To enlarge the export of dishes that the royal porcelain factories produced, the following obligations were placed upon Jews: When the *Schutzjude* enrolled his eldest son in the register of the "privileged" he had, for this "grace," to purchase from the royal porcelain factory merchandise of three hundred thalers and export it outside the country. When a Jew was endowed with "general privileges" he was obliged, in addition to all other payments, to purchase porcelain for five hundred thalers. If a Jew bought a house or transferred his house to another Jew—it made no difference whether the residence was large or small—he was obliged to purchase porcelain for three hundred thalers and to sell it outside the country. The same applied in every purchase, in every permit, that the Jew obtained: as part of the transaction he had to purchase porcelain for a definite sum from the royal factories.[3]

At first glance it might seem that, for the Jew to be able to pay such taxes, he would have to be granted the necessary material opportunities. But precisely under Frederick II the civic rights of the Prussian Jews became even more limited. They were not only forbidden to engage in agriculture and to produce spirits or beer, but in the realm of trade they also ran up against ever new prohibitions. The Jew was forbidden to deal in almost all raw materials. According to the regulations of 1750, he could not trade either in domestic or imported cattle, wool, untanned hides, tobacco, groceries, herring, butter, cheese, salt, soap, vegetables, eggs, candles, any kind of fish, etc. Nevertheless, the actual economic needs of the kingdom compelled Frederick to relent at least in one area and to endow the hated Jews with certain "privileges."

"Finances are the most important nerve of the kingdom,"

2. See D. Friedländer, *Aktenstücke*, 1793, 57–58.
3. *Ibid.*, 68.

the king categorically declared. But he understood very well that in an industrially backward country it is extremely difficult to strengthen this "most important nerve." And it was precisely Prussia that was extremely retarded in industrial development. The first factories and textile looms were established in the country only at the end of the seventeenth century —and this thanks to the Huguenots who had been driven out of France. To develop the industry of the country as quickly as possible was one of the major tasks Frederick set himself. He realized quite well that factories for the manufacture of luxury items were the highest level of contemporary economic development. Hence, he did everything to establish as many silk and velvet factories as possible. For this, however, men of broad initiative and entrepreneurial drive were required. The old-fashioned Prussian middleclass or bourgeoisie of that time included very few such persons. Frederick, therefore, had no alternative but to turn to the Jewish ghetto and make use of the entrepreneurial spirit of its residents. Already in the 1730's virtually the entire trade in colonial merchandise (coffee, tea, foreign tobacco, etc.) was exclusively in the hands of Jews. Frederick II also opened wide to them a new realm; he bestowed upon them the "privileges" of building factories, and, to strengthen the industrial development of the country, was not chary of special "protection decrees" for his "velvet Jews," "silk Jews," and "mint Jews."[4]

When the Jews of Berlin, after the Seven Years War, submitted a petition requesting that the abovementioned privilege which Frederick had taken away from them be restored and that every *Schutzjude* obtain the right to transmit his *Schutzrecht* to at least two of his older children, they received the following reply from Frederick: He was prepared to grant their request, but only on the condition that the *Schutzjude's* second son obligate himself to establish a new factory.[5]

For industry to be able to develop normally and without hindrance it was, furthermore, essential to have an extensive credit system. Hence, in this area also Frederick could not do without Jewish financiers. Indeed, it was to the Jews residing in Berlin that he was indebted for the fact that banking and credit enterprises burgeoned so rapidly in the city. Thus the king, against his own will and under the pressure of purely

4. See Joseph Kulisher's work on "Jews in the Prussian Silk Industry" (Russian), *Yevreyskaya Starina*, IX, 1924, 129–161, where Frederick's decrees regarding Jewish manufacturers are given.

5. See L. Geiger, *op. cit.*, I, 65; II, 91.

economic factors, contributed much to the fact that the leading ranks of the *haute bourgeoisie* in his capital city were occupied, alongside the French whom he so revered, by the Jews whom he so despised.[6] According to the "General Privileges" of 1750, it was rigidly determined that the Jewish population in Berlin should not exceed 152 families. Nevertheless, the number of Jews increased greatly, and at the end of the 1770's there were already in Berlin, which then had 138,719 inhabitants, no less than 4,245 Jews. "In order to advance the growth of trade, commerce, textile production, and factories," Frederick decreed that "as many rich Jews as possible ought to be drawn to the country, but common artisans, teachers, cantors, artists, and employees ought to be forbidden to marry and establish a family."

Frederick generously bestowed privileges on rich Jews. His "mint" Jews Veitel Ephraim, Daniel Itzig, and Abraham Marcus obtained in 1761 the same "freedoms" as Christian bankers. But when Moses Mendelssohn,[7] who was already then renowned as an esthetician and philosopher, submitted a request that he be granted the residential right of a *Schutzjude*, he did not even receive a reply to his petition. Only through the intercession of the Marquis d'Argens, who was extremely popular at court, did he finally (in 1763) obtain the limited right of an *ausserordentlicher Schutzjude*. But Frederick did not find it possible to grant Mendelssohn's petition (in 1779) that his right of residence be awarded also to his children. Mendelssohn, after all, was at that time only an employee in a silk factory, not a factory owner.[8]

Thus, as a result of the unique, selective system, the total of wealthy Jews—bankers, factory owners, court-contractors and mint-masters—continued to grow in Berlin. As early as the 1730's there were only ten among the one hundred twenty members of the community whose capital amounted to less than one thousand thalers. Among the rest there were many whose fortune was estimated in the tens of thousands.[9] Frederick II with his industrial policy significantly assisted the Prus-

6. The famous Mirabeau who visited Berlin in Frederick's times declares with astonishment: *On peut même assurer que ce sont (les juifs) le seuls negociants ou fabricants à grandes fortunes, qu'il y ait dans les provinces prussiennes. Il en est des millionnaires* (we quote according to Heinrich Graetz, *Geschichte der Juden*, Vol. XI).

7. See Dubnow's *Die Weltgeschichte des jüdischen Volkes*.

8. Only after the death of the factory owner Isaac Bernhard did Mendelssohn become a partner in the firm.

9. See L. Geiger, *op. cit.*, I, 43.

sian Jews, especially those of Berlin, to accumulate large capital and to become a prominent economic force. The Seven Years War, which ruined the country but provided the possibility for many Jews to become rich through supplying the military and through financial enterprises, magnified the social weight of Berlin Jewry, which became the harbinger of the new capitalist-bourgeois era.

Together with economic power, intellectual growth became discernible in the Jewish colony of Berlin. The Jewish merchants and bankers, the velvet and silk manufacturers, had close relations with foreign countries and came into frequent contact with the highest German nobility, which at that time especially distinguished itself by its self-deprecation before the "foreign," especially before everything coming from France. As is known, German literature of the seventeenth and eighteenth centuries imitated French models in all details; and Frederick II, who greatly desired to win fame with his French "poems," regarded everything produced in the language of his own country with contempt. The rich Jewish houses of the Prussian capital also came into friendly contact with their close neighbors—the large[10] French colony residing there, which then constituted the majority of the industrial-entrepreneurial and progressive, intellectual circles in Berlin. The youth of the Jewish bourgeoisie thus had opportunity to become familiar with the new ideological tendencies which appeared at that time under the influence of the Encyclopedists and Enlighteners.

An interesting portrait of how this familiarity came about is provided us by Henriette Herz in her memoirs:

The first who began to learn French were the daughters of the wealthy Jewish elements. The parents interposed no objection to this because of utilitarian reasons; with the aid of the French language, after all, one could connect himself with the whole of the civilized world. At first the Jewish daughters used their French to carry on gallant conversations with officers and cavaliers of the court who used to come visit their fathers on financial matters. Later, however, they began to employ the French language for more important purposes: to acquaint themselves with the French classics and the newer writers in the original.[11]

Solomon Maimon relates in his *Lebensgeschichte* how young Jews who came to Berlin and there engaged in study devoted

10. At the end of the 1770's the French colony in Berlin consisted of 5,346 members.
11. See *Henriette Herz, Ihr Leben und ihre Errinerungen.*

themselves mainly to learning French.[12] Characteristic also in this respect are the numerous Yiddish letters which the young Moses Mendelssohn wrote from Berlin to his bride in 1762.[13] These letters are filled with French expressions that were apparently taken into the vernacular. Mendelssohn writes, for example: *vi ambarasirt ikh bin; zikh mokiren; komoditet; distinktzia; pretext; deranzhirt; resulfirt;* etc. He does not tire of always reminding his "beloved Fromet" that she should, by all means, diligently study French, "which can almost become the mother tongue here."[14]

The bearers of ideas of the youthful class bubbling with fresh powers, whose stormy steps were heard ever more loudly in the historical arena, necessarily made a tremendous impression, with their fiery preachings, on the residents of the ghetto suffering severe civic disabilities. The latter heard in these preachments the tidings of liberation and the grant of equal rights for all "citizens of the world," the promise of the destruction of all caste privileges. It is no wonder, then, that the ideas of the French "enlighteners" found a sharp resonance in certain Jewish circles.

Old-fashioned rabbinic Judaism, rigidified in its customs, was unable to check these new ideological tendencies. To be sure, the rabbis and the supervisors of Judaism stood on guard. They endeavored to fence off their congregations from alien ideas, from everything that could arouse suspicion of heresy. In the 1740's the ancestor of the Bleichroeders, then a poor *yeshivah*-student, was driven out of Berlin because a charity *gabbai* of the community caught him with a German book under his arm.[15] But twenty or thirty years later, for the rising generation, for the children of the Jewish bankers, manufacturers, and leading citizens, a bridge had already been thrown across to European culture. Among these young people the supreme authority was the freethinker Voltaire, whose clever aphorisms and sallies went from mouth to mouth; and Bleichroeder's friend—also a poor *yeshivah*-student and the one for

12. *Lebensgeschichte,* p. 393 (we quote according to A.J. Goldschmidt's Yiddish translation).

13. The letters are published in the sixteenth volume of the Mendelssohn Jubilee Edition (1929).

14. *Ibid.,* 21. In subsequent letters he asks many times: "How goes it with the French, dear Fromet?" (p. 38). In one of the last letters Mendelssohn writes with great satisfaction, "That you continue with French is extremely dear to me" (p. 98).

15. S. Bernfeld (*Dor Tahapuchot,* p. 32) declares this an "invented, fabricated story." The fact, however, is reported by Bleichroeder himself in his memoirs (see *Gedenkblatt,* 1929, No, 9, p. 440).

whom, in fact, the young Bleichroeder carried the forbidden German book and was punished for it—occupied a central position in the German literature of that time and was the acknowledged standardbearer of the Enlightenment era for German Jewry. This *yeshivah*-student was named Moses ben Menaḥem Mendel of Dessau.

For generations Mendelssohn was regarded as the "father of Haskalah," the founder of the era of enlightenment. While he was still alive, he was enthusiastically declared the "third Moses" who "raised us from deep mire to honor and glory,"[16] the redeemer who "liberated the people of Israel from spiritual and intellectual enslavement and led them on the radiant way of culture and education."[17]

Immediately after Mendelssohn's death, *Ha-Meassef* declared that "the truth and the correct interpretation of the Torah were veiled in darkness for generations until God commanded: Let Moses appear. Then suddenly it became light."[18] And a Christian writer, Karl Philipp Kranz, lamented Mendelssohn's death in a long poem which ends as follows:

> Und du, die ihn geboren, Germania!
> Sei stolz, dass du die Mutter des Weisen warst.
> Du wirst ihn ewig ehren, den du
> Ehrest dich selber in deinen Söhnen![19]

16. Abraham Meldola of Hamburg writes in *Ha-Meassef* (December, 1784): "The man who stands in its midst like a sapphire and a topaz, a man of great eminence. And who is there like him, perfect in every science and wisdom? He is glorified among kings, and his sheaf stands upright [like the biblical Joseph's], he is exalted among sages and has no peer . . . And who has heard this and does not know that this man Moses bar Menaḥem is the light of our generation, the glory of our people, and the light of our eyes, and that from Moses unto Moses there arose no wise and understanding man like Moses? Happy are ye, O men of Berlin, that you have been privileged to have him, and happy art thou, O Israel, that a man such as this is like a wall and a shelter amidst our congregation. Every wise and understanding man is familiar with his books . . . Together they say: Long live the man Moses! For he is a holy man of God . . . Was it not this man Moses who raised us from the clinging mud to honor and beauty?"

17. See Jost, *Die Geschichte des Judenthums und seiner Sekten*, Part Three, 296: "Moses Mendelssohn appeared and, with him, a third Moses was sent to the Israelites to raise those who were bowed down and to free the fettered." See also Dr. Friedländer, *Geschichtsbilder aus der nachtalmudischer Zeit*, Part Four, 1, *et al.*

18. *Ha-Meassef*, 5546, p. 177.

19. Also the then well-known German poet Karl Wilhelm Ramler lamented Mendelssohn's death in a special mourning cantata in which Eusebia (the Christian populace) assures her sister Shulamith (Jewry) that she feels equally with her the greatness of this loss (see *Penei Tevel*, pp. 237–238, and Euchel in his *Toledot Ha-Rambeman*.

Some seventy-five years after Mendelssohn's death the talented poet Moritz Rapoport celebrated him in the following emotive lines:

> In Nacht und Stumpfsinn war das Volk versunken,
> In's Grab der Ahnen zog er sich zurück;
> Da naht ein Moses mit den Geistesfunken
> Als Flammensäule dem erstaunten Blick,
> Er zieht voran ihm mit den milden Strahlen.
> Und Israel folgt treu der lichten Spur,
> Und führt es durch das Meer uralter Qualen
> In das gelobte Land hin der Kultur.[20]

Not only in the generation of the Meassefim in the era of the Berlin enlightenment, but even as late as the end of the nineteenth century, Mendelssohn was considered the great reformer, the spiritual father of the cultural efflorescence of the Jews, and much was said about his "school" and his "disciples." "If we were asked," says the historian of culture Ludwig Geiger, "to whom the Jews of Berlin are indebted for the fact that they became members of cultured society, to whom they owe the fact that they became Germans, we must name Mendelssohn." His contemporary from Russia, Professor Bakst, goes even further in his enthusiasm. He sees in Mendelssohn

the man who, with his life and activity, contributed more than all others to the liberation of our people in modern Europe; the man who, with the power of his genius, conducted Jews out of the narrow labyrinth of ritual-theological casuistry on to the broad field of human culture; the man whose name became the banner of all progressives, who led to the spiritual and intellectual revival of the Jewish people in the course of the last hundred years.[21]

Also those who came forward as decisive opponents of the "false enlightenment of Berlin" poured out their wrath, above all, on Moses Mendelssohn, for they saw in him the founder of the direction which cultural development among the Jews of the West assumed in the nineteenth century.[22]

In point of fact both Mendelssohn's admirers and opponents are mistaken in their estimate of his role and significance for

---

20. *Am Todestage Moses Mendelssohn,* Leipzig, 1860.
21. Bakst, *Pamyati Moiseya Mendelsona.*
22. It is sufficient to mention Smolenskin's *Et Lata'at* which, in its day, made a great impression.

the history of Jewish enlightenment. *Meine Gemütsart ist nicht für Neuerungen,* "My kind of disposition is not for innovations," Mendelssohn candidly admits.[23] In character and temperament he was certainly no reformer or stormer, and much that is credited to him, both by his admirers and his detractors, was done not only without his will but definitely against his will. Mendelssohn himself presents, in his modest fashion, a quite accurate estimate of his character in his well-known preface to Menasseh ben Israel's *Vindiciae Judaeorum:* "I have always lived in seclusion, never had any impulse or vocation to mix into the quarrels of the active world, and my whole intercourse has always been limited to the circle of a few friends who followed the same ways as I."[24] Even so ardent an admirer of Mendelssohn's as Ludwig Geiger must confess that he was "a sober, extremely cautious man, who arrived at his convictions quite slowly and gradually and did not always have the courage to fight for these convictions obtained through so much effort; he was not a battler."[25]

In this respect Mendelssohn was the complete antithesis of his friend Gotthold Ephraim Lessing. The latter was a restless spirit, a born fighter by nature. His entire life was spent in indefatigable and heroic struggle against the obsolete, against everything that smacked of routine, of congealed tradition. He regarded with hatred and contempt everything that was called *Staat* by the German Philistine, the thoroughgoing *Spiessbürger.* A truly bohemian nature, he was a constant wanderer, a gambling cardplayer; always associated with the pariahs of society —actors, Jews, soldiers; lived all his years in poverty; and did not have the capacity or patience to attain the slightest material success, the minimum comforts of life.

Mendelssohn, however, was the calm, sedate man and approved of the householderly *Staat.* In his youth a poor *yeshivah* student who, during the first years after his arrival in Berlin,[26] had to take his meals on different days of the week at the homes of various families and frequently went hungry, he no longer knew of poverty or want after 1750. At first he was a tutor in

23. *Gesammelte Schriften,* 1843, Vol. V, p. 351.
24. *Ibid.,* Vol. III, p. 180.
25. See *Voskhod,* 1897, IV, p. 90.
26. Mendelssohn was born September 6, 1729, in Dessau, into the family of a poor scribe named Menaḥem Mendel. He studied the Talmud and its commentaries with the local rabbi David Fränkel who acquired renown with his commentary on the Jerusalem Talmud. When, in 1743, David Fränkel was invited to occupy a rabbinic post in Berlin, his pupil, the fourteen-year-old Moses ben Menaḥem, followed him there.

the home of the rich silk manufacturer Bernhard, afterwards (from 1754 on) bookkeeper and correspondent, and later also partner in the business and renowned in industrial circles as one of the great experts and specialists in the production of silk. Mendelssohn also had outside income, even dealt at one time in *etrogim* or citrons, and on occasion earned some fees through marriage brokerage. He notes with pleasure that he came of a very distinguished family, that he was a descendant of the author of the *Mappah*, Rabbi Moses Isserles. He also had a great longing for the honorary rabbinic title *ḥaver* and even applied on this matter to the famous Rabbi Jonathan Eybe-schütz.[27]

In his sympathies and world view Mendelssohn had considerable affinity with the group of "predecessors of Haskalah" who undertook efforts before his time to lead their brethren in peaceful, gradual fashion "out of the narrow labyrinth of ritual-theological casuistry."[28] Indeed, one of these "forerunners of Haskalah," Israel Zamosc, who is already known to us,[29] was the first who familiarized the still quite young Mendelssohn with Maimonides' *Guide for the Perplexed* and awakened his critical, speculative thought. Zamosc was also the teacher of the extraordinary man who had such a large influence on Mendelssohn's intellectual development—the physician Aaron Emerich Gumperz.[30]

Gumperz was six years older than Mendelssohn. Zamosc aroused his interest in mathematics, philosophy, and the natural sciences. In 1751 Gumperz took examinations to qualify as a doctor of medicine but, being a well-to-do man who did not have to be concerned about earning a living, never practiced as a physician. A great influence on the young Gumperz was exercised by Frederick II's friend the Marquis d'Argens, author of the *Lettres Juives*, who served the king for a time as secretary. Thanks to the marquis, Gumperz obtained acquaintance with the literary and scientific circles, became a member

---

27. See Eybeschütz's letter printed in *Kerem Ḥemed*, III, 224–25; reprinted in the Mendelssohn Jubilee Edition, 1929, Vol. XVI, pp. 2–3. Eybeschütz denied Mendelssohn's request under the pretext that he was still a young, unmarried man. Only a year later (1762) did Mendelssohn marry Fromet Guggenheim of Hamburg who was, according to his own report (in a letter to Lessing) "neither beautiful nor learned" (*Gesammelte Schriften*, 1844, Vol. V, p. 166).
28. See our *History*, Vol. VI, Part Two, Chapters Four to Eight.
29. *Ibid.*, pp. 244–45.
30. For a discussion of Aaron Emerich Gumperz, a grandson of the famous Glückel of Hameln, see Kaufmann—Freudenthal, *Die Familie Gumperz*, 1907, pp. 164–200.

of the "Learned Coffeehouse" society of Berlin, and also a habitúe of the "Monday Club," which became the focus of the Berlin enlighteners. There Gumperz became acquainted with Gotthold Ephraim Lessing, Friedrich Nicolai, and others.

Under the influence of these circles, Gumperz decided to occupy himself with "enlightening" work in his own environment. He undertook to write a large work in Hebrew that would embrace all the sciences: however, he lacked the necessary power of creation,[31] and his projected work remained unfinished. He published, in 1765, only the introduction,[32] in which he provides—in clear, comprehensible form—a general overview of all of the sciences, and endeavors to demonstrate to his readers the great utility of general secular knowledge. He also stresses that only foolish, ignorant persons can perceive a threat to the faith in this.[33] The cultured physician attempts to convey to his readers, raised on *pilpul* and scholasticism, the vast importance of the experimental scientific method. We must, he declares, follow the way laid down by such eminent scholars as Maimonides, Ibn Ezra, Gersonides, and Joseph Solomon Delmedigo, who were equipped with comprehensive knowledge and indefatigably struggled against the ignorant fools who persecuted the bearers of wisdom and science.

To Gumperz belongs the merit of having been the first to reveal to the young Mendelssohn the broad world of European culture. He diligently studied the civilized European languages, French and English,[34] with him, and also introduced him to Lessing, who had such an enormous influence on Mendelssohn's literary development and activity.[35] "It can rightly be asserted," declares Mendelssohn's biographer Kayserling,[36] "that without Gumperz Mendelssohn would not have been

31. Gumperz was a sickly man and died at the age of forty-seven.
32. Under the title *Maamar Ha-Madda*, as a supplement to his work *Megalleh Sod* (explanations to Ibn Ezra's commentary on the five biblical scrolls).
33. "And it will protect it [the faith] from the blasphemers, the ignorant rabble among the people, malicious, evil-thinking persons who scheme to slay men honest and perfect in researches in Torah studies, for the fanatacism in their hearts burns like a fire and therefore there is no sense among them; they do not understand and will not be wise."
34. Mendelssohn studied Latin with the physician Abraham Kisch and Greek with the director of the gymnasium Damm.
35. Mendelssohn himself points this out with his customary honesty. In one of his letters to Lessing he notes: *Mein Geist ist ohne alle Bewegung, wenn Sie nicht seine Triebfedern aufziehen.* To be sure, Mendelssohn for his part, also helped Lessing a good deal with his literary work. So, for instance, he supplied Lessing with much essential material when the latter wrote his celebrated *Laokoön.*
36. *Mendelssohn, Sein Leben und seine Werke*, 1862, p. 22.

Mendelssohn." Mendelssohn himself writes in one of his letters to his bride Fromet: "To him alone [Dr. Aaron Gumperz] I am indebted for everything that I have attained in the sciences."[37] In his autobiographical notice also Mendelssohn deems it necessary to point out: "Then and there I gained through association with the later doctor of medicine, Herr Aaron Gumperz, a taste for the sciences, and also obtained from him an inspiring first instruction" (*Gesammelte Schriften*, 1843, Vol. V, p. 526).

The case of Aaron Gumperz shows in the clearest way how exaggerated and unjustified is the accepted view that Mendelssohn was the first among the German Jews who reached the upper levels of European culture. On the other hand, however, Mendelssohn actually was the first Jew who came forth as an important, universally recognized writer and who, as a master of literary style and language, inscribed his name in the history of national German literature. It was he, the son of the Torah scribe Menaḥem Mendel of Dessau, the *ausserordentlicher Schutzjude*, who was the first German writer to treat the profoundest philosophical problems in such elegant and lucid style. It was he, the son of the disenfranchised and rightless ghetto, who was given the honorific title "the Socrates of Berlin" and with whom crowned princes and the most eminent scientists and thinkers of that age were eager to become acquainted. It was he who in 1743, as a poor fourteen-year-old *yeshivah* student, had knocked with great trepidation on the Rosenthaler Gate (the only gate through which a Jew could enter Berlin), and to whom twenty years later the Prussian Academy awarded its first prize for his philosophical essay *Abhandlung über die Evidenz in metaphysischen Wissenschaften*.[38] One must also take into consideration Mendelssohn's gentle character, the remarkable grace of his sympathetic personality. All this illuminated his name with great glory and extraordinary radiance and created the Mendelssohn legend, the emotive legend about the "third Moses" who "led the Jewish people out of the night of spiritual and intellectual enslavement."[39]

37. *Ketavim Ivrim*, Volume XVI, p. 16.
38. The second prize at that time was received by Immanuel Kant, the great revolutionary, the future destroyer of the "metaphysical sciences." Mendelssohn's prize composition later also appeared in Hebrew translation (*Ha-Berur Ha-Pilosofi*, 1866).
39. The first historian who attempted to give a more objective picture of Mendelssohn's literary and social activity was Simon Bernfeld in his *Dor Tahapuchot* (1897). Before Bernfeld, as early as the 1880's, David Frishman, in his well-known *Michtavim Al Devar Ha-Safrut*, noted that not only Mendelssohn's admirers but his opponents as

In fact, however, Mendelssohn in temperament and world view was very little suited to become the standardbearer of a reform movement. He himself admits in a letter to Lessing[40] that the very term *Freigeist* (free thought) arouses terror *(erweckt Schauder)* in him. He is astounded by the news that his friend of many years, the author of *Nathan the Wise*, was inclined in his last years toward the atheistic world view which denies the existence of the First Cause governing the world. Mendelssohn was bound with his whole heart to the old Jewish way of life and loyally maintained the traditions of the religious customs. His rationalistically-minded followers, who consider themselves his disciples, always attempt to show that this was merely external. Such a view, however, is refuted not only by his *Jerusalem*, of which we shall speak later, but also by many of Mendelssohn's private letters.

Thanks to them we learn, for example, that when he was *en route* traveling in Brunswick, he did not seize the opportunity of visiting his friend Lessing only because this would involve desecration of the Sabbath.[41] He interrupts his letter to Abbt in the middle because "the Sabbath is approaching."[42] "The Sabbath is drawing near and I must close," Mendelssohn writes on another occasion to the same Abbt.[43] He also declines to drink the cup of wine Lessing gives him because it is *yayin nesech* (the wine of idolaters).[44] "I rejoice," he candidly admits, "in every religious custom that does not lead to intolerance and hatred of men, rejoice as with my children in every ceremony that has something true and good at its foundation."[45] The Biblical Book

---

well provided a quite onesided and false picture of Mendelssohn and his activity. To those who spoke with such indignation and bitterness of "Mendelssohn's Haskalah," Frishman argued: "What sense does it make to associate everything with Mendelssohn's name and then come with pretensions that all this is pernicious and evil? Who demands of you that you declare Mendelssohn the creator and chief leader of the Berlin Haskalah, and then complain that his intellectual heirs pursue evil ways and that the Haskalah they preach is of very slight value? Who bade you take a man who was still so closely associated with the tradition of the fathers, a man who dwelt quietly in his tent, who in fact had such a slight relationship to the events of that time, and then come to him with complaints that those events were bad and their consequences still worse? I, for instance, have never over-estimated Mendelssohn's importance or idolized him and, therefore, I did not need to hurl him down from his pedestal later on."

40. *Gesammelte Schriften*, 1843, Vol. V, p. 82.
41. *Gesammelte Schriften*, 1843, Vol. V, p. 191.
42. *Ibid.*, p. 326.
43. *Ibid.*, p. 334.
44. Kayserling, *Moses Mendelssohn*, p. 143.
45. *Gesammelte Schriften*, Vol. V, p. 649.

of Psalms was precious to him not only as a literary monument of great value, but chiefly as a book of prayers in which he poured out his religious feelings. "They (the Psalms) sweeten my heavy mood," Mendelssohn wrote to Sophia Becker a week before his death, "and I recite and sing them whenever I feel a need to pray and sing."[46]

When Mendelssohn was already renowned as a brilliant writer and aesthetic critic in the German literary world, he remained, in the Jewish milieu, the traditional *talmid ḥacham*, or sage, who strictly observed all the commandments of the Torah, had an attitude of profound reverence for the rabbis of his time, and even requested the greatest of them to bestow on him the honorary title *ḥaver*. Here there can be no thought of hypocrisy on Mendelssohn's part, born out of fear of persecution by the rabbis. He himself notes in his well-known reply to Lavater: "What can prevent me? Fear of my coreligionists? Their worldly power is all too slight for them to be able to arouse fear in me."[47]

Mendelssohn's intimate world and his entire philosophy are most clearly disclosed in the work which made him so renowned in the general intellectual circles of his day—*Phaedon: Oder über die Unsterblichkeit der Seele.* This work written in German which, in style and external form, is so closely associated with the literary creation of the great Greek thinker Plato,[48] is, in content and theme, a typically Jewish work and in direct affinity with the chief problems that occupied such an important place in Hebrew religious-philosophical literature. Not without reason did Mendelssohn at first plan to compose his work in Hebrew.[49] "Numerous weighty factors," he notes, however, "did not permit me to carry this through and compelled me to write my projected work in a language of the nations of the world, as many greater and more important men

---

46. *Ibid.*, p. 650.
47. Kayserling, *Moses Mendelssohn*, Vol. III, p. 41.
48. Mendelssohn was especially enchanted by Plato as an incomparable stylist. "There is virtually no one as eloquent as he among the sages of the nations and their rhetoricians," he writes in one of his letters. In Mendelssohn's literary remains there was a manuscript of his German translation of the first three books of Plato's *Republic.*
49. See his letter to Naftali Herz Wessely in *Ketavim Ivrim*, 1929, Vol. XVI, p. 119–188: "Originally I intended to write it in Hebrew . . . and I wished to turn away from the path of Plato entirely and to write a book by myself on the origins of the soul and its immortality, and to base my doctrine on the sayings of the rabbis in the *Aggadot* and *Midrashim*, for the majority of them agree very much with what I explained in the way of truth, so that it does not oppose the truth in any way."

than I did in their day when they composed their works in Arabic."[50]

The motives that impelled Mendelssohn to write his *Phaedon* in German were, indeed, quite serious. The entire Enlightenment era bears a sharply individualistic character. The bourgeoisie struggling for power issued forth in the name of the individual, of the personality proudly demanding its rights, its recognition in society. "Man was born to enjoy happiness"— this was the slogan of the newly rising class which wished to base itself not on family pedigree but on the personal merits of each individual member. Furthermore, the philosophical system to which Mendelssohn was devoted all his life, the system of Leibniz in the reworking of his disciple Baron Christian von Wolff, was thoroughly optimistic. It was Leibniz' firm conviction that the world is conducted according to the order of a preestablished harmony. The existing world is the best of all possible worlds, and through it alone can the goal of the world-creation be realized. The system of Leibniz and Wolff did, indeed, continue to carry a certain theological vesture. However, the rationalist ideas which greatly aided the personality to liberate itself from the spiritual enslavement remaining as a legacy from the old way of life powerfully undermined the religious world view, with its firm belief in reward and punishment and in the immortality of the soul. There was, above all, an inconsistency with the optimistic *Weltanschauung:* Man is born to enjoy happiness in the best of all worlds ruled through the "preestablished harmony," but human life—alas—is so brief, so filled with pain and suffering; death lies in wait for man, and he soon disappears like a shadow, dissolves into earth and dust.

Hence, it is not surprising that in the period of the *Aufklärer* so much attention was devoted to this problem, and that men occupied themselves with such painful interest with the question of the immortality of the human soul. It suffices to mention the greatest German writer of that era, Gotthold Ephraim

---

50. Soon after *Phaedon* appeared Mendelssohn wrote in a letter to the mathematician Raphael Levi: "I intend to write in Hebrew a treatise on the 'immortality of the soul.' *Phaedon* does not allow itself to be translated; at least in Hebrew it would cease to be understandable. Of this I am convinced. For this reason I would gladly give it another vestment, in order to make the matter more comprehensible to our co-religionists" (*Gesammelte Schriften*, Vol. V, p. 449). And, indeed, Mendelssohn partially fulfilled his desire; he made a Hebrew summary of his *Phaedon* in the Hebrew treatise *Ha-Nefesh* which Friedländer published in 1787. A year earlier Beer-Bing's complete Hebrew translation of *Phaedon*, which was later reprinted several times, appeared in print.

Lessing. This bright and free spirit was a convinced rationalist. "We now live in a time," he declares with complacency, "when the voice of common sense rings loudly." Lessing—and in this he was diametrically opposed to Mendelssohn—was blessed with a historical sense.[51] He considered the historic religions definite stages in the history of the education of the human race, and was strongly persuaded that "if the human race would be helped thereby," it is absolutely necessary that the revealed religions should develop into *Vernunftwahrheiten*, or "truths of reason."[52] But even Lessing devotes his greatest attention to the question of the immortality of the soul. The fundamental difference between Judaism and Christianity, which Lessing regards as distinct stages "in the education of the human race," is perceived by him exclusively in the fact that the Torah of Moses still does not know of the immortality of the soul, whereas one of the basic dogmas of the Gospels is the belief in immortality. In this last work of his, which Lessing published several months before his death, the convinced rationalist concludes with a tender, emotive paean to the belief, already well known to us from the Kabbalah, in transmigration of the soul. "Why," he asks, "can every single person also not have been in this world previously more than once? Is this hypothesis so ridiculous because it is the oldest? Why should I not come here again, as also sent to obtain new knowledge, new skills? Why not?"

Why not?—This doubt-filled question disturbed many spirits of that time. "Without God, Providence and immortality," declares Mendelssohn, "all the goods of life have in my eyes negligible value."[53] The popular preacher Johann Joachim Spalding wrote a special work *Über die Bestimmung des Menschen* (on the Destiny of Man).[54] Not all, however, were satisfied and calmed by it. The youthful and clever Abbt pours out his sorrow before Mendelssohn and expresses to him his grievous hesitancies "about the fate of man." Mendelssohn attempted to remove Abbt's doubts in a short treatise, but a definitive answer

---

51. He expresses, for instance, the following thought which is highly interesting for that time: *Viele von den kleineren Staaten würden ein ganz verschiedenes Klima, folglich ganz verschiedene Bedürfnisse und Befriedigungen, folglich ganz verschiedene Gewohnheiten und Sitten, folglich ganz verschiedene Sittenlehren, folglich ganz verschiedene Religionen haben* (Ernst und Falk, Zweites Gespräch).

52. *Die Erziehung des Menschengeschlechts*, Section 76.

53. *Morgenstunden*, 147 (Vienna edition, 1838).

54. See Mendelssohn's *Gesammelte Schriften*, 1843, Vol. V, pp. 279–313.

was given to Abbt and all the other doubters of that generation in his *Phaedon* (published 1767).[55]

The enormous success of this work is due not so much to its brilliant style and ingenious dialectic as to the profound and firm belief, with which it is permeated, in the graciousness of the Creator who is "the Supreme Good and the Supreme Wisdom."

"Man was born to enjoy happiness"—this motto shimmers from the pages of Mendelssohn's *Phaedon* with an artless and gentle light. To Mendelssohn Leo de Modena's notion that God condemned the crown of His creation, man, to unremitting suffering seemed arrogantly wild. The agonies endured in life cannot be without recompense. Creation, which is permeated with God-consciousness, cannot be transformed into "dust, mold, and decay *(Staub, Moder, und Verwesung)*." Mendelssohn puts into the mouth of Socrates his own credo when he has the Greek philosopher declare:

As far as I am concerned, I am content with the conviction that I will always be under divine protection, that a holy and just Providence rules over me in *this* life as in the other, and that my true happiness consists in the beauties and perfections of my spirit, and that these are justice, freedom, love, goodness, acknowledging God, promoting His decrees, and surrendering myself with my whole heart to His holy will. These beatitudes wait for me in that future to which I hasten. More I do not need to know to be able to walk the way that will carry me there with a calm spirit.[56]

What a tender faith is reflected in Mendelssohn's words: "We men here below—we are like sentries and must therefore not leave our posts until we are relieved."[57]

Not only Socrates' pupil Simias but also Mendelssohn himself believe unshakeably in the dogma that man's soul is immortal. He is only doubtful of the *vernunftmässiger Erweislichkeit*, the rational demonstrability, of this belief. "But I," Mendelssohn declares in the name of Simias, "accept with my whole heart this consoling doctrine, not simply in the form that we have obtained it as a legacy from our ancient sages, but with the exception of a few possible falsifications that poets and fabulists have devised and added to it."[58] Also without

55. A certain role was also played here by personal circumstances. In 1766 Mendelssohn lost his father and his son, and in the same year was himself also dangerously ill.
56. *Phaedon*, 1869 edition, the Third Discourse, p. 101.
57. *Ibid.*, p. 34.
58. *Ibid.*, p. 62.

logically "unassailable grounds" does Mendelssohn firmly believe in the immortality of the soul, for he is deeply permeated with the conviction that the love of the Creator for His creatures is boundless. "I know," he affirms in the name of Socrates, "that not everything ends for us with death; another life follows."[59]

This faith of Mendelssohn's is not founded on logical demonstration but on moral consciousness. Leibniz based the immortality of the soul on his theory of the "preestablished harmony," and his follower Mendelssohn comes to the following conclusion: It cannot be that the human spirit, like the body, should end with death. Otherwise all of life would be a melancholy play of scoffers, and the tradition of the fathers would be lies and swindlery. "If our spirit is ephemeral," exclaims Socrates' pupil Simias, "then our lawgivers and the founders of human societies have deluded either us or themselves; if all of human society decided so to propagandize a false notion and to hold in great honor the name of the deceivers who fabricated this idea, then a community of free, thinking persons is nothing more than a flock of ignorant beasts."[60]

Not with the aid of experiment, not through our external senses, do we obtain our conceptions of wisdom, goodness, and perfection, but thanks to our innermost consciousness, which confirms with the highest force of persuasion that these conceptions are the truly correct ones, the actually existing ones —or, as one of Socrates' pupils expresses it in Mendelssohn— "are real in the supreme degree." And it is these concepts that compel us with their whole being to apply our constant reflection and thought to the highest of all conceptions, which is "pure truth, pure goodness, pure perfection."[61] Mendelssohn deems it necessary to stress in this connection that, in obtaining these highest concepts in which the supreme beatitude and the loftiest achievement on man's way consist, the body with its senses is "not only a useless but actually a troublesome partner *(nicht nur ein unnützlicher, sondern auch ein beschwerlicher Gesellschafter)."*

The following point is characteristic. So convinced a rationalist as Gersonides considered it necessary to emphasize that the "acquired intellect"—which is the individually immortal element in man, the product of the universal "active intellect" —is closely associated with the senses, with the organs of feel-

59. *Ibid.,* p. 37.
60. *Ibid.,* p. 62.
61. *Ibid.,* p. 41.

ing and sensation.[62] This Aristotelian and rationalist had to acknowledge that the concepts of the thinking and inquiring person do not yield a completely accurate and valid picture of the nature of the objects which the human mind must investigate, for man—this creature of flesh and blood—does not possess so completely "pure" an intellect that it is capable of receiving and grasping the absolute and abstract, the general and universal, without the aid of feelings and sensations. To grasp in full measure the universal spirit, to unite perfectly with the active intellect—this, for the acquired intellect, is impossible, for its knowledge is, after all, dependent on man's limited feelings. We can only strive as far as possible to *approximate* the truth and perfect knowledge. After a person's death, however, his spirit, his acquired intellect, can no longer enrich his knowledge; he is no longer capable of gaining new concepts, for he now lacks the senses which are the instruments necessary for man to obtain knowledge.

Mendelssohn's attitude toward this question is quite different. As a faithful adherent of the Leibnizian-Wolffian philosophical system,[63] he considers the soul or mind as independent to a certain degree of the body, and agrees with Leibniz that the human mind actually obtains nothing from the external, material world. Our senses can give our consciousness only vague, incorrect ideas and representations. "We thus obtain," Mendelssohn declares, "merely shadows instead of reality." The goal of our strivings, actual knowledge, may be obtained by man, according to his philosophy, only after death. "Only then can we succeed on the path of our search for truth. Only then will we be in a position to grasp everything according to its actual essence, and not judge it according to the notion that our senses give us of it *(die Dinge nach der Wirklichkeit, nicht aber nach dem Sinnenschein beurteilen)*.[64]

As a follower of Leibniz, Mendelssohn decisively rejects the basic principle of the materialists and sensationalists that *nihil est in intellectu quod non fuerit in sensu,* i.e., that our intellect can obtain no conceptions without the perceptions of our senses, since the senses alone produce for the human mind the raw material which man's highest critical understanding then refashions. Mendelssohn does not believe in the truth of this

62. See our *History*, Vol. III, pp. 135ff.
63. That he agrees in this matter with the "men of Leibniz's school" Mendelssohn himself stresses in his Hebrew summary of *Phaedon.*
64. *Phaedon*, p. 48.

principle. How, he asks, did men arrive at this conclusion?—
Only from the experience that here in our life we cannot think
without impressions obtained from our senses.[65] But one must
not forget in this connection that when our intellect liberates
itself from the body rigidified by death, our soul continues to
exist and develop according to other, natural but *non-earthly*
[italicized by Mendelssohn] laws that are not bound up with
the notions of time and space.[66]

Mendelssohn considers the accepted view that sensation and
perception are the exclusive property of the body erroneous.
He even sets forth the following principle: *Das Vermögen zu
empfinden ist keine Beschaffenheit des Körpers,* "The capacity to
experience or perceive is no quality of the body." The soul,
however, is superlatively endowed with the property of willing and thinking.[67] Only after death, when the soul, endowed
with feelings and will, frees itself from its heavy corporeal
chains, can it devote itself without hindrance to everything for
which it yearned most when it still wandered about on earth:
beauty, virtue, and ardent desire to explore the truth. Only
then is it capable of fulfilling the supreme goal of the creation
of the world: to raise itself from level to level in the loftiest
distances that lead to the most exalted primordial being, the
original source of wisdom and knowledge, the prototype of
true beauty and perfection.[68]

A contemporary of Holbach and the other materialists, Mendelssohn, who remained faithful to the Leibnizian-Wolffian
system all his life, struggled with special force against the
materialist world view. "The first thing that appears to us as
the really true and actual," he writes, "is our body and its
functions. These functions dominate our attention and our
feeling so powerfully that we are originally inclined to the
notion that the material is the only thing which exists and that
all things outside it are merely its qualities."[69] Mendelssohn,
however, considers this an enormous mistake and does not tire
of demonstrating that "matter cannot think."[70]

Yet—and herein lies the irony of that most interesting and
contradictory period—despite the fact that Mendelssohn could

---

65. *Ibid.*, p. 57: *Ist es nicht bloss die Erfahrung, dass wir hier in diesem Leben niemals ohne
sinnliche Eindrücke denken können?*
66. *Ibid.*, p. 58.
67. *Das Vermögen zu denken und zu wollen nenne ich Seele.*
68. *Phaedon,* pp. 58–59, 93.
69. *Das materielle Dasein für das einzige, und alles übrige für Eigenschaften desselben halten.*
70. *Gesammelte Schriften,* Vol. V, p. 18.

in no way agree with many assumptions of the Encyclopedists, he was attracted to them as faithful fellow-battlers in the area of some highly important problems of life. Of this we shall have occasion to speak in the later chapters. Now, however, we must dwell on the phenomena associated with the tremendous impression that Mendelssohn's *Phaedon* evoked in the literary world of that era.

Mendelssohn's Translation of the Torah and His Jerusalem

[The extraordinary success of Mendelssohn's *Phaedon*—Mendelssohn's controversy with Lavater—Mendelssohn's reply—His attitude towards Christianity and Judaism—His journal *Kohelet Musar*—His commentary to *Ecclesiastes*—Mordecai Schnaber against Mendelssohn—Schnaber as a physician—His *Maamar Ha-Torah Veha-Hochmah*—His radical views—His *Yesod Torah*—Faith and knowledge—The role of sensations in the process of inquiry—The exchange of correspondence between Mendelssohn and Jacob Emden—Mendelssohn and Solomon Dubno—Mendelssohn's translation of the Pentateuch and his *Biur*—Mendelssohn the rationalist and the thoroughgoingly stubborn Jew—His attitude toward religious ritual—His *Jerusalem.*]

E HAVE quoted Mendelssohn's words: "I have always lived hiddenly and quietly, never had either desire or capacity to become involved in public, social affairs." His fate, however, brought it about that he was borne out of his hidden corner into the open marketplace of boisterous life and that his name resounded over the whole world. The success of Mendelssohn's *Phaedon* was unparalleled in contemporary German literature. In a period of four months the entire first edition was sold out, and one edition followed another. In a short time the work was translated into virtually all the European languages, and the modest bookkeeper of the Jewish silk manufacturer became the true "guide of the perplexed" of his time, the pointer of the way for persons lost and in doubt. The members of the society that had just been awakened from pious religious slumber threw themselves restlessly from freethinking rationalism to sentimental romanticism, but they could not allay the painful doubts in their hearts.

With bated breath these restless and perplexed persons listened to the calm and sedate conversations, carried on in the classic form of Plato's dialogues and grounded with logical, rationalist arguments, about the immortality of the human soul and about its tireless striving toward the heavenly spheres of beauty and divine harmony. The short, hunchbacked Jew, Moses of Dessau, was transformed into the "Jewish Socrates" and the "Plato of Berlin." From dukes and scholars, monks and writers, Mendelssohn received enthusiastic letters of gratitude for the cup of consolation that he handed to doubting hearts. He was celebrated in prose and in song, and Issachar Falkensohn (Behr), the first Jew who climbed the German Parnassus,[1] addressed the author of *Phaedon* in his paean with the following verses:

Allauslöschend verschont, Mendelssohn, dich die Zeit,
Der du, ewig zum Ruhm von dem Unendlichen
Auserkosen, die Todesfurcht
Von den Menschen vertilgt hast.

Welchen heiligen Trost leihest du jeglicher
Seele, welche zu stolz sich mit vergänglichen
Erdengütern zu täuschen,
Nach Unsterblichkeit stets sich sehnt?[2]

The Berlin Academy decided to elect Mendelssohn to its membership. The "tolerant" Prussian king Frederick, how-

---

1. Falkensohn (Behr) was born in Zamosc in 1746. Already the father of a family, he set out for Koenigsberg to study medicine. From Koenigsberg he later moved to Leipzig, but on the way spent some time in Berlin where his townsman and relative, Israel Zamosc, introduced him to Mendelssohn, Lessing, and other writers of Berlin. In 1772 he published his collection of German poems *Gedichte von einem pohlnischen Juden*. In 1773 Falkensohn settled in Haasengott where he spent all his life as a practicing physician. On Falkensohn, see Kayserling's article in Wertheim's *Wiener Jahrbuch* for 1863; *Ha-Melitz*, III, No., 40, pp. 633–637; *Historishe Shriftn*, 1929, I, p. 343.
2. *Gedichte*, 68.

ever, could not bear this and erased Mendelssohn's name with the note: "I wish to have neither priests nor Jews in my academy." Intellectual tourists, both German and foreign, whoever came to Berlin, considered it a duty to make the acquaintance of the "Jewish Socrates," the author of *Phaedon*. On a certain Benedictine monk Peter Adolph Winkopp (1759–1813), *Phaedon* made such an enormous impression that he came from his monastery to Berlin and revealed all his doubts and struggles to Mendelssohn. The effect of the latter with his gentle, comforting words on the monk was so vast that Winkopp afterwards gratefully asserted: "If I am virtuous, it is through Mendelssohn's teaching and principles; I enjoyed the happiest hours in association with him."[3]

A certain incident which greatly agitated the literary world of the time and had a rather large influence on Mendelssohn's further literary activity is associated with one of these visits. This is the well known "Lavater controversy." Johann Caspar Lavater, a clergyman and preacher of Zurich who also acquired a certain reputation as a writer, made the acquaintance of the "Jewish Socrates" on one of his visits, was a guest in Mendelssohn's home, and carried on intimate discussions on religious subjects with him. One must remember the contempt and hatred that the Christian clergy at that time had for Jews; they perceived in them "blasphemers of Christ," "narrow-hearted fanatics." And here Lavater witnessed a literally marvelous phenomenon—a Jew who adheres to the school of Christian philosophers, is acquainted with Christian scholars, writes with such tender sentiment on so Christian a theme as immortality (the "Old Testament," after all, knows very little of this matter), and in private conversations with himself speaks with greatest respect about Jesus Christ and his ethical significance.

For the clergyman from Zurich it was clear that in Mendelssohn resides a Christian soul which, unfortunately, requires "correction," and that the obligation rests on him, the Christian minister, to restore this soul to its source, to bring it "under the wings of the Church" through holy baptism. The fanatical missionary was aroused in the learned cleric. He translated into German the French work of the scholar of Geneva Charles Bonnet, entitling it *Untersuchung der Beweise für das Christentum*, for, in Lavater's view, this book contained the most cogent proofs of the truth of the Christian faith. Lavater

---

3. *Gemeindeblatt*, 1929, No. 9, p. 437.

published his translation in 1796 with a special appeal to Mendelssohn, urging the latter either to come forward publicly with a response to Bonnet's work and refute his arguments, or to recognize their truth and consequently do what wisdom, candor, and true love demand—as a Socrates would have done in such a case, had he recognized what is logical and true.

Lavater's unanticipated challenge struck Mendelssohn like a thunderbolt in a bright, clear sky. Quite unexpectedly he realized how fearfully great was his error when he believed that there, in the realm of spirit and reason, in modern Christian intellectual circles, the dark shadows of the Middle Ages had been overcome, and that he was regarded therein not as the disenfranchised *ausserordentlicher Schutzjude* with a yellow patch on his shoulder, but as the equal fellow-battler for culture and science. Suddenly he realized that even those with whom he used to carry on intimate conversations on philosophical and literary subjects can in no way comprehend how it is possible that a man of European culture who concerns himself with philosophy and literature should remain faithful out of conviction to such a "superstitious" religion as Judaism. He who strove "to live in hiddenness" was now forced to issue forth, as his ancestors had been in the Middle Ages, into the battle arena, to enter publicly into a religious disputation, and to give Christian society an account of why he remains loyal to the faith of his fathers and refuses to convert to Christianity. He, the tenderly, delicately feeling man, was arrogantly summoned to disclose his most private experiences to the whole world.

Mendelssohn was stunned by this but not terrified. Courageously he took up the challenge to battle, and in this battle showed most clearly that the author of *Phaedon* was not only a brilliant German writer but also a significant personality of extraordinary moral power.

Proudly Mendelssohn declares in his reply to Lavater[4] that he will remain loyal to the faith of his fathers to his last breath because he is firmly persuaded of the truth and unassailability of its foundations.[5] "To be sure," he admits, "I will not deny

4. Mendelssohn first had to submit a petition to the consistory for permission to publish his reply to Lavater, for he would have to touch on religious questions without the proper censorship on the part of the religious authorities. The consistory granted his petition, noting that it relied "on his tact and understanding."

5. "I do not understand," Mendelssohn adds in this connection, "what could keep me chained to a religion so overly strict by all appearances and so commonly despised, were I not convinced in my heart of its truth."

that I see in my religion extraneous later additions which unfortunately obscure its glory." But—Mendelssohn addresses
Christian intellectual society, the *Aufklärer* of his generation—
who of those who wishes to hold faithfully to the truth is in
a position to boast that *his* religion is free of extraneous human
additions? We are all familiar with the poisoned breath of
hypocrisy and superstition. For my part, however, I take pride
in the consciousness that my religion is distinguished from
others by the fact that it relies not on assumptions that are
inconsistent with reason and logical thought. The Jewish religion, Mendelssohn adds sarcastically, has the further virtue
that it does not seek to make proselytes, does not set itself any
missionary goal, does not dispatch its emissaries to India and
Greenland to "capture human souls" there. And if a Confucius
or a Solon were to live in my generation, I could love him on
the basis of my religion and appreciate the great man in him
without at all conceiving the wild idea that I must absolutely
persuade him to adopt my religion.[6]

Lavater was greatly moved by Mendelssohn's masterly and
calmly restrained reply, and publicly declared that he regret-
ted the fact that he had caused distress to the "noblest man" of
his generation. However, the controversy did not end with
this; others promptly became involved in it. The controversy
continued for all of two years and, as one of the participants
in it asserts, disturbed many spirits in German literary circles
far more even than the Seven Years War. Charles Bonnet himself, the author of the work through which Lavater hoped to
persuade Mendelssohn of the truth of the Christian dogmas,
came forth, as did many others.[7] Among those who attacked
Mendelssohn, particular notoriety was attained, through his
crude attacks and insults, by the jurist Johann Balthasar
Kölbele.

Some accused Mendelssohn of clinging to the Jewish faith
not out of conviction but out of purely material motives, because he derived a livelihood from Jewish men of wealth. Others again argued that he was not at all capable of considering
the question of Judaism and Christianity objectively, since he

6. *Gesammelte Schriften*, 1844, III, 44.
7. In his letter to Avigdor Levi of Glogau, Mendelssohn writes (March 1770): "After
I began to speak and reply to the words of that impetuous man, all the people of that
religion and its supporters set upon me from all around. One came in his wrath, and
another with soft, kind, smooth words; one was angry, another mocking. For this is
their way, and in any case they harassed me with their words and their dreams"
(*Gesammelte Schriften*, 1929, Vol. XVI, p. 139).

was not free of "prejudices" in regard to his faith. Not to be free of "prejudices"—this, naturally, was considered the greatest defect among the rationalists of that generation. Mendelssohn, himself a rationalist who, since his very earliest years, had been an ardent admirer of Maimonides' *Guide for the Perplexed*, was not greatly moved by this accusation and gave the following pregnant reply to it: "If I really have 'prejudices' in regard to my faith, I am not the authority to determine this, as little as I can determine whether my breath has a bad odor." Mendelssohn, as we shall see further, was not endowed with a particularly keen historical sense. Nevertheless, he felt intuitively and unconsciously that his "Jewishness," and Judaism in general, are what Jehudah Halevi had proclaimed in such remarkable fashion in his *Kuzari*—not merely a religious community, but also a psychologically unique folk-individuality with an enormously rich social-historical, spiritual-cultural heritage.[8] Mendelssohn felt deeply but, as a child of his generation, was not, as we shall see further, in a position to explain it properly:—He is a Jew because he is such and not something else. The words he addresses to Charles Bonnet are moving: "Love for the religion of our fathers is stronger than death and misery."

However, it was not only from Christian Kölbeles that Mendelssohn had to suffer but also from the "Kölbeles of our own people," as he puts it in one of his letters. The strictly orthodox Jews were delighted at the annoyances that the "heretic of Dessau" who writes German books had to endure from the gentiles with whom he had associated all his years. The Berlin "city fathers," the *parnassim* and rich men, for their part, always reminded Mendelssohn that he must not anger the "gentiles," that—God forbid—much animosity and harm for the Jewish community may result from this controversy.

Characteristic in this respect is the letter Mendelssohn wrote on November 16, 1770, to a relative of his, Elkan Herz:

You ask me why I entered into the dispute. I only wish that I had entered into it more. But, praise God, I have no regrets about it. I pay no attention to scribblings that are issued against me. Whoever has any sense at all in his head knows that they are words without reason. If I once more obtained such an opportunity, I would again do what I have done now. Some would have recommended remaining silent in the face of all this. I do not believe so. When I consider what one

8. See our *History*, Vol. I.

is obliged to do to sanctify God's name, then I do not at all understand how some of our people always cry that, for God's sake, I should write no more about this. I did not—God knows—willingly desist from the dispute. I nullified my will before the will of others. Had I had my own way, I should have given a quite different reply.[9]

This "quite different reply" Mendelssohn had no desire whatever completely to silence. He did, indeed, have great respect for the founder of Christianity and stressed the moral power of his personality, but his attitude toward Christianity itself was quite different—and this not as a Jew, but as a rationalist. We have noted[10] that the Jewish rationalists from Maimonides to Mendelssohn were all extremely hostile to the fundamental dogmas of the Christian religion because these dogmas are difficult to explain through sober common sense.[11] Not having the opportunity to state his position on this question publicly in an essay written for the German public, Mendelssohn decided to do so in a special work which he very probably wrote in Hebrew. Of this we are informed by his letter of November 15, 1771, to his friend and cousin Elkan Hertz:

You request, in your last letter, my manuscript against the religion of the Christians. But I must tell you, first of all, that it is not now possible for it to be read by anyone else, since everything in it is still so disorderly and diffuse. Secondly, I must also tell you that I firmly intend never to let it out of my hands and certainly not to send it out abroad. If God restores my health to me, I shall see what is to be made of it.[12]

The fact that Mendelssohn was not in good health, as he here indicates, was also a direct consequence of the two-year Lavater controversy. Mendelssohn did, indeed, triumph in this battle, but he paid dearly for his victory. We have noted that he was not at all a fighter by nature. Given the weakness of his sickly body, he required a calm, strictly regulated mode of life. The Lavater affair, however, demanded of him enormous intel-

9. Mendelssohn Jubilee Edition, 1929, Vol. XVI, p. 148.
10. See our *History*, Vol. II, p. 109, Note 24.
11. Spinoza also underscores in his letter to his friend Henry Oldenburg that "the Christians argue only on the basis of miracles, i.e., ignorance, which is the source of all hatred and baseness" (we quote according to the Russian translation, 1932, p. 215).
12. Jubilee Edition, Vol. XVI, p. 153. We do not know whether this manuscript is preserved in Mendelssohn's archives and whether it will be published in the complete Jubilee Edition.

lectual exertion, and his weak nervous system did not hold out. The two-year struggle completely ruined his health. For years afterwards he suffered severe pains. Reading and writing required the most extreme exertion, and he would frequently suffer from sharp attacks of dizziness.

In May, 1779, he complained that it was now already more than eight years since his powers had been greatly weakened and that he could no longer come and go or work as he had formerly.[13] Also in the introduction to his *Morgenstunden*, which appeared in the last year of his life, Mendelssohn notes: "For some twelve to fifteen years now I have found myself in the condition of not being able to expand my knowledge. Some kind of nervous weakness from which I have been suffering since that time does not permit me any intellectual exertion." Thus in the course of the last fifteen years of his life Mendelssohn's power of creativity was significantly diminished. He decided to devote the capacities that remained to him after the Lavater affair no longer, as before, to German culture, but to the culture and needs of his brethren. Indeed, only as a result of his activity in the last fifteen years of his life, did he become the recognized standard-bearer of the Enlightenment in German Jewry, and only because of this was the "Mendelssohn legend" to which we referred previously created. For the fact is that what Mendelssohn produced in the field of Jewish culture and knowledge before the 1770's has relatively slight value.

Most important was the interesting attempt in 1750 made by the still very young Mendelssohn to establish, together with his friend Tobias Baum, a Hebrew weekly called *Kohelet Musar*, for the purpose of arousing among the Jewish youth love for the Hebrew language and interest in elegant style. *Kohelet Musar* is written in purely Biblical language with a great deal of rhetorical ornamentation, and Talmudic expressions are very rarely encountered in it.[14] The young authors[15] address their readers with the challenge to devote more attention to the beauties of nature, which produce so much sincere joy for man,

13. "It is now eight years and more that I am greatly weakened in strength and can no longer go out and come in as of old" (Jubilee Edition, Vol. XVI, p. 253).
14. *Kohelet Musar* is extremely rare. We have used a handwritten copy of the copy in the Strashun Library in Vilna. In modern times (1928) M. Adelstein reprinted *Kohelet Musar* in a photographic copy in the *Jubelschrift* of the Budapest Rabbinical Seminary.
15. The most important segment of the articles in *Kohelet Musar* were composed by Mendelssohn. Three of these articles, which appeared in the first number, are reprinted in *Ha-Meassef*, 1785.

and deplore the fact that Jews take so little trouble to learn the splendid, incomparable national language.[16]

Aside from original articles, the first number also published a fragment of Edward Young's *Night Thoughts* in Hebrew translation.

This first Hebrew journal, however, did not enjoy long life; no more than two numbers appeared. Mendelssohn's first biographer Isaac Euchel (and after him G. Mendelssohn and M. Kayserling) assert that responsible for its demise were the "fanatics" who were greatly displeased with the style and tone of *Kohelet Musar*.[17] The very fact that *Kohelet Musar* was a new phenomenon "that our fathers had not thought of" was highly suspect. Apparently the leading figures of the community forbade the young and then unknown *yeshivah*-student of Dessau to continue issuing the journal, and Mendelssohn, who was not a fighter by nature, humbly obeyed the edict.

After this attempt Mendelssohn abandoned Hebrew literature for many years. He did, indeed, write a commentary to Maimonides' *Millot Ha-Higgayon,* but he did not think of publishing it, and gave the manuscript away to a certain emissary from Jerusalem, Samson Klier, who published the commentary (in 1761) under his own name. Only in 1769, when his name already resounded throughout the European world as the author of *Phaedon,* did he also provide the Jewish reader with a work—a commentary on Kohelet, or the Book of Ecclesiastes. In this work, however, it is hard to recognize the "standard-bearer" and "enlightener."

When one reads the introduction, written in the old-fashioned style, about the four "ways" of Bible-exegesis—*Peshat, Derush, Remez,* and *Sod*—with the remark that all of them are "the words of the living God," it is difficult to believe that the author is the European-educated writer who had acquired

---

16. *Kohelet Musar,* Gate Two: "I saw our brethren the children of Israel abandon our holy language, and it greatly angered me; I did not know how this evil happened. What did they see to do this, and what came over them: to cast to the ground the crown of their majesty, the glory of their beauty? Is it not the choicest of languages, and did not the Lord speak in visions to his servants, the prophets, in the Hebrew language, and did not the Lord prepare and form His world in it? . . . And no man strengthens himself to restore the language to its pedestal, according to the original order. And if it be said that the face of the Lord has scattered us to the four winds of heaven in the lands of the nations who do not understand our language, this answer will evaporate as the chaff of the mountains is scattered before the east wind. Lo, our ancestors were sold as manservants and maidservants in the house of Egypt; nevertheless, they did not forget their language, as is said in the *Mechilta,* "*Shemot.*"

17. *Toledot Ha-Rambeman,* 1789, p. 13.

a great reputation for himself in German literature with his critical aesthetic works. The commentary is written in a strictly conservative spirit, and it is interesting that one of the harbingers and pioneers of the Haskalah movement, a contemporary of Mendelssohn's, found it necessary to write, in opposition to it, a new commentary on the renowned pessimistic book of the Bible. The polemic character of this commentary is detectible in its very title *Tochaḥat Megullah* (A Reproach Laid Bare).[18] Its author is Mordecai Gumpel ben Jehudah Leib Schnaber, in his time a very well known doctor, who used to sign his scientific works in European languages with the name Marcus Georg Levisohn, from his father's name Leib. This half-forgotten but interesting figure certainly deserves to have his name noted in the history of Jewish literature and enlightenment.

Mordecai Gumpel Schnaber was born in Berlin into a prominent family. The year of his birth is unknown. It can only be conjectured that he was approximately the same age as Mendelssohn. Schnaber studied the Talmud and its commentaries with Mendelssohn's teacher Rabbi David Fränkel.[19] As was the case with the author of *Phaedon*, so also Schnaber's first guide in the realm of science was Maimonides' *Guide for the Perplexed*. He assiduously studied philosophy, the natural sciences, and especially medicine. To complete his training as a physician he went in the 1760's to London where he worked with the well known surgeon John Gunther.[20] In the years that Schnaber spent in London he published several medical works in English (the best known of them is *An Essay on the Blood*) and also an essay on religion.[21] Schnaber acquired such an outstanding reputation in the medical world that the Swedish king Gustav II invited him to Uppsala where he occupied a chair at the university. At the command of the king, his medical works were translated from English into Swedish. Schnaber, however, spent only several years in Sweden. In 1781 he returned to Germany, settled as a practicing physician in Hamburg, and there lived out his life. He died in 1797.

Despite his intensive medical practice and his scientific work in medicine, Schnaber found time to occupy himself with en-

18. Mendelssohn is not mentioned by name in this work but as "the sage of Berlin."
19. See *Tochaḥat Megullah*, folio 2a.
20. See *ibid.*, folio 3b.
21. See *Yesod Torah*, p. 3: "In my book *Ruaḥ Ha-Dat* (The Spirit of Religion) which I composed in English."

lightening tasks among his brethren. While still residing in
London he projected a rather large work in Hebrew on scientific matters and religious philosophy.[22] The first part of this
work appeared in London in 1771 under the title *Maamar Ha-
Torah Veha-Ḥochmah*. Here is given, in popular form, general
information about mathematics, astronomy, and physics. Especially interesting is the preface to the *Maamar*. Basing himself
on Maimonides (*Guide for the Perplexed*, Part III, Chapter 41),
Schnaber insists that the explanations for the commandments
of the Torah, the indications how each particular precept is to
be fulfilled, were all given by Moses orally in order that the
sages of later generations might have the opportunity to make
their own improvements on them, to create "fences" or to
annul them entirely, according to the demands of the time and
the prevalent conditions. Had it not been so, had the Oral
Torah from the beginning been firmly established and reduced
to writing, Schnaber notes, everything would have been rigidified and the sages of later generations would be bound at every
step and would not have been able to make any correction
whatever, for the common people would have wanted to take
account only of the firmly established written word. Now, however, the people are obliged to follow their spiritual leaders, to
whom the right has been given to interpret, according to the
thirteen hermeneutical principles, all the rules and laws of the
Torah, taking into consideration the requirements of the time.[23]

The same point of view is expressed by Schnaber in the
second part of his work which he published many years later[24]
as a commentary to Maimonides' "Thirteen Principles of
Faith." All of Jewish dogmatics, all the items of faith and
principles of the Jewish religion, are condensed by Schnaber
into one basic principle: acknowledgement of the existence of
God, of a single Creator. Only this commandment, he asserts
from his rationalist point of view, is the firm foundation of the
Torah, while all the other commandments may be altered in

22. At that time he also composed a work *Sefer Refuot* which remained in manuscript
(see *Tochahat Megullah*, folio 12b).

23. It is also worth underscoring this point: Like the majority of the first *maskilim*,
Schnaber deplores the fact that, because of the bad system of education, only rarely
are any of the Jewish youth "familiar with the Hebrew language"; the language of the
Bible is forgotten and they speak in a "tongue of stammerers." Thereby we are
barbarized and have become foolish, and with mockery and laughter all the peoples
say of us: "What a foolish and petty nation this is."

24. In Hamburg in 1792 under the title *Yesod Torah*. This work was written much
earlier (see *Tochahat Megullah*, folio 9b).

time. This is because the basic principle about the sole Creator is a universal truth that is eternally valid. Other commandments, however, belong to the realm of *belief*, and matters of faith change with the time, so that "it happens that we believe today in things in which we did not believe yesterday and it may be that we will again cease to believe tomorrow."[25]

In complete opposition to Mendelssohn, Schnaber is firmly convinced that man is capable of exploring the truth only with the aid of his senses, and that thanks to them he obtains his conceptions. The senses provide the essential raw material which man's reason utilizes for its conclusions and logical ideas.[26]

The following point is also characteristic. Mendelssohn, as we previously noted, remained faithful all his life to the Leibnizian-Wolffian philosophy.[27] To be sure, he regarded the *alles zermalmenden* Kant with the greatest respect, but Kant's *Critique of Pure Reason*, which appeared in 1781, he did not—as he himself candidly admits—understand at all.[28] Schnaber, however, for his part, deems it necessary to familiarize his readers with Kant's fundamental idea that time (and space also) is neither an objective, existing reality, nor an abstract concept, but the basic condition according to which man's reason is able to rework synthetically, into ideas and concepts, the material which it obtains from the senses.[29] Indeed, Schnaber also sets

25. *Yesod Torah*, 2: "In my view there is an essential difference between this principle of the existence of God and all the other commandments . . . for all the rest of the commandments may be changed in time, being only a matter of faith. But this principle cannot be changed even for an hour, being the truth." *Ibid.*, 13: "For a matter of truth does not fall under the rule of time and is not changed, and what is true in it now will be true forever . . . The existence of the Creator Blessed be He is true . . . But from the word faith . . . it may be that the faith is in matters that will change and its subject will fall under time, and we shall sometimes believe something today that men did not believe yesterday and we shall not believe tomorrow . . ."

26. *Ibid.*, 11: "For we have no other means of knowing the truth save the combined perception of the senses, because the basis of the judgment of reason made when the soul is still in the body is the information obtained through the senses." *Ibid.*, 91: "For, following the view of the sage Plato that abstract ideas inhere in the human soul, one cannot deny that man's knowledge in this existence does not come save through the grasp of the senses."

27. Mendelssohn himself notes in his *Morgenstunden*, which he composed in the last year of his life, that because of his long-standing nervous ailment, he is not fit to occupy himself with philosophy. "For me," he adds, "this science [philosophy] therefore now stands at about the same point it was around the year 1775."

28. See his letter to Elise Reimarus: "For my part, I must admit that I do not understand him [the author of the *Critique of Pure Reason*]" (*Gesammelte Schriften*, Vol. V, p. 706).

29. *Yesod Ha-Torah*, Chapter Nine; *ibid.*, 43: "The sages of our time explain that time in itself is not anything, but only a value that is sensed and perceived consecutively by the percipients, that is to say, a form which the human soul fashions."

forth this basic condition as a ground for his conclusion that divinity is beyond any association with the notion of time. Basing himself on Kant's philosophical assumptions, Schnaber also endeavors to explain to his readers that man, with the help of his senses, obtains merely phenomena but not "the essence of each thing" *(das Ding an sich).*[30]

As we have observed, Schnaber was not satisified with Mendelssohn's commentary to the Book of Ecclesiastes and wrote his own, in which the influence of Kant's critical philosophy is discernible in places. Schnaber's polemical work, in fact, is the only response that Mendelssohn's commentary evoked in Hebrew literature. The Lavater controversy, which so catastrophically affected Mendelssohn's health, is also of the greatest significance for his subsequent literary activity. After this controversy he came to the conclusion that henceforth he would no longer devote his weakened powers to German literature but to the enlightenment, and the fulfillment of the cultural needs, of his brethren.[31]

Just at the beginning of the 1770's the drive for enlightenment and education became significantly more marked in the wealthy Jewish circles of Berlin, and the voice of the radically-minded youth became ever bolder. Mendelssohn also became more audacious, and this is discernible in the position he took on the question of burying the corpses of Jews on the day of death which arose in 1772 as a result of the edict issued by the duke of Mecklenburg-Schwerin that year forbidding the burial of a body before the third day after death.[32] The Jewish communities in the duchy saw in this a grievously oppressive decree, for it was contrary to the Jewish custom of burying the dead as quickly as possible. They therefore applied to Mendelssohn, requesting him to write a petition in their name to the government for nullification of the decree, so that Jews should not be compelled to violate the tradition of their fathers.

Mendelssohn, however, declined to act as their intermediary simply because he did not see any "oppression" in the government edict. He even attempted to prove with numerous quotations from the earlier rabbinic codifiers and the sages of the Talmud that not to inter the dead on the day of death is by no means inconsistent with the tradition of the fathers. At this point the zealous Rabbi Jacob Emden[33] came forth and entered

---

30. *Tochaḥat Megullah,* folios 2b, 11a.
31. Interesting in this respect is Mendelssohn's letter of June 29, 1779, to Hennings (printed in M. Kayserling, *Moses Mendelssohn,* 1862, p. 552).
32. For the text of the duke's orders, see *Ha-Meassef,* 5545, p. 155.
33. See our *History,* Vol. VI, pp. 205ff.

into a long dispute with Mendelssohn regarding this question, and the author of *Phaedon* manifested great skill in the unique responsum-style.[34] Emden, in his irascible fashion, demanded that Mendelssohn prevail upon the officials to annul the bitter "decree," so that "God's people should not be compelled to imitate the customs of the nations of the world." Mendelssohn, however, shows in his calm and sedate reply that in this question one must, above all, take account of the competent view of the physicians.

Mendelssohn understood very well that one could not convince the opposite side, those who remained with both feet in the old medieval world view, through disputations and debates. He, the son of the enlightenment era, saw only one remedy for this—education, raising the young generation not in the old-fashioned way, but in the modern European spirit. Through his initiative the first Jewish model school *"Ḥinnuch Nearim"* (*Jüdische Freyschule*) was founded in 1778. Here not only Talmud and the Bible, but German, French, and general secular subjects were studied. Mendelssohn also composed, together with David Friedländer, a special textbook for the school.[35]

In the same year Mendelssohn also began that literary enterprise which was of the greatest cultural-historical significance for German Jewry—his German translation of the Pentateuch. In a sample bearing the title *Alim Li-Terufah* (published in 1778), he declares:

When God gave me sons and the time came to teach them Torah and to familiarize them with God's living word, as is written in Scripture, I began, for the sake of my dear children, to translate the five books of the Torah into the pure German language, as it is spoken at the present time . . . God brought it about that I should become acquainted with Rabbi Solomon of Dubno, and I invited him to teach my only remaining son[36] grammar for an hour each day. And when Rabbi Solomon learned of my Torah translation, he was very pleased with it and begged me to permit him to publish it, in order to profit the young people in schools. I agreed to do so.[37]

Mendelssohn repeats this in virtually the same terms in a private letter, dated May 25, 1779, to Avigdor Levi of Glogau.[38]

---

34. This responsum-letter was published by Mendelssohn in *Ha-Meassef*, II, p. 155, and reprinted in *Gesammelte Schriften*, 1929, Vol. XVI, pp. 154–168.

35. See *Gemeindeblatt*, 1929, No. 9, pp. 432, 436.

36. His second son died at that time.

37. *Or La-Netivah*, XXVIII (we quote according to the Vilna edition, 1849).

38. *Gesammelte Schriften*, Jubilee Edition, 1929, Vol. XVI, p. 162.

However, it is beyond doubt that the cautious author does not here tell the whole truth. He expresses more clearly and definitely what he intended with his translation in another letter written in the same year but addressed to a Christian friend, August von Hennings:

After much reflection, I have come to the conclusion that with the powers that remain to me I can benefit my own children and also a significant part of my nation by giving them a good Bible translation with the proper commentary. *This will be the first step to enlightenment, from which my nation is, unfortunately, still so far removed that one begins at times literally to despair of the future of the Jewish people.*[39]

It is beyond doubt that Mendelssohn set himself a double goal with this literary undertaking: (1) to facilitate the acquisition, on the part of the German Jews, of the literary German language by means of his Bible translation, which was to be printed in Hebrew letters; and (2) through his precise translation and the clear, systematic *Biur* or commentary, to give the rising generation the opportunity to become familiar with the classic poetic beauties of the Biblical text and with the grammatical pecularities of the Hebrew language, to awaken in the Jewish youth the desire to turn away from tortuous *pilpul* and arid scholasticism and to return to the Bible and the Biblical style. Indeed, for this reason, at the same time that Mendelssohn was translating the Pentateuch, he was also deeply engrossed in translating the Book of Psalms. We observed previously how powerfully these prayers preserved from remote antiquity worked on Mendelssohn's religious sentiments. However, he also esteemed them highly as prime examples of lyric poetry and, in his letters to various friends[40] stresses, indeed, that his translation of the Psalms is intended primarily to accustom the reader to perceive in the prayers of the Psalms, above all, a model of the classical "lyrical poetry of the Hebrews . . . without seeing the prophetic and mystical elements that Christian as well as Jewish interpreters find in the Psalms only because they have sought them there, and sought them only because they were neither philosophers nor connoisseurs of art."

Mendelssohn had another purpose in his translation of the Bible: to remove from Jewish life "the Judeo-German way of speaking," i.e., the Yiddish dialect, and to push out from the

---

39. Kayserling, *Moses Mendelssohn*, 1862, p. 522.
40. See, for example, his letter to Michaelis (*Gesammelte Schriften*, 1844, Vol. V, pp. 505–506).

school and family the Old-Yiddish Bible translations, e.g., that of Yekutiel Blitz[41] which, in Mendelssohn's view, was written "in a corrupt and distorted language that will disgust the soul of any reader who knows how to speak cleanly and correctly." In Mendelssohn's eyes the Yiddish "jargon" was only a mechanical mixture of Hebrew and German. "I am afraid," he writes in August, 1772 to his friend Ernest Ferdinand Klein,[42] "that this jargon has contributed not a little to the moral barbarization of the common man *(hat nicht wenig zur Unsittlichkeit des gemeines Mannes beigetragen)* and I hope the fact that, in recent times, my brethren have begun to employ pure German will have a good effect." "But let there be no mixing of language!"—with this Mendelssohn concludes his letter.

This goal was to be not insignificantly advanced by his classic German translation of the Pentateuch, which he decided to print in Hebrew letters. To effectuate the second of the above-mentioned purposes—to arouse in the Jewish youth interest in the Hebrew language and its grammar—Mendelssohn deemed it necessary to draw into this work the previously mentioned grammarian and philologist, Solomon Dubno.

This man, whom Mendelssohn considered the most suitable and essential person to assist him in his important literary undertaking, deserves to be better known. Solomon ben Joel Dubno was born in the old Volhynian city of Dubno on October 12, 1738. Interest in Biblical exegesis and everything pertaining to Biblical philology was awakened in the young Dubno by the author of *Mirkevet Ha-Mishneh*, Solomon ben Moses Chelm (1717–1781). As a token of gratitude to his beloved teacher, Dubno published (in 1766), with important notes and a long poem of praise preceding it, Chelm's study on the pointing and musical cantillation of the Biblical text, *Shaarei Ne'imah*. To that period also apparently belongs his first independent work, a collection of Hebrew poems, written in Biblical style and entitled *Yuval Ve-Na'aman*.[43]

Dubno also wrote a certain number of didactic and satirical poems. In them, however, the spark of the true poet is not

41. On Blitz's translation of the Bible, see our *History*, Vol. VII, pp. 137ff.
42. *Gesammelte Schriften*, 1844, Vol. V, pp. 505–506.
43. In one of his letters to Wolf Heidenheim, Dubno writes about this work: "It is a little composition written completely in the rhetorical style of the Bible; I wrote it in my youth when I was still young and vigorous." The bibliographers Fuerst and Zeitlin even note that this collection was published by Dubno in the 1770's. S. Stanislavsky, however, has shown that this report is not correct and *Yuval Ve-Na'aman* remained in manuscript (see *Voskhod*, 1893, X–XI, p. 246).

discernible.[44] His great merit in neo-Hebrew poetry consists in the fact that he reprinted Moses Ḥayyim Luzzatto's allegorical drama *La-Yesharim Tehillah*, which until that time remained completely unknown to the general reading public because the poet had published it in 1743 in only fifty copies. Dubno first became familar with the work during the years 1767–1772, which he spent in Amsterdam, where he worked in the local libraries. Charmed by Luzzatto's masterpiece, he decided to reprint it, so that, as he notes in the introduction, it might arouse in Jewish youth love for the Biblical tongue, and so that they might become convinced, from the magnificent beauties of this work, that the holy language is still vivid and fresh and filled with the power of youth.[45]

When Dubno later moved from Amsterdam to Berlin he became friendly with Mendelssohn. He was also a frequent visitor in Mendelssohn's home since, for a certain period, he gave the latter's son instruction in Hebrew. Undoubtedly Dubno so strongly urged that Mendelssohn's translation of the Pentateuch be published as quickly as possible because he was in full agreement with the translator in regard to the "Judeo-German dialect." He, too, hoped that the translation would succeed in displacing the "despised jargon."

In this connection one must not forget that philology, the discipline that explores language and the word as the creator and bearer of human thought, was at that time still in its infancy. Wilhelm von Humboldt, the future great scholar who some decades later was to express the idea[46] that no people can enliven and fertilize an alien tongue with its own spirit unless it reworks this language into a completely different one, was then still a ten-year-old child growing up in a knightly castle. As a learned philological purist of the old school, Dubno especially insisted that "every man, no matter what language he may employ, is obliged to protect it from distortion and may not permit himself anything that is inconsistent with the

44. Franz Delitzsch, however, speaks in his well-known work (*Zur Geschichte der jüdischen Poesie*, p. 118) of Dubno's poems with a certain enthusiasm: "His poems are really Hebrew in expression, Biblical in imagery, medieval in rhyme and verse form, and also mainly Jewish in subject matter."

45. *La-Yesharim Tehillah* actually had a great influence on neo-Hebrew poetry, and numerous works were produced using it as a model.

46. In his *Über die Verschiedenheit des menschlichen Sprachbaues*, p. 203.

laws of grammar."[47] He regarded Judeo-German not as a dialect but as a German language that Jews had corrupted and distorted.

Solomon Dubno gladly accepted Mendelssohn's proposal that he write for his edition of the Pentateuchal text a commentary *(Biur)*, and also supply it with a special *tikkun soferim* (scribal emendation). Mendelssohn himself testifies that "Dubno completed his work with extraordinary skill . . . and did everything possible in order that a *davar metukan*, a perfect thing, should leave his hands."[48]

In 1778, as we have noted, there appeared a prospectus and sample of Mendelssohn's translation of the Pentateuch in Amsterdam under the title *Alim Li-Terufah*. In it are printed fragments of the German translation and of the *Biur*, with a lengthy introduction by Solomon Dubno setting forth the character and purposes of the entire edition.

Alim Li-Terufah made a very great impression in the intellectual circles. The apostate Christian Gottlieb Mayer even reprinted the entire work in German (1780) under the title *Probe einer jüdisch-deutschen Übersetzung der fünf Bücher Moses*. The attitude of the orthodox elements, however, was quite different. Despite the fact that the rabbis of Berlin gave their *haskamot* or approbations to Mendelssohn's translation,[49] the orthodox

47. See Dubno's *haskamah* to the exemplary edition of the *Maḥzor* for Shavuot (1805) published with explanations and a German translation by the distinguished grammarian Wolf Heidenheim: "And he who reads any language ought to guard himself against the corrupted words in that language, and he ought to be as precise in that language as he is in the holy tongue."

48. *Or La-Netivah*, XXX.

49. Mendelssohn published the *haskamot* when the translation of the Book of Exodus appeared. We have had occasion to see the autographs of these *haskamot* because they were contained, along with many of Dubno's manuscripts, in Samuel Joseph Fuenn's archives, and from there passed to the historian S. Ginsburg who lived in Leningrad until recently. It is interesting that the Berlin rabbis, Tzevi Hirsch Levin and his son Saul Berlin, of whom we shall speak later, also consider it necessary to deplore, in their *haskamot* to the work, the fact that the German Jews speak a corrupted language and cannot speak "in the language of the country." Hirsch Levin writes: "And we, the children of the people of Israel, for whom the language of each country is not fluent on our tongues as it is properly written, and especially the residents of these lands, all of whom are "Germans" with the name of "Jew" . . . we speak in laughable language . . . and there is not among us any understanding person and one who knows precisely and properly how to exposit his speech in a foreign tongue . . ." His son Saul Berlin complains: "When the shame of Israel is revealed among the nations, who mock us upon seeing teachers of the Bible for whom it is not enough that the book of the law of God is too deep and concealed for them, but, even more, their speech in the language of the country is vile."

rabbis viewed the edition with great suspicion. Leading the opponents who attacked Mendelssohn's translation and the *Biur* were three rabbinic figures: Ezekiel Landau of Prague; the rabbi of Hamburg, Raphael Kohen (Gabriel Riesser's grandfather); and Tzevi Hirsch Jacob Harif of Fürth, of whom Solomon Maimon speaks so enthusiastically in his *Autobiography*.

These rabbis perceived in Mendelssohn's edition something of a "desecration of a holy thing." They believed that "the German translation of the Pentateuch by Moses of Dessau" was not so much intended to provide the possibility of understanding the sacred text better and more easily, as mainly to utilize the Torah of Moses so that the young should become acquainted with the German language all the more quickly, and, through it, familiarize themselves with the culture of the nations of the world; this, in their view, would undoubtedly lead to neglect of, and contempt for, the Torah.[50] The fanatical Raphael Kohen even wished to attack Moses of Dessau's undertaking with the weapon of the ban, or excommunication. Mendelssohn, however, managed through his friends in Hamburg to bring it about that the king of Denmark, under whose sovereignty Hamburg then was, signed up as a subscriber to his edition. Naturally, the rabbi could no longer dare ban a work which the king himself favored with his subscription.

Soon, however, a controversy broke out between the two major participants in the edition itself. As may be gathered from Dubno's letter to Mendelssohn of September 22, 1780,[51] already in 1780 a certain tension existed between them. Mendelssohn, who appreciated Dubno's collaboration in the enterprise, was prepared to make all possible financial concessions and to renounce all the profit that the edition might bring in Dubno's favor.[52] Material benefit, however, could not alter Dubno's decision; he was generally extremely scrupulous in

50. This is expressed most clearly by the rabbi of Prague Ezekiel Landau (*Ha-Meassef*, 1786, p. 143). See also Landau's *Tziyyun Le-Nefesh Hayyah* on *Berachot*, folio 28b.

51. The letter is published in Kobak's *Jeschurun*, III, 85–88; reprinted in *Ha-Meassef*, 5544, Letteris' edition, 1862, pp. 120–122, 180–182; and also in the Mendelssohn Jubilee Edition, Vol. XVI, pp. 258–261.

52. See D. Friedländer's letter to Joseph ben Elijah Peseles in Vilna: "I personally was present at the legal proceedings (*din Torah*) that Mendelssohn and Solomon Dubno had at the court of the rabbi of Berlin. There it was decided that Dubno was obligated to continue participating in the Pentateuch edition, and that the entire sum collected from the subscribers should be transferred to Dubno's account, aside from a small part owing to Mendelssohn's brother Saul" (*Ha-Karmel*, VII, 36).

money matters, notwithstanding his dire economic situation.[53]
In the spring of 1781 the two partners finally went their separate
ways. "I do not know," Mendelssohn writes, "why Dubno
decided to leave me and return to his native land."[54]

Whether Mendelssohn really did not know the reason for
which Dubno departed is difficult to say. In any case, Dubno
himself speaks of it quite explicitly (to be sure, after Mendelssohn's death) in his letter to his friend, the grammarian Wolf
Heidenheim. "Since I left Berlin," he writes,[55]

I have no dealings with Mendelssohn's heirs. The teacher and master
of my youth, the rabbi of Dubno, Naftali Herz, in traveling through
Berlin, reproached me saying: "Because thou hast joined thyself with
Ahaziah, the Lord hath broken thy words."[56] He reproached me for
working with men whose entire thought is to uproot the Oral Torah.
His words had a great effect on me, and I promised him that I would
remove myself from these people and leave Berlin. Mendelssohn's
translation is, indeed, a highly successful and useful one, and I endeavored to see it published, but some of those who were invited to
participate in this very important edition are extremely suspicious
persons, for they have completely cast off the yoke of the Torah, and
of them it has been said, "Turn away from the tents of these wicked
men . . . lest ye perish through all their sins" (Numbers 16:26).[57]

Leaving Berlin, Dubno nevertheless did not abandon hope
of publishing his commentary *(Biur)* to the Pentateuch.[58] He

53. Characteristic in this respect is Dubno's above-mentioned letter to Mendelssohn.
54. *Or La-Netivah*, XXX: "A change of mood came over him. I do not know what
happened to him that he left me and went back to his land."
55. This letter, written on the eighth of Sivan 1789 in Amsterdam, was first published
in German translation by B. Auerbach in his *Geschichte der israelitischen Gemeinde Halberstadt*, 1866, pp. 179–183. The Hebrew text was printed by A.D. Liebermann in *Asefat
Ḥachamim*, 1878, p. 13.
56. The meaning of this historic phrase (Chronicles II, 20:37) is: As you have become
friends with wicked men, God will turn away from you."
57. *Asefat Ḥachamim*, 1878, 13: "And from the time I removed myself from Berlin I am
no longer on friendly terms with the heirs of Rabbi Moses Mendelssohn . . . My teacher
and master from my youth, the rabbi of Dubno, Naftali Herz, passed through Berlin
and warned me: "Because thou hast joined thyself with Ahaziah, the Lord hath broken
thy works." For I was doing my work with those all whose thought was to uproot the
Oral Torah. His words prevailed upon me and I gave my word that I would separate
from this group and remove myself far from Berlin . . ." After mentioning, with praise,
Mendelssohn's translation, Dubno concludes: "And yet some of the people who were
attached to aid in this honorable work were a breed of suspect persons, for they had
thrown off themselves the yoke of the Torah, and of men such as these it is said in truth
and righteousness: 'Turn away . . .'"
58. In Mendelssohn's edition only Dubno's commentary to the book of Genesis was
published.

set out for Vilna where, under the influence of Elijah Gaon, interest in exploring the language of the Bible and its grammar had been aroused. Dubno was welcomed in extremely friendly fashion in the house of the son-in-law of the rabbi of Vilna, the wealthy philanthropist Joseph ben Elijah Peseles,[59] and the entire circle of the Gaon's disciples and associates in Vilna very warmly received his project of issuing the Pentateuch with his commentary.

Approbations or *haskamot* for this edition were obtained by Dubno not only from Joseph Peseles and the chameleon-like Moses Meisels but also from the great scholars Rabbi Ḥayyim Volozhiner, the founder of the *yeshivah* of Volozhin, and from his brother Rabbi Zelmele, who was endowed with an extraordinary, truly remarkable memory.[60]

To obtain the financial resources required to undertake the projected edition, Dubno set out on a tour of many cities to enlist subscribers. He visited Amsterdam, Hannover, Copenhagen, Prague, and numerous other places. For this tour numerous prominent acquaintances provided him with letters of recommendation,[61] and he managed to gather more than seven hundred subscribers on the journey. Nevertheless, this was too small a number for such a costly edition, and Dubno's *Biur* to the entire Torah remained in manuscript.[62]

On the other hand, Mendelssohn, despite all difficulties, managed to carry his edition through to the end. After Dubno left him, he had to seek out new collaborators for his *Biur*. He himself wrote the *biur*, or commentary, to the Book of Exodus and last two *sidrot* of Deuteronomy, in which he dwells especially on their poetic style. The commentaries to the remaining books were written by three of Mendelssohn's associates of whom we shall speak in later chapters. In the period 1780–1783 Mendelssohn's classic translation of the Pentateuch, supplied

59. On the role that Peseles played in the well-known struggle between the community council of Vilna and Rabbi Samuel ben Avigdor (this *History*, Vol. VI, pp. 219ff), see our work "Milḥemet Ha-Kahal Beha-Rav Ha-Aharon" in *He-Avar*, II (1918). His exchange of correspondence with Friedländer was published by Samuel Joseph Fuenn in *Ha-Karmel*. When *Ha-Meassef* began to appear in Koenigsberg, Peseles subscribed for two copies.

60. About Rabbi Zelmele's phenomenal memory many legends are told. For a discussion of him, see his biography *Toledot Adam*, written by the *maggid* Ezekiel Feivels.

61. We have had occasion to see these letters of recommendation because they also are in the archives of S. Ginsburg. In them it is frequently stressed that "the great grammarian" Solomon Dubno intends to issue the five Books of the Torah with a new commentary but "without the German of Rabbi Moses Dessau."

62. Solomon Dubno died in Amsterdam June 23, 1813. He left an extremely valuable library. The catalogue of its books, *Reshimat Sifrei Rashad*, was printed in 1814.

with a new commentary and an excellent introduction, appeared under the title *Netivot Ha-Shalom*.

The translator's considerable literary talent and fine aesthetic taste are displayed here in all their brilliance. The hand of a true master who understands how to render the incomparable beauties of the Book of Books into another language is discernible in the translation. Mendelssohn takes pains to follow the way of literal interpretation, to render the text verbatim and faithfully. However, he also manages skillfully to weave in at various places the traditional interpretation, enlivened by *derush*, homiletical and customary explanation, and withal not to destroy the general style. It is beyond doubt that, among the numerous translations of the Bible, Mendelssohn's *Netivot Ha-Shalom* occupies a very honored place as a result of its precision, its polished form, and its harmonious simplicity. The extensive Hebrew introduction, bearing the title *Or La-Netivah*, is also a great literary achievement. Here there is no longer any remnant of the mellifluous, highly rhetorical style that is so strongly discernible in Mendelssohn's youthful *Kohelet Musar*. With its clear, measured, and elegantly composed language, *Or La-Netivah* reminds one of the classical style of Maimonides' *Mishneh Torah*.

Hence, it is no wonder that *Netivot Ha-Shalom* evoked such enthusiasm in the progressive circles and was celebrated in prose compositions and in emotive poems of praise. This work was destined to form a significant stage in the cultural history not only of German Jewry but also of the Jews of Eastern Europe.[63] In the course of two or three generations Mendelssohn's translation, along with the *Biur*, was the major, if not the sole, source thanks to which young Jews not only learned to appreciate the poetic beauties of the Biblical text and lovingly to explore the Hebrew language and its grammar but, at the same time, also became familiar with the German language and thereby obtained the possibility of approaching European culture.

In his letter to Avigdor Levi of Glogau Mendelssohn wrote on April 22, 1784: "Unfortunately, the customary method of studying the words of the prophets and sacred singers has led us so far away from the correct feeling of beauty and exaltedness that I can barely count on a few people *(ehad be-ir u-shenaim*

---

63. Mendelssohn's Torah translation was especially reprinted for Polish-Russian Jewry in Warsaw in 1836–1838 and later, together with the translation of the whole Bible, in Vilna in 1848–1853.

be-mishpaḥah)."[64] He therefore announces that he intends "also to issue the Prophets and the Hagiographa, if God so decrees and His grace be upon me."[65] But he was not fated to realize this wish. In the last ten years of his life the sickly Mendelssohn had to devote his weakened powers to other literary enterprises, all of which, with one exception, are closely associated with exclusively Jewish interests and problems.

When the Prussian government demanded of the Jewish community that it provide a suitable handbook for familiarizing government officials with the religious laws and customs of Judaism the rabbi of Berlin requested Mendelssohn to write the work. To this end Mendelssohn composed his *Rituellgesetze der Juden* (1778), a kind of abbreviated *Shulḥan Aruch* in German. In consequence of the great reputation Mendelssohn had obtained in the Christian world as a writer and thinker, various Jewish communities (and not infrequently also private persons) applied to him in time of difficulty, requesting that he serve as their intercessor. And, indeed, Mendelssohn quite frequently managed to help Jewish communities avoid grievous oppressions, such as expulsions and blood libels.

Typical in this respect is the letter[66] the community of Dresden dispatched to him in September 1777, when a decree of expulsion hung over it. In this letter special emphasis is placed on Mendelssohn's renown, thanks to which the nations of the world can no longer mock Jews and declare arrogantly that they are wild, ignorant people with a crude, distorted, and unclear language. Now they see, after all, that we are not inferior to them, and that among us there are men who stand on the highest levels of European culture. ("In thee we glory, for thou hast removed from us the shame of many nations, who always reproached us, saying: Shame on you, mockery on you, O people of incomprehensible language, dumb sheep, uncouth speakers without understanding! And now it is made known to the peoples before our eyes that Israel is not forsaken, that it is not inferior to their masses.")[67]

---

64. Jubilee Edition, 1929, Vol. XVI, p. 292.
65. *Ibid.*, 296.
66. Jubilee Edition, 1929, Vol. VI, p. 236.
67. Characteristic also is the introduction with which Wessely's disciple David Wagenhaar begins his letter to Mendelssohn: " 'Guide of the perplexed' *(Moreh Nevuchim)* in the 'duties of hearts' *(Ḥovot Ha-Levavot)* and 'stone of help' (Ibn Ezra) and 'enlightener of eyes' *(Me'or Einayim),* and 'source of life' *(Mekor Ḥayyim)* is he to thousands and tens of thousands . . . the prince of God in our midst, the crown of our nation, the intercessor for us, who lightens the yoke of our exile, master of disputation

In 1779 the Jews of Alsace addressed Mendelssohn with the request that, on the basis of materials which they were sending him, he compose a memoir, i.e., a thoroughly worked-out petition, which they wished to submit to the French National Assembly concerning the grant of equal civic rights to the Jews of France. The philosopher apparently felt himself little suited to write such official documents. However, he hit upon the happy idea of drawing to this work his young friend, the capable government official Christian Wilhelm von Dohm. Dohm, who, as a result of his close acquaintance with Mendelssohn, was extremely tolerant toward Jews, agreed to the latter's proposal. However, he considerably deepened the task put to him and, out of a special petition to the French National Assembly, grew an independent work, *Über die bürgerliche Verbesserung der Juden*,[68] an interesting cultural monument of the Enlightenment era in which the first attempt is made to consider the Jewish question objectively and systematically from the historical point of view.

Mendelssohn acclaimed Dohm's work with great warmth but found it necessary to protest against two of the theses his friend had set forth: (1) that, because of their civic disabilities, the Jews are at a low moral level; and (2) that, as the government recognizes the Jewish faith, the Jewish religious administration must be given the right to exclude rebellious and disobedient members.[69] Again, at Mendelssohn's suggestion, his friend Dr. Marcus Herz translated into German Menasseh ben Israel's apologetic work *Vindiciae Judaeorum (Die Rettung der Juden)*. To this edition, which appeared in 1782, Mendelssohn wrote an extensive introduction in which he dwells at length on the abovementioned propositions of Dohm. With bitter sarcasm he speaks of the hypocrisy of Christian society, which robs Jews of all human rights, bars to them all paths leading to cultural and useful occupations, and then puts forth the backwardness and barbarization resulting therefrom as a reason for further oppressions. Mendelssohn indignantly writes: "They drive us out and remove us from all arts and sciences and other useful callings and occupations of men, bar to us all roads to beneficial improvement, and then make our lack of

---

and performer of righteousness with all flesh and spirit . . . divine philosopher, understander of incantations and wizard, privy counselor and sage, the choicest of men . . ." (*ibid.,* 206).

68. First published in 1781.

69. *Über die bürgerliche Verbesserung d. Juden,* 1781, 124: "*So wie jede kirkliche Gesellschaft müsste auch die jüdische das Recht der Ausschliessung auf gewisse Zeiten oder immer haben.*"

culture the reason for our further oppression. They tie our hands and reproach us for not using them."[70]

In regard to the second of Dohm's theses, Mendelssohn can in no way understand how one can seriously speak of "ecclesiastical rights, ecclesiastical power and force." How can there be any talk whatever of compulsion where it is a question of "things committed to the heart," of opinions and ideas regarding "eternal truths"?[71] The true divine religion will not permit itself to use force and instruments of punishment in regard to convictions and opinions. Its power and weapon are the living word, the spiritual force of persuasion. And it is regrettable that all peoples to the present day are still in grievous error and believe that religion can rule and prevail only through iron power, that men can be brought to beatitude only through persecutions and oppressions, and that the idea of divine love can be preached and disseminated with the aid of persecution and hatred.[72]

A tremendous impression was made on Christian society by the slogan that Mendelssohn publicly put forth to the effect that the church may not employ any kind of coercion in relation to its members, for in the realm of religious convictions complete freedom must prevail. In the same year (1782), shortly after *Die Rettung der Juden* came off the press, there appeared an anonymous brochure, *Das Forschen nach Licht und Recht*, in which the unknown author notes that Mendelssohn with his slogan undermines the foundations of the Torah of Moses, in which faith rests—according to the author's view—mainly on the coercive power of the state. And as Lavater had done in his time, he puts to Mendelssohn the sarcastic question: "Does this not show that you are now quite close to the Christian faith?"

Mendelssohn promptly replied to the challenge of the anonymous author, and in 1783 his fundamental work *Jerusalem*, with the subtitle *Über religiöse Macht und Judenthum*, appeared. Before we discuss the content of this work, it is necessary, however, to dwell on several points of Mendelssohn's world outlook and his attitude to the enlighteners and rationalists of his age.

At the close of the first chapter we noted that, despite the fact that Mendelssohn could absolutely not agree with many assumptions of *"der Herren Enzyklopädisten,"* he was nevertheless

70. *Gesammelte Schriften*, 1844, Vol. III, p. 183.
71. *Ibid.*, 197.
72. *Ibid.*, 202.

attracted to them as loyal fellowbattlers in the realm of highly important problems of life. He was attracted to the French rationalists and freethinkers of his time because their doctrine shattered the old medieval fortress and led rigorously to the proud proclamation of full human rights, to the exhilarating and promising slogan: Freedom, equality, and fraternity for everything that bears a "human form." This slogan had to ring in the ears of the Jews with their civic disabilities like a harbinger of redemption, for it carried in itself, as a logical consequence, the recognition of human rights also for every Jew as an equal member of the universal human family. Mendelssohn gives thanks to Providence that he has been privileged to arrive, toward the end of his years, at the "happy point of time" when the *"rights of humanity"* (italics Mendelssohn's) are recognized in their "true scope,"[73] when all prejudices are rejected and men endeavor, above all, "to consider men as men."[74]

The newly rising capitalist class fought against the restraints and walls of the old feudal order and endeavored to build a free, liberal, individualistic society. The bourgeois strata struggling for their political and human rights battled against hereditary family distinctions and historical privileges in the name of the individual endowed with full rights—the central pillar of human society. "The human species," Mendelssohn wrote to Hennings, "is not an entity that exists in itself; it consists rather of single persons." And all "single persons" are equal! This rang like a revelation. To be sure, the enlighteners gave quite abstract forms to the "individual," to the concept of "man." The thesis was put forth that human nature is "good and rational from birth." It was crippled and distorted only by the prejudices and mendacious hypocrisies of the priests and representatives of the religious cult.

Completely in the spirit of the French enlighteners, Mendelssohn also declares: "Man seeks after truth, approves the good and the beautiful, wishes everything good and does the best."[75] Fighting for the slogan that all those who bear a "human form" are equal, the rationalists and enlighteners of that age did not wish to take note of the uniqueness and specific forms which his historical past, the cultural-national milieu in which he has grown up, place upon the individual. They were content with stressing the separation and alienation to which religious hatred and fanaticism have given birth. This naive,

73. The first sentence in the preface to *Rettung der Juden.*
74. See his letter to Lessing, *Gesammelte Schriften*, 1844, p. 195.
75. *Morgenstunden*, p. 146 (*Gesammelte Schriften*, Vienna edition, 1838).

anti-historical mixture of quite different phenomena and concepts is expressed most clearly in one of the loveliest and noblest cultural monuments of that era, Lessing's *Nathan der Weise*. Feelingly the wise Nathan addresses the Knight Templar:

> Wir haben beide
> Uns unser Volk nicht auserlesen. Sind
> Wir unser Volk? Was heisst den Volk?
> Sind Christ und Jude eher Christ und Jude,
> Als Mensch? Ach! wenn Ich einen mehr in Euch
> Gefunden hätte, dem es g'nugt, ein Mensch
> Zu heissen!

It is from this that the dissonances and contradictions in Mendelssohn's world outlook derive. He remains firm in defense of religious ritual. He perceives in the observance of the *mitzvot*, in the act of will expressing itself in religious ceremonies, a great educative power, a link that unites the Jewish community. But along with this, he considers it necessary to put forth a rationalist-utilitarian motive: this must be done for the sake of the Jewish people's special mission, which consists in their battle with the *Plagegeister der Vernunft*, the "tormentors of reason," with anthropomorphism and belief in polytheism. Generally, he adds in purely rationalist fashion, customs must have a rational substratum and the text of Holy Writ which has become imcomprehensible "through hypocrisy and priestcraft"[76] must be explained anew and made understandable.

Intuitively Mendelssohn arrives at the conviction that, in matters of faith, the chief role is played not by logical reason and rational theories but by the heart and the sentiments. He acknowledges the necessity even of such ritual precepts as have lost their utility, for he finds that they have not thereby forfeited their significance "as a bond of unity."[77] At the same time, however, he remains a faithful disciple of Maimonides and is under the influence of his own contemporaries—the French enlighteners. In their fashion he always appeals to the "plain, natural, healthy common sense of man" and deplores the fact that "superstition and priestcraft" have "brought sound human common sense into confusion."[78] Hence he seeks

76. See his interesting letter to Homberg (*Gesammelte Schriften*, 1844, Vol. V, p. 669).
77. *Ibid.*
78. *An die Freunde Lessings*, p. 511 (*Sämtliche Werke*, Vienna edition, 1838).

to demonstrate, in the rationalist manner, the utility and reasonable nature of Jewish ritual.

The tradition of the fathers, the Jewish religion with its customs, is precious to him—the rationalist and admirer of Maimonides. And the great miracle occurs: he discovers, in the Torah of Moses and Judaism, the purely rational, the entire world outlook and philosophy of the Wolffian-Leibnizian system. Proudly Mendelssohn declares, at the time of his controversy with Lavater and Bonnet, that in the Jewish religion there are no dogmas that are inconsistent with human reason and understanding.[79] He even concludes that such a freethinker as Spinoza could, with his philosophical system, peacefully remain "an orthodox Jew," and that the Spinozist doctrine is much closer to Judaism "than the orthodox doctrine of the Christians."[80] Mendelssohn discovers in the Torah of Moses the supreme ideal of the enlighteners—the "religion of reason." Especially interesting in this respect is the letter he sent during the Lavater controversy to his relative and friend Elkan Herz on July 22, 1771.

In the second volume of our work (page 110) we mentioned the rationalist of the thirteenth century Nissan bar Moses of Marseilles and noted how he mockingly related that the Christian scholars reproach him in a polemic that "everything your teacher Moses says in his Torah" is also "believed and asserted by the philosopher." "They intend thereby," Nissan bar Moses concludes, "to degrade our Torah. They do not understand that, on the contrary, they thereby exalt it, for religion and reason were both given by one God, not as the Christians in their great folly believe—that the essence and content of every religion consists precisely in having to believe in wild, crude tales which reason must deny." In virtually the same tone Mendelssohn also writes his letter[81] to Elkan Herz, in which he touches upon the polemic attacks of the pamphleteer Kölbele:

Christians in general and especially theologians used to charge people with Deism, for their revealed religion (i.e., the Christian), which transcends and is contrary to reason, was very much afraid of natural

---

79. "*Unsere Vernunft kann ganz gamächlich von den ersten sieben Grundbegriffen der menschlichen Erkenntnis ausgehen und versichert sein, am Ende die Religion auf eben dem Wege anzutreffen. Hier ist kein Kampf zwischen Religion und Vernunft, kein Aufruhr unserer natürlichen Erkenntnis wider die unterdrückende Gewalt des Glaubens*".

80. *An die Fruende Lessings*, p. 504 (*Sämtliche Werke*, Vienna edition, 1838).

81. Jubilee Edition, 1929, Vol. XVI, pp. 150–151.

religion. But blessed be God who has given us a Torah of truth. We have no principles that are opposed to reason or beyond reason. We do not add to natural religion anything other than commandments, precepts, and righteous ordinances—praised be God. The principles and foundations of our religion, however, are based on the pillars of reason and agree with inquiry and true thought from all sides, without any contradiction and controversy whatever. And this is the superiority of our true and divine religion above all other false religions. The Christians will charge all our principles with Deism or naturalism . . . and I will not enter at length into this, for in all such matters words are superfluous. The sons of our people should fairly recognize all this by themselves. For this is our praise and our beauty, and all the books of our sages are filled with it.

Mendelssohn's generation in general had a very limited understanding of historical development. A son of a typically anti-historical era, Mendelssohn himself totally lacked historical perspective, the feeling for historical evolution, and with the candor that is so characteristic of him he laments in a letter to Abbt: "What do I know of history? Whatever so much as has the name of history, political history, intellectual history, never wanted to enter my head."[82]

In this connection it must be remembered that in the generation of the enlighteners the entire historical process of human cultural development was regarded as a sorry mistake, a regrettable turning away on false paths over which the human species had wandered in confusion. Only now—the enlighteners consoled themselves and others—after the fundamental qualities of human nature have been explored, has an end finally been made to all the melancholy errors and confused wanderings. The absolutely correct order has now been discovered and explained through clear human reason, and all prejudices, all injustices, will disappear before the bright rays of eternal reason and eternal justice. It seemed at the time that free, critical thought had thoroughly destroyed the old theological structure. All the foundations of social life, all beliefs and ideas, were investigated anew and their worth calculated. The new forces that appeared in the arena of social life came forth under the banner of positive science. Their slogan was—enlightenment; their highest divinity—reason. Emotional factors were given scant attention. These, it was considered, are only in the substratum and play a rather subordinate role. Absolute reason alone was recognized as the sole ruler and commander. And

---

82. *Gesammelte Schriften*, 1844, Vol. V, p. 342.

everything that wishes to live, to struggle for its further existence, must, first of all, give an account before this supreme sovereign and demonstrate the *rational motives* of its existence.

It should, therefore, occasion no surprise that Mendelssohn, who felt himself firmly bound to traditional Judaism, was nevertheless, under the conditions of that time, not in a position to illuminate historical Judaism scientifically. He perceived in it not a product of a complex historical process, not a living, national world outlook which changes its forms in the course of its organic development, but a congealed phenomenon, firmly established and rigidly delimited for all times. Nevertheless the ideas and assumptions that he expresses in his *Jerusalem* have not lost a certain interest, and this work undoubtedly has considerable cultural-historical value as a monument of that unique, though contradiction-filled, era.

In the first part of his work Mendelssohn dwells on the role of the power of the state and the church, respectively, in human society. He sharply emphasizes the boundaries of their competence and their functions. The state, Mendelssohn notes, demands of its members actions, deeds; religion, however, requires ways of thinking and inward convictions. It is obvious, he concludes, that in matters "committed to the heart," in inward convictions and beliefs, there can be no talk whatever of commandments, of coercive methods. The only weapon the church may employ is the word—the word of love, of comfort, of persuasion. Clearly and definitely Mendelssohn sets forth the principle that the state must be completely separate from the church, and, in this connection, underscores most sharply that the government must not be at all interested in the beliefs and religious views of its citizens and that differences in religion can in no way be considered a bar to the enjoyment of civic rights. For him it is clear that the state must put forth as its motto complete tolerance, freedom of thought and belief; and the church must not claim any earthly riches *(masset sich auf kein irdisches Gut ein Recht)* and has the right to employ no force other than the force of persuasion.[83]

In the second part of his work Mendelssohn particularly stresses the profound difference between the Christian and the Jewish religions. Christianity is the religion of faith, Judaism the religion of deed. Christianity, which proceeds from the assumption that the individual can be saved only through faith, places the chief emphasis on dogmas and perceives in them the

83. *Gesammelte Schriften,* 1844, Vol. III, p. 283.

major factor of universal, exclusive importance. Judaism, however, is the religion of real life and activity; its laws and rituals are merely symbols of acts of will. The Torah of Moses distinguishes itself radically from Christianity, in Mendelssohn's interpretation, by the fact that it does not command that one believe in any specific dogmas. It commands only the fulfillment of laws and precepts that exalt man's life, inscribe in the human memory the divine will, and awaken the drive toward the proper deeds which lead to temporal and eternal happiness.[84] "Among all the precepts and ordinances in the Torah of Moses," he insists, "there is not a single one that ordains, You shall believe or you shall not believe, but all say, You shall do or you shall not do."[85] The Torah issues forth with curses and punishments not for unbelief *(Unglaube)* but for nonfulfillment, for criminal acts *(Unthaten)*.[86]

Mendelssohn asserts that the mistake is too frequently made of confusing quite different notions: the *legislation* disclosed in a supernatural fashion is taken as a supernatural *religious revelation*. Judaism, however, does not know of any religious revelation, in the sense accepted in the Christian world. The Jews possess only a divine legislation; their ancestors were merely given religious laws, commandments, and principles of life that lead man to beatitude.[87] These laws do, indeed, make it easier to grasp the "eternal truths"; these truths, however, have no need of being confirmed through miracles and wonders, and they were not especially given to the Jewish people through revelation. They were given to the whole of civilized mankind forever through the religion of nature,[88] through the consciousness that rests in the heart of every rational person. These eternal laws must not be merely *believed;* they are "laws of reason," they rest on the human understanding. And Mendelssohn proudly declares: "I refuse to recognize any eternal truths other than those that human reason not only is able to grasp, but that can also be confirmed and fulfilled through human powers."[89]

84. *Gesammelte Schriften,* 1844, Vol. III, p. 311.

85. *Ibid.,* p. 321.

86. *Ibid.,* p. 352.

87. See also Mendelssohn's *An die Freunde Lessings:* "Judaism also is not a *revealed religion* but a *revealed law*" (*Sämtlichte Werke,* Vienna edition, 1838, p. 510).

88. *Ibid.,* p. 311: *Diese offenbaret der Ewige uns, wie allen übrigen Menschen, alle Zeit durch Natur und Sache, wie durch Wort und Schriftzeichen.*

89. *Ibid.: Ich erkenne keine andere ewige Wahrheiten, als die der menschlichen Vernunft nicht nur begreiflich, sondern durch menschliche Kräfte dargethan und bewährt werden können.*

Mendelssohn's ideological opponent, the emotive and mystically-minded Johann Georg Hamann, is not completely unjustified when he so frequently stresses Mendelssohn's ambiguity. On the one side, a "rationalist and sophist," a "rational enlightener," and on the other, a typically pious Jew (*Stockjude*). As an enthusiastic admirer of Maimonides and a contemporary of the enlighteners and rationalists, Mendelssohn attempts to demonstrate that in Judaism there is no contradiction between reason and faith. He endeavors, in purely rationalist fashion, to establish the necessity and "rationality" of Jewish ritual. He speaks in the rationalist manner about the distortion and misunderstandings produced through the "folly of men" (*Thorheit der Menschen*), but at the same time stresses that the "laws, precepts, commandments and rules of life" of the Torah of Moses must remain unalterable and are obligatory forever on every member of the Jewish people, for the legislator is God Himself—not as God the Creator and Ruler of the world, but as the God of Israel, the Ruler and Commander of the Jewish community with whom He entered into an eternal covenant and to whom He gave His laws publicly in an extraordinary, marvelous way.[90] And because God the Creator is also the Lord and Commander of the Jewish people, in the Jewish community the civic has a holy and religious vesture, "and every civic service is at the same time a true service of God."[91]

Mendelssohn further notes that even now after the Jewish people has lost its civic-political independence, the laws in question cannot be abolished, notwithstanding the possibility that originally they bore a thoroughly temporal character. For —"what God has bound, man cannot loose."[92] Mendelssohn the rationalist candidly admits: In truth I do not see how those born into the house of Jacob can "in any conscientious way" free themselves from the divine law which they have obtained as a legacy from their ancestors.[93]

Naturally, everyone can inquire into and consider each individual law, express his own conjecture that it was *perhaps* bound up with a specific place, time, and circumstances and may *perhaps*, with the passage of time, in another place, and

---

90. *Gesammelte Schriften*, Vol. III, p. 350: *Und er gab seinen Gesetzen die feuerlichste Sanction, öffentlich und auf eine nie erhörte, wundervolle Weise, wodurch sie der Nation und allen ihren Nachkommen als unabänderliche Pflicht und Schuldigkeit auferlegt worden sind.*
91. *Ibid.*, pp. 350–352.
92. *Gesammelte Schriften*, 1844, Vol. III, p. 356.
93. *Ibid.*

under different circumstances, also be changed, but—"weak and shortsighted is man's eye." Who can say "I have come into the sanctuary of God, completely investigated the system of its intentions, and determined what weight and goal and limit to define for it"?[94] God alone, who made His covenant with our ancestors and publicly commanded His laws to them, can "make us know His will on these matters."[95]

Mendelssohn the enlightener and Mendelssohn the "typical Jew" knows very well that he stands on the threshold of a new era when unprecedented tendencies and circumstances put forward the strict demand that the Jewish world view and the Jewish way of life be adapted to the requirements of modern cultural life. And he, the man who stands at the crossroads of two worlds, finds that the "house of Jacob" can have "no wiser counsel" than the following:

Adapt yourself to the mores and order of the land in which you live, but hold fast also to the religion of your fathers. Bear the double yoke as well as you can. Certainly it is difficult for you to fulfill all the requirements of civic life while remaining faithful to the commandments of the religion. Moreover, the fulfillment of the religious commandments under very different times and circumstances is now felt as a considerably heavier burden than in previous generations. Nevertheless hold firm. Despite all this, stand on watch unmoved, and fulfill the tasks that Providence has laid upon you.[96]

Mendelssohn's work, in which the slogan of tolerance and freedom of belief is proclaimed in the sharpest way, made a powerful impression in the Christian world. The most important thinkers of that time welcomed it enthusiastically. Mirabeau declared that Mendelssohn's *Jerusalem* "deserves to be translated into all languages," and Immanuel Kant wrote to Mendelssohn shortly after the appearance of his work: "I consider this book the promise of a great reform which will, to be sure, only gradually and slowly be realized not, however, in regard to your nation alone but for all other peoples."[97]

In Hebrew literature Mendelssohn's *Jerusalem* found rather

---

94. Already at the time of his controversy with Lavater-Bonnet, Mendelssohn declared: *Andere Völker können ihre Gesetze nach den Zeiten, Umständen, Bedürfnissen und Bequemlichkeiten abändern, aber mir hat der Schöpfer selbst Gesetze vorgeschrieben, sollte ich, schwaches Geschöpf, mich erdreisten nach meinen Dünkel diese göttlichen Gesetze abzuändern?*
95. *Gesammelte Schriften*, Vol. III, p. 358.
96. *Gesammelte Schriften*, Vol. III, p. 355.
97. *Ich halte dieses Buch für die Verkündigung einer grossen, obzwar langsambevorstehenden und fortrückenden Reform, die nicht allein ihre Nation, sondern andere treffen wird.*

slight resonance in its own time. Only Abraham Meldola, mentioned in the first chapter of this volume, sang a paean of praise to it in *Ha-Measseƒ*,[98] and Isaac Euchel in his monograph on Mendelssohn reported the content of *Jerusalem*.[99] It was only later, after Mendelssohn's death, that critical comments on his ideas concerning the nature and significance of the Jewish religion were heard from Jewish writers. Mendelssohn's work appeared in Hebrew only in the second half of the nineteenth century.[100]

98. *Ha-Measseƒ*, 5545, p. 84.
99. Euchel's complete Hebrew translation of *Jerusalem* did not find a publisher and remained in manuscript.
100. By Gottlober in 1867 and by Grünbaum-Fedorov in 1876.

CHAPTER THREE

Naftali Herz Wessely and the Meassefim

[The cultural significance of Mendelssohn's translation of the Pentateuch—Naftali Herz Wessely as philologist and grammarian—Joseph II's Edict of Toleration—Wessely as fighter for Haskalah—His summons *Divrei Shalom Ve-Emet*—His program for the education of children—The battle of the orthodox against Wessely's summons—The Koenigsberg society *Doreshei Leshon Ever* and its journal *Ha-Meassef*—The program of the Meassefim—The significance of the journal—*Ha-Meassef* is transferred from Koenigsberg to Berlin.]

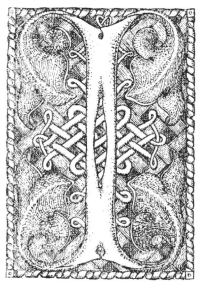 N THE previous chapter we noted the cultural-historical significance of Mendelssohn's translation of the Pentateuch. It became the ground for the new shoots that appeared in the Jewish quarter in the second half of the eighteenth century, the first major stage in the history of the Haskalah movement. The tendencies that are so prominent in Mendelssohn's undertaking—reforming the system of education, implanting love for the language of the Bible, and arousing the drive for European culture and education—became the basic theses, the most important items in the credo of the battlers for Haskalah. At Mendelssohn's initiative there was founded in Berlin as early as 1778 the *Jüdische Freyschule (Ḥinnuch Ne'arim)*, where the children studied German, French, and other secular subjects in addition to the Bible and Talmud. And at the same time as Mendelssohn's translation of the Pentateuch appeared, one of the collaborators who assisted him in completing the *Biur* after the departure of Solomon Dubno,[1]

---

1. See above, pp. 40ff.

Naftali Herz (Hartwig) Wessely, published a small brochure of two printer's sheets that is justly considered the original manifesto of the youthful Haskalah movement, the first foundation of the new Hebrew enlightenment literature.

Naftali Herz Wessely's[2] family originated in Poland. His great grandfather Joseph Reis of Bar (in the region of Podolia) was miraculously saved when his entire family perished at the time of the terrible Cossack massacre in 1648.[3] Joseph Reis settled in Amsterdam where he became wealthy. His last years were spent in the Brandenburg town of Wesel (hence the family name). Naftali Wessely's grandfather Moses, as well as his father Issachar Baer, were wealthy court purveyors ("They used to stand before kings," he writes about his father). Naftali Herz was born in Hamburg, but when he was still a small child the whole family moved to Copenhagen. Issachar Baer, the rich purveyor to the court of the king of Denmark, gave his son a traditional education, and at the age of five the little Naftali already studied *Gemara*—in fact, the difficult tractate *Kiddushin*.[4] Fortune brought it about that just in 1735, when he was ten years old, the wandering scholar and author of *Tzohar Ha-Tevah*, Solomon Zalman Hanau,[5] settled for a time in Copenhagen. Hanau familiarized the young boy, who had a deep thirst for knowledge, with the principles of grammar and aroused in him love for the language of the Bible. A certain influence was also exerted on the young Wessely by the renowned Rabbi Jonathan Eybeschütz in whose *yeshivah* he studied in his youth.

The style of life of the wealthy court Jews and the extensive business contacts the Wesselys had with dukes and lords brought it about that Issachar's eldest son Naftali Herz also obtained a certain amount of secular knowledge. He himself relates in his *Divrei Shalom Ve-Emet* how once in his youth his father opened a map of Europe and familiarized him with the geographic location of various cities and countries. As an associate in his father's business, the young Wessely became familiar with several European languages—German, French, Danish, and Dutch.[6] To be sure, his knowledge of these languages

2. The most important sources on Wessely's life and activity are noted in our article in the Russian-Jewish Encyclopedia (V, 528). To be added are: J. Klausner, *Historyah Shel Ha-Safrut Ha-Ivrit Ha-Hadashah*, Vol. I, pp. 88–130; and L. Levin, "Aus dem jüdischen Kultur-Kampfe" (*Jahrbuch des jüdische literarische Gesellschaft*, XII, pp. 165–197).
3. See *Divrei Shalom Ve-Emet*, II, p. 54 (we quote according to the Vienna edition of 1827); *Gan Na'ul*, I, Introduction.
4. *Divrei Shalom Ve-Emet*, II, p. 55.
5. See our *History*, Vol. VI, pp. 149–50.
6. See David Friedrichsfeld, *Zecher Tzaddik*, Amsterdam, 1909, p. 2.

was quite superficial. How little competence he had even in German is attested by his crude and very erroneous Hebrew translation of Mendelssohn's reply to Lavater.[7] But while still quite young, Naftali Herz, participating in his father's business, acquired a reputation as a skilled and capable merchant. He found favor with the well-known court banker of Berlin, Veitel Ephraim, and the latter, traveling through Copenhagen, appointed Wessely as his agent in the great mercantile city of Amsterdam. There he became acquainted with Moses Ḥayyim Luzzatto's disciple, the poet David Franco-Mendes, and through him established close relationships with the Spanish-Portuguese community. He was enchanted by the Sephardic schools for children where the young obtained a far more normal education than in the German-Polish communities.

As Veitel Ephraim's representative, Wessely had occasion to visit Berlin, where he became personally acquainted with Mendelssohn in 1761.[8] The intellectually curious Wessely did not wish to content himself merely with business affairs; he also dreamed of becoming a Hebrew writer. He was in love with the language of the Bible and devoted all his free time to philology. In 1765–1766 appeared the first parts of his philological work *Ha-Levanon* (which also bears the title *Gan Na'ul*)[9] on synonyms in the Bible. But even in his beloved realm of philology Wessely remained no more than a dilettante, and his philological investigations had, even for that time, very limited scholarly value. Their sole virtue is the language, which is light, clear, and simple. But even this virtue is lost through the author's enormous loquaciousness. The slightest idea is literally drowned in a sea of superfluous words, unnecessary arguments, and exaggerated hypotheses. Moreover, he always calls the attention of the reader to it, saying with a naive mien, "And superfluous words I despise."

Wessely achieved great success in business at Amsterdam; as a skilled connoisseur of precious stones he gained a substantial fortune. Later he left his position in Veitel Ephraim's business, established his own, and at the end of the 1760's joined his father in Copenhagen, where shortly afterwards he married

---

7. On this, see J. Klausner, *op. cit.*, pp. 48–49. The same thing is discernible in Wessely's translation (at the end of the second part of *Divrei Shalom Ve-Emet*) of the closing sentences of Mendelssohn's introduction to Menasseh ben Israel's apologetic work *Teshuat Yisrael*. Mendelssohn's phrase *Noch keine Geistlichkeit so aufgeklärt* is translated by Wessely: *Hokerei ha-ruḥot aden lo hitaharu le-maddai.*

8. See Mendelssohn, Jubilee Edition, Vol. XVI, p. 61.

9. The third part, as well as Wessely's other philological works, *Mayan Gannim* and *Migdal Ha-Levanon*, remained in manuscript.

and became the head of a family. Several years thereafter, however, Wessely lost his fortune in a financial crisis, again had to accept a position in the Veitel Ephraim firm, and for this purpose moved in 1774 to Berlin. In 1775 he there completed his commentary to the Mishnaic tractate *Avot* entitled *Yein Levanon*. He obtained a great reputation as a Hebrew "rhetorician" and philologist, however, with another work that appeared several years later. While still quite young he had become familiar, through Luther's translation of the Bible, with the apocryphal *Wisdom of Solomon*. The young Wessely was highly enchanted by the work. He had no doubt whatever that the *Wisdom of Solomon* was written by none other than King Solomon himself. He therefore decided to restore the work to its original source, "from the profane to the holy," and with great diligence translated it from French[10] into classical Biblical Hebrew. He accompanied the text with an extensive commentary entitled *Ruaḥ Ḥen* and published it in Berlin in 1777.[11]

In Berlin Wessely entered into close association with Mendelssohn and his friends. He was greatly charmed by the reformed Jewish school *Ḥinnuch Ne'arim* that had been established there, and when Mendelssohn decided to issue the prospectus *Alim Li-Terufah* for his translation of the Pentateuch in 1778, Wessely published in it an enthusiastic article "Mehallel Re'a" with a long poem of praise in which he deplores the wild order of educating children prevalent among Jews in the German-Polish communities. Youngsters are taught difficult and profound matters even before they obtain any knowledge of the Hebrew language; moreover, in instructing the children, the teachers do not employ the language of the country but the corrupt jargon that is incapable of transmitting the beauties of the sacred writings. Wessely hopes, however, that Mendelssohn's translation, complemented by the *Biur*, will help greatly to arouse in the hearts of the Jewish youth love for the Hebrew language and to awaken their interest in the poetic values of the Bible.

For their shepherds will rely on you,
According to the pace of your work the flocks will follow,
And from the well you have dug they will drink water.

10. See Friedrichsfeld, *op. cit.*, p. 14.
11. Friedrichsfeld, *op. cit.*, p. 14. According to Benjacob and William (Ze'ev) Zeitlin, the work appeared in 1780. (Is this perhaps the second edition?). The work was reprinted a number of times. In 1822 *Ḥochmat Shelomoh* was published in Shklov along with a Yiddish translation.

The grace of your words will be like a skylight to them,
The eloquence will become pure as the sky in its
   brightness.
Now they will set themselves to studying Hebrew.

At just that time Wessely lost his position in the Veitel
Ephraim firm (which closed its business), and he and his large
family[12] were reduced to poverty. The wealthy David Friedländer, as well as Mendelssohn with his translation of the Pentateuch, came to his aid in this situation. After Solomon Dubno's departure, Mendelssohn proposed to Wessely that he
write the *Biur*, or commentary, to the Book of Leviticus. Wessely's *Biur*, which came off the press at the end of August 1781,
suffers, like all the author's earlier works, from the same defect
—a flood of superfluous verbiage. One of his critics[13] notes
quite justly that "where Rashi and Ibn Ezra were content with
one or two words, Wessely takes many pages." Nevertheless,
his commentary found considerable favor in the enlightened
circles. Incomparably greater success in these circles was
achieved, however, by another work of Wessely's that appeared several months later. This short composition,[14] which
produced such enormous excitement in the rabbinic world, is
closely connected with the emperor Joseph II's Edict of Toleration, issued on October 19, 1781.

Like his contemporary, Frederick II of Prussia, Joseph II of
Austria was a typical representative of "enlightened absolutism" or "benevolent despotism." In the name of humanism and
enlightenment he attempted forcibly to impose German culture on all the peoples speaking various languages who lived
under his sovereignty. As an adherent of the Physiocratic system, which taught that only the earth contains good fortune
and blessing, that agriculture, which endows man with the
gifts of nature, alone is the source and foundation of the state's
economic life, Joseph II regarded the Jews, who did not till the
soil with their hands, as a pernicious and useless element. In
order to prevent this "harmful" element from growing in
numbers, he issued the strictest edict that no Jew had the right
to marry without the permission of the higher officials.[15] For

12. Wessely was burdened with six children.
13. Mendelssohn of Hamburg, *Penei Tevel*, 140.
14. It contains altogether sixteen pages in thirty-two°.
15. "Thus all Jews are hereby prohibited in the most rigorous manner, also under
penalty of confiscation of all possessions and, according to circumstance, corporal
punishment, be it within or without *huppah*, to contract marriages, without previously
receiving permission from the local government and paying the prescribed fee."

this permission Jews had to pay a large head-tax, and whoever violated the edict had his entire fortune confiscated.[16] To protect the welfare of the peasants who worked the soil, Joseph II expelled all the Jewish lessees from the villages and issued an order prohibiting Jews from leasing not only estates but also mills, breweries for beer and mead, etc. In this way a third of the Jewish populace in Galicia was ruined at one stroke.

At the command of the same "enlightened" emperor all the "beggar Jews," i.e., all who were unable to pay the special poll-tax *(Toleranzgebühr)*, were driven out in 1773. Every year a new segment of the Jews was declared "beggars" and expelled from the country.[17] To be sure, Joseph II formulated the project of settling Jews on the land and making "useful" citizens of them. The impoverished Jewish masses responded enthusiastically to this project, and in the course of several years thousands of Jewish families applied to the government with the request that they be granted the opportunity to transfer to agriculture.[18] However, the sums required for this were not assigned, and the avaricious and untalented civil servants were hostile to the whole enterprise,[19] with the result that nothing came of it.

Thus, in the course of Joseph II's ten-year reign (1780–90), the economic foundations of the Jewish populace in Galicia were ruined. No new foundations were created, and this brought it about that for generations frightful poverty prevailed in this unhappy country. To be sure, for the Jews who were prepared to assume German culture, to throw off the "superstitious" Jewish faith with its "wild" customs, and to become "useful" fellow-citizens, Joseph II was a "gracious king." He opened the doors of the better government schools for them. Jewish doctors and lawyers obtained equal rights with their Christian colleagues; they could even hope to occupy an official position in the government.

It is therefore not surprising that when the Holy Roman Emperor's Patent of Toleration appeared, with the project of reforming the education of children among Jews, establishing special Jewish normal schools with German as the language of instruction, and teaching the children the foundations of ethics

16. For a discussion of this, see Dr. A. Brawer's thorough work "Yosef Ha-Sheni Ve-Yehudei Galitzie" (*Ha-Shiloaḥ*, XXIII, pp. 35–38).

17. In the course of the first year after the *Toleranzpatent* (in 1782), 1192 persons were driven out as "beggar Jews" (see Brawer, *op. cit.*, p. 39).

18. M. Balaban, *Yidn in Poiln*, pp. 38–43.

19. See Brawer, *op. cit.*, pp. 334, 338–342.

and practical morality on the basis of textbooks especially produced for this purpose, not only the orthodox circles but even the author of *Phaedon* and *Jerusalem* regarded it with suspicion. In the edict of the Austrian emperor that was bedecked with humanistic phrases, the perspicacious Mendelssohn discerned a hidden tendency toward forced assimilation and missionary "fraternization." "What good are normal schools for us," writes Mendelssohn, "when we cannot pursue trades and may have no occupations? Much thanks for all tolerance when, through this, they always work for a *unification of religion.*"[20] In another letter Mendelssohn returns again to the same question:

Of the tolerance which is so very prevalent in all pages of the journals, I have not by far the favorable opinion that they derive from it. As long as the *system of unification* hides in the background, this tolerance—hypocrisy seems to me more dangerous than open persecution . . . Hence it becomes all the more necessary in this case that the small handful of those who do not convert others, but also refuse to be converted, should band together and cling firmly to one another.[21]

Quite different was the attitude of the naive, good-natured Wessely. In his world view he belonged, in fact, to the right wing of the *maskilim*. He was a pious Jew; in his commentaries to the text of the Bible he holds faithfully to the accepted tradition. He was quite cool to the rationalist ideas of that era and himself noted: "The old suspect me of being an innovator, and the new regard me as a follower of the old."[22] To a certain degree he was a man of sentiment with excited nerves and with a fair amount of naive feeling and sentimental effusiveness. Moreover, he grew up in the environment and traditions of the court Jews with their enormous self-deprecation before lords and dukes. The Austrian emperor's Patent of Toleration brought Wessely into great ecstasy. He, who was certain that "to direct the erring aright, one man of great intellect is sufficient" and that "when a wise man rules, the people ceases to be barbaric,"[23] at once saw realized before himself his ideal of reforming the education of children, in which he perceived the true salvation of the Jewish people. In cumbersome, somewhat wooden verses, he immediately betook himself to celebrating

---

20. *Gesammelte Schriften*, 1844, p. 671. Italicized by Mendelssohn himself.
21. *Ibid.*, pp. 676–677.
22. *Penei Tevel*, p. 241.
23. In Wessely's paean in honor of Joseph II, *Ha-Meassef*, 5544, pp. 164, 175.

the Austrian emperor's goodness and his "love" for the people of Israel, whom he wishes to free from servile shame:

You also, House of Jacob, note the kindness of Joseph!
For he has remembered the poor people, the leavings
   remaining to him,
And said: Return, I will remove your disgrace from you . . .

Wessely, however, refused to be satisfied with this. He also considered it his duty to enlighten the Jews of the Austrian provinces, so that they would understand with what joy they ought to greet the new normal schools, and how grateful they ought to be to the humane emperor who desires to liberate them "from the darkness of ignorance."

Early in 1782[24] Wessely published his booklet *Divrei Shalom Ve-Emet*,[25] which is rightly considered the first public manifesto of the youthful Haskalah movement. In this brochure appear quite prominently both the virtues and the defects of the Haskalah literature of the initial period: emotiveness and enthusiasm for enlightenment and European education, on the one side, and on the other, self-deprecation before the representatives of secular power, a firm belief in the humanitarian, progressive role of "enlightened absolutism." Wessely speaks very enthusiastically about the graciousness of the enlightened monarchs of his time—the Holy Roman Emperor Joseph II, Frederick II of Prussia, and Catherine II[26] of Russia who corresponded with the French Encyclopedists and were not chary with phrases about equal rights for all and love of mankind.

One must take into consideration in this connection that, under contemporary social conditions, the industrial-capitalist classes, as well as public opinion, did not at that time represent any political force in the German lands.[27] Hence the Jewish

---

24. Neither a date nor the place of printing is indicated on this edition. However, it is known that the battle against Wessely's tract was already so sharp in the month of March that the Minister of Education considered it necessary to intervene. We also know that two weeks after Passover (the 10th of Iyyar), Wessely's second tract, which contains all of five printers' sheets, was already finished. When one takes into consideration the rather slow circulation of mail and books in that time, he must come to the conclusion that Wessely's first tract appeared no later than January 1782.

25. The full title: *Divrei Shalom Ve-Emet Le-Kehal Adat Yisrael, Ha-Garim Be-Artzot Memshelet Ha-Kesar Ha-Gadol Ha-Ohev Et Benei Ha-Adam U-Mesame'ah Et Ha-Beriot, Yozefus Ha-Sheni Yarum Hodo.*

26. *Ibid.*, pp. 57–58. We have employed the first edition of *Divrei Shalom Ve-Emet*, but, since it is not paginated, we quote according to the Vienna edition of 1827.

27. How the "enlightened" Frederick II regarded public opinion is attested by the following lines in his letter to Voltaire: *Mais les hommes ne sont pas faits pour la verité.*

bourgeoisie and intellectual circles had to place all their hope for the improvement of their civic status only on the "gracious kings," on the humanitarian sentiments of the "enlightened" sovereigns. This explains the servile, exaggerated patriotic tone so characteristic of the entire literature of the Haskalah, the tone in which Wessely's pamphlet is written. Also the well-known motto of the later Haskalah literature which found its classic statement in J.L. Gordon's dictum "Be a man in the outside world and a Jew at home," already finds quite clear expression in *Divrei Shalom Ve-Emet*, where it is explained that "the Hebrew language is a thing in itself, and *Leshon Ashkenaz* (Judeo-German) a different thing; the former is for the sacred matters of religion and the Torah, and the latter for secular affairs, business matters, interpersonal relationships, and the practical, natural and learned sciences." The education of children, Wessely explains, must be divided into two separate parts. The first is study of the Torah of man. One must first familiarize the child with the secular studies without which no person can get along, i.e., the ways of morality and virtue, then elementary information, both for practical life and for investigating the Torah with its laws, about important branches of science, such as history, geography, mathematics, astronomy, botany, chemistry, medicine, etc.

This information is essential to every man and without it he is not worthy of bearing the name man. Unfortunately, Wessely notes, there is a people in the world, precisely the people that was once called "a wise and understanding people," which is now sunk in darkness and ignorance. To be sure, it is not we who are responsible therefor. This is the legacy of the bitter exile, of the hatred and terrible persecutions we had to endure in the course of many generations. But now we have lived to see quite different times. Now we find ourselves under the rule of righteous kings who act lovingly toward all peoples without distinction of faith. Behold how there sits on the "Roman throne" a great and humane emperor who makes his subjects happy with laws of graciousness and compassion and who, with his vast grace, has also not forgotten the persecuted people of Israel and has decided to help them out of their spiritual barbarism and degradation.

As a merchant and businessman, Wessely at every step notes how important it is to know the language of the country and to be in a position to carry on business correspondence in this

---

Je les regarde comme une horde de cerfs dans le parc d'un grand seigneur, et qui n'ont d'autre fonction que le peupler et remplir l'enclos.

language.[28] Raised in a family of wealthy court Jews, he does not tire of repeating how vital it is to command German in order to be in a position to appear in the ducal courts and to communicate with high officials and lords.[29] He knows very well the contempt that the "courts of the princes" and also the homes of the common German "Philistines" have for the Jewish idiom, for "Moshele." We, he laments, have become a scorn and an object of ridicule among all peoples, for we are "stammerers." We make ourselves ridiculous whenever we speak with the nobles or with the merchants of the peoples of the world.[30] Every page of *Divrei Shalom Ve-Emet* is filled with bitter hatred and contempt for the Yiddish "jargon." Like Mendelssohn, Wessely considers the language of the Ashkenazic Jews not as a special dialect but as a sullied and distorted German, as a melancholy factor of frightful spiritual demoralization. "The House of Israel are of uncircumcised lips," he exclaims bitterly. The pure German language has become corrupted in our mouths. How—he argues—is any normal education possible, when among us both the pupils and the teachers are inarticulate and employ a crude, spoiled mixture of crippled and distorted words?[31]

Wessely's hatred for the corrupted "jargon" was so vast that he occasionally forgot to take account of certain universally known facts. So, for example, he asserts that while we speak the language of the country in which we live, the Jewish child does not understand a single Hebrew word.[32] In this connection he pretends to be ignorant of the fact that in the despised "jargon" that "we speak" there are many hundreds of Hebrew words. *Tedabberu me-attah tzaḥut*, Wessely emotively exclaims; "Henceforth you must speak a pure language." This slogan resounds through all the pages of *Divrei Shalom Ve-Emet*. Only with the aid of a pure, cultured language, the author asserts, can one first thoroughly learn the Hebrew that ought to be, according to his program, the foundation-stone of the second part of the studies in the normal schools—the Torah of the Lord. The boorish jargon, Wessely declares, is not capable of rendering the beauty and poetic power of the language of the Bible. Therefore, he stresses a number of times, as soon as the child obtains elementary knowledge of the secular sciences in

28. *Divrei Shalom Ve-Emet*, pp. 49ff.
29. *Ibid.*, pp. 11, 17ff.
30. *Ibid.*, p. 50.
31. *Ibid.*, p. 19.
32. *Ibid.*, p. 28.

the normal schools projected by the emperor Joseph II, he should be taught the Torah of Moses with the aid of Mendelssohn's excellent, poetic German translation. Thanks to this translation, the child will become thoroughly familiar with both languages.[33]

Wessely also deems it necessary to stress how right and useful is the demand put forth in the Patent of Toleration that special textbooks (catechisms) to familiarize the children with the foundations of the Jewish faith and ethic be produced for the Jewish normal schools. In our Written Torah and Oral Torah, he explains, these foundations are presented in such profound and hidden form that they are too difficult for the childish understanding. He also finds unsuitable for this purpose all of the old books of *musar*, or moral instruction. Hence, new "books of *musar* according to the philosophy that agrees with reason" must be produced for this purpose;[34] with their aid the children will become familiar with the light of the Torah and with the treasures of "wisdom and morality."[35]

Wessely's *Divrei Shalom Ve-Emet* was received with great enthusiasm in the progressive circles. It was promptly translated into French,[36] and later Elijah Morpurgo translated it into Italian[37] and David Friedländer into German.[38] The Italian communities, which were under Austrian sovereignty, at once

33. *Ibid.*, pp. 12, 15, 18, 20ff. Wessely, however, was mistaken. The "enlightened" Joseph II precisely did not wish that the Jewish children in the normal schools should be taught the Pentateuch with Mendelssohn's translation and *Biur*. The reason for this was that the "Roman emperor" suspected Mendelssohn of being a "naturalist," and Joseph was decisively opposed to "his Jews becoming naturalists."

34. "And, furthermore, for this our community needs to compose new books about [religious] beliefs and opinions."

35. Wessely himself, in fact, soon composed such a textbook (printed in Berlin in 1784) under the title *Sefer Ha-Middot Ve-Hu Sefer Musar Ha-Sechel*, in which he endeavors to explain the "paths of the soul" and the "powers of the soul" according to "the laws of man's sound reason that is implanted in all of us." Wessely's work is certainly free of the medieval superstition with which the *Sefer Hasidim*, for instance, is so filled. It is also free of the leaden melancholy and fearful dread that hangs over such works as *Shevet Musar* or *Kav Ha-Yashar*. It also lacks, however, what the older morality books possess in such great measure—tender feeling, the ecstasy of devotion. Wessely's *Sefer Ha-Middot* is in general "neither hot nor cold." It is genteelly utilitarian, sedately rational, and watered down with nine measures of rhetorical speech, as was his style.

36. In Paris, 1782.

37. In Gorizia, 1783. In the battle which broke out after the appearance of *Divrei Shalom Ve-Emet*, Elijah Morpurgo played an active role as Wessely's ardent defender (on this, see Rivkind's article in the collection *Studies in Jewish Bibliography . . . in Memory of Abraham Solomon Freidus*, New York, 1929, pp. 138–59).

38. Berlin, 1798.

responded to Wessely's summons and declared that they were prepared to establish normal schools among themselves. On the other hand, in the rabbinic circles of the Polish communities, Wessely's summons evoked enormous excitement and tumult.

We noted earlier the reasons for which the well known rabbi of Prague, Rabbi Ezekiel Landau, issued forth against Mendelssohn's translation of the Pentateuch.[39] Since this translation was written in modern, literary High German, a tongue that is too difficult and incomprehensible for Jewish children, much time would have to be spent first in teaching them this language and its grammatical principles. The study of Torah would therefore be set aside as a secondary matter, and the German language would be the chief thing.[40] Now the orthodox rabbis perceived in Wessely's pamphlet a confirmation of Rabbi Ezekiel Landau's view. According to Wessely's program, one ought first to study secular subjects (*nimusiyyut ve-derech eretz*), and the Torah of Moses is also to be taught the children through Mendelssohn's translation, so that, with its aid, the pupil might learn both languages—Hebrew as well as German.[41]

The orthodox rabbis were particularly incensed by an extremely tactless phrase of Wessely's. We noted previously that the author, in his philosophy and world outlook, was a pious, religiously-minded person. His knowledge of the scientific disciplines was quite superficial and unsystematic. But as a typical dilettante and autodidact, he was so enchanted by European culture and secular knowledge that in his summons he permitted himself, paraphrasing a well-known Talmudic dictum, to make the following statement: A scholar who is quite competent in Talmudic knowledge but has no knowledge in *nimusiyyut ve-derech eretz*, i.e., in everything pertaining to secular culture, is worse than a *nevelah*, an unclean carcass.[42] This explains why the orthodox rabbis, especially the rabbis of the Polish territories,[43] perceived in Wessely's summons not

39. In his *haskamah* to Zussman Glogau's translation of the Pentateuch.
40. See above, p. 43f.
41. See above, p. 69.
42. *Divrei Shalom Ve-Emet*, at the end of the first chapter: "Every scholar (who knows the laws of God and our Torah) and who has no knowledge (of secular subjects), a carcass is better than he . . . for he disgraces his Torah and is despised by the creatures."
43. See Mendelssohn's letter to Wolf: "From all regions of Poland the arrows of the ban arrive here together, hurtling one on top of the other" (*Gesammelte Schriften*, 1844, No. 602).

"words of peace and truth" but enormous impudence, wickedness, and heresy. Backward, old-fashioned, ideologically isolated from the surrounding world and its demands, they saw in his appearance the greatest threat to the survival of the religion, and they considered his summons the most explosive material, which might ruthlessly destroy the entire ancient way of life hallowed by generations. Therefore, they considered it their duty to gird up their loins and issued forth against the dangerous enemy.

Leading Wessely's opponents were the previously mentioned rabbi of Prague, Rabbi Ezekiel Landau, and the rabbi of Lissa, David (Tevele) ben Nathan, both of whom several years previously had given *haskamot* or approbations to Wessely's *Yein Levanon*, in which they were not chary of praises and laudations of the author, as was the fashion in *haskamot*.[44] But Wessely's antagonists found themselves in an extremely difficult situation. The rabbi of Prague, as an Austrian subject, could not issue forth openly and high-handedly against his emperor's Patent of Toleration. Also the rabbi of Lissa, as a subject of Frederick II, was afraid of coming forward publicly against projects which aimed to reform the old-fashioned Jewish school. Hence, they were virtually silent about the basic question of establishing normal schools and only noted that it is, indeed, a duty to know the language of the country and immediately afterwards attacked Wessely as a "sinner in Israel" and a seducer and misleader, employing in this connection the same weapons that Jacob Emden had used in his battle against Jonathan Eybeschütz—insults, curses, and excommunications. The sermon which the rabbi of Lissa delivered against Wessely is filled to overflowing with such epithets as "wicked man," "a man poor in knowledge," "the most common of the common," "poor and dishonorable," "misleader of children," "fool," "wicked and impudent man," etc.

David Tevele and his collaborators also considered it necessary to request the rabbi of Berlin, Tzevi Hirsch (Hirschel) Levin, to induce Wessely to repent; otherwise, he was to be punished. Rabbi Levin was a tolerant man and not at all belligerent. The author's tactless expression about the "scholar who has no knowledge or understanding," however, apparently enraged him greatly. In addition, for special reasons, he also

---

44. Some scholars (L. Levin, J. Klausner, and others) even assert that leading Wessely's opponents was the Gaon of Vilna. However, we view this assertion with certain doubts.

deemed it necessary to issue forth in this matter in a highly militant fashion. His own son, as we shall see further, was "tainted," secretly agreed with the *maskilim,* and came forth with a rabid pamphlet against Wessley's opponents. The aged rabbi, therefore, endeavored to show that he himself stood faithfully on guard and was prepared to battle against the "breakers down of the fence." He proposed to the *parnassim* and leaders of the city that if Wessely continued to come forth with his appeals he should be forced to leave Berlin.

Mendelssohn writes (April 17, 1782) of this to David Friedländer with indignation: "I leave everything aside, and I will not enter into speculations about who is right here. I only think: What will the Christians say of this? What will they think when they see that we persecute a writer in this way and prevent him from openly expressing his thoughts?"[45] And to another acquaintance, the secretary of the community of Trieste, Joseph Gallico, Mendelssohn pours out his bitter heart concerning the persecutions that his "dear friend Rabbi Herz Weisel" has to endure: "This man has always walked in the ways of truth, has never allowed himself either by word or deed to turn aside on seductive paths, and now, as soon as he attempted with his *Divrei Shalom Ve-Emet* to strengthen slack hands and to awaken those sunk in the slumber of lethargy, belligerent men have risen against him, embitter his life, and persecute him as if he wished—God forbid—to turn the whole Jewish community aside from their God in heaven. So far has the folly of the benighted persons, who have no conception of what is happening around them, gone."[46]

Wessely, however, did not remain without protectors. The "enlighteners," the battlers for European education, came to his aid. Though they were not at that time very numerous, they were in a more advantageous position than their opponents, the orthodox. We know how in ancient times, when the controversy between the Maimunists and their opponents broke out, the freethinkers considered it appropriate to apply for help in their battle of ideas to the government.[47] What occurred in Provence at the beginning of the fourteenth century recurred at the end of the eighteenth century in the capital city of Prussia. "We," David Friedländer declares many years later with great smugness, "brought all the rabbis to silence, not

45. Mendelssohn, *Gesammelte Schriften,* 1844, Vol. V, p. 594.
46. Jubilee Edition, Vol. XVI, pp. 281–82.
47. See our *History,* Vol. III, pp. 128–29.

through arguments and proofs, but through fear."[48] The en-lightened applied to the Minister of Education Baron Karl Abraham von Zedlitz with the request that he intervene and not allow Wessely to be persecuted. At first Zedlitz contented himself with a private letter to the head of the Jewish commu-nity, the wealthy Daniel Itzig, requesting the latter to explain to him why the author was being harrassed; after all, it is not just that a man be oppressed merely because he has written a useful book.[49]

Shortly thereafter, Wessely himself came forward. Not at all a fighter by nature, he was greatly frightened by the excite-ment and tumult that his pamphlet had evoked in the orthodox circles. Shortly after Passover, 1782, he issued another docu-ment *Rav Tuv Le-Veit Yisrael*[50] in which he endeavors to defend himself by saying that, with his statement about "a scholar in whom there is no understanding," he in no way intended to insult the Talmudic scholars who do not possess general educa-tion. This document was ostensibly written as a reply to a letter in which the representatives of the community of Trieste are supposed to have inquired of him why the Polish rabbis are so enraged by his *Divrei Shalom Ve-Emet*.[51]

In a calmer tone Wessely repeats the same theses he had put forth in his first pamphlet. He cites arguments from the words of the Talmudic sages and from such great figures of the Mid-dle Ages as Maimonides, Abravanel, etc. to the effect that it is permissible to occupy oneself also with secular sciences, and that to know the language of the country and not speak in a corrupted jargon is both highly useful for trade and other business matters, as well as a means of winning favor and great honor among the peoples of the world. As proof Wessely notes how highly revered among the princes and great scholars are such cultured men as Moses Mendelssohn, Dr. Herz, and the like.

Nevertheless, the second writing did not calm moods. Testi-

---

48. *Gesammelte Schriften*, 1844, Vol. V, p. 593.
49. See M. Kayserling, *Moses Mendelssohn*, 1862.
50. Under the following full title: *Teshuvah Le-Anshei Hayil Yere'ei Elohim, Hachamim U-Nevonim, Ketzinim Ve-Rozenim, Ha-Kahal Ha-Kodesh Me-Aheinu Venei Yisrael Asher Be-Ir Trieste—Yechonenehah Elyon Amen—Al Ketav Yosher Asher Katevu Lanu, Be-Higia Aleihem Michtavenu Divrei Shalom Ve-Emet. Ve-Shem Ha-Teshuvah Ha-Zot Rav Tuv Le-Veit Yisrael, Me-Et Naftali Hirtz Vaizel.*
51. That this inquiry on the part of the community of Trieste is something that never was is clear from Wessely's letter of justification which he sent to the leaders of this community (the letter is published in *Kerem Hemed*, I, pp. 5–7).

mony to this is provided by the official rescript which the minister Baron von Zedlitz deemed it necessary on July 4, 1782 to address to the elders and representatives of Berlin Jewry. He notes how he has been informed that the author of *Divrei Shalom Ve-Emet* is being persecuted. The minister writes further:

I have investigated this matter, but have not managed to obtain the truth. Since I am certain that the representatives of the community undoubtedly understand how highly such a useful and cultured man, who preaches knowledge and enlightenment, must be esteemed, I request you to inform me about the status of the matter, so that we shall know how to regard such a man who has set himself the task of spreading culture and proper education among Jews.

After this rescript the rabbis lost the courage to enjoin Wessely from printing his propaganda pieces. In 1784 Wessely issued in Berlin, without hindrance, his third appeal *Ein Mishpat*[52] in which he published the "verdicts" wherein the rabbis of five Italian communities declare that they agree with him on the question of educating children. Some of the Italian scholars were so enthused that they celebrated Wessely in poems, and the author printed these poems, together with his reply—also in verses of the same meter.

Soon afterwards Wessely's fourth propaganda piece *Reḥovot*[53] appeared. In this he discusses his program of education at greater length and carries on a long polemic with his energetic opponent, the rabbi of Lissa, David Tevele ben Nathan.[54]

The struggle that broke out over Mendelssohn's translation of the Pentateuch and Wessely's *Divrei Shalom Ve-Emet* was the strong signal which encouraged the *maskilim* and enlighteners

---

52. The full title of the tract: *Michtav Shelishi Katuv Le-Aḥeinu Venei Yisrael Be-Chol Mekomot Moshevoteihem, Adonai Yagen Aleihem, Ketuvim Bo Mishpetei Emet, Mi-Pi Shivah Meshivei Ta'am, Kullom Ḥachamim Gedolim, Geonim Ve-Rabbanim Kollelim, Morim Hora'ot Be-Kehillot Kedoshot Italya—Yechonenem Elyon Amen—Asher Shafetu Be-Ḥochmat Libbom Be-Devar Ha-Telunot She-Hillinu Mi-Ketzat Me-Aḥeinu Venei Yisrael Al Michtevenu Divrei Shalom Ve-Emet.*

53. The full title: *Michtav Revi'i Katuv Gam Hu Le-Aḥeinu Venei Yisrael, Adonai Yagen Aleihem, Hu Yifrosh Divrei Ha-Michtav Ha-Rishon, Ve-Yoreh Ki Amarav Tzadeku Yaḥedav, Ein Ba-Hem Niftal Ve-Ikkesh, Ve-Yosef Le-Dabber Od Be-Inyan Seder Ha-Limmud Ve-Giddul Ha-Banim Ule-Fi Sheba-Kore Bo Yithalech Bo Bi-Reḥavah Gam Attah Hirḥiv Adonai Lanu Al Pi Edutan Shel Ḥachamim Ve-Soferim Ha-Nizkarim Be-Michtav Ha-Zeh "Reḥovot." Me-Et Naftali Hirtz Vaizel, Berlin, Bi-Defus Ha-Institut Ḥinnuch Ne'arim, Berlin.*

54. In the later editions all four tracts are printed together under the general title *Divrei Shalom Ve-Emet.*

to unite and organize around a definite center. It was then that there ripened among them the idea of creating a periodical that would serve as a platform for the younger generation, with its new requirements and aspirations. The representatives of these new strivings derived in the main from two social strata: (1) wealthy young people, children of Jewish bankers, manufacturers, and great merchants; and (2) teachers and tutors in wealthy Jewish homes and in the new Reform synagogues.

Typical representatives of the first group are the brothers Friedländer of Koenigsberg; of the second, Isaac Euchel, a teacher in the Friedländer house, Aaron Wolfsohn, a teacher in the Wilhelm-Schule, and Herz Homberg who, for three years, was a tutor in Mendelssohn's home.

At the beginning of 1783 (the seventh of Tevet, 5743) a group of young men in Koenigsberg established an association called *Ḥevrat Doreshei Leshon Ever* (Society of Exponents of the Hebrew Language), for the purpose of producing a Hebrew monthly[55] following the pattern of the then very popular *Berliner Monatsschrift*. Several wealthy Jews of Koenigsberg gave financial aid to the enterprise.[56] First of all, the *Doreshei Leshon Ever* applied to the author of *Divrei Shalom Emet*. They considered it necessary immediately to demonstrate to him, as a collaborator in Mendelssohn's *Biur*, that they would faithfully follow Mendelssohn's summons to return to the Bible and its language and, following his example, occupy themselves as "Biurists," exponents and interpreters of the Biblical text. "Not long ago," they explained in their letter,

there gathered a group of young *maskilim*, some of whom are Torah scholars and some command foreign languages—Greek and Latin, as well as modern—and are competent in various branches of knowledge, and together they decided to set themselves the task of comprehensively exploring the characteristics of the Hebrew language, illuminating and explaining the text of the Bible in a direct, common sense way . . . Their entire goal and wish is to spread our holy language among our people as much as possible and to demonstrate its beauty to all nations.

In order to realize this, they write further, they have decided to establish a periodical and are applying first of all to him, the

---

55. At first they projected a weekly, but, following Wessely's advice, they decided to issue a monthly journal.

56. See *Naḥal Ha-Besor:* "Some precious rich men of our community who give generously to the people agreed to provide a definite sum to support this society."

acknowledged master, with the request that he favor them with his poems and philological works. Wessely greeted their enterprise with joy but, recalling his own sad experience, warned the young editors to take great care not to print any erotic poems of the type written by Immanuel of Rome or love stories, and, for God's sake, not to publish any satirical items that ridicule and mock anyone. "Let milk and honey be under your tongue."

A few months later the prospectus of the new journal *(Naḥal Ha-Besor)* appeared with the following signatures: Isaac Euchel, Simeon Friedländer, Mendel Bresselau, and Zanvil Friedländer.[57]

The prospectus informs "every *maskil* (enlightened person) who thirsts after truth and seeks knowledge" that soon there will begin to appear a monthly called *Ha-Meassef* which will consist of the following five divisions: (1) poems and poetic articles (in this connection the editors consider it necessary to stress that they will not publish any erotiç poems; also no place will be found in their journal for poems in which Greek and Roman gods are mentioned by name, following foreign patterns); (2) treatises on philology, exegesis, and other sciences, as well as on moral and physical education; (3) biographies of great men of "our nation;" (4) news of events in Jewish life in various lands; and (5) reports about new books that have appeared.

Naḥal Ha-Besor concludes with a summons to the Jewish youth:

Know, our dearly beloved brethren, that not for the sake of honor and also not for financial purposes are we producing our journal. We have only you in mind; we wish simply to be of assistance to you. Come toward us, then. Do not remain deaf to the demands of the new time, the time of education and enlightenment. Read our journal attentively, be its loyal friends. See how all people strive after knowledge, think day and night about raising children, about education for their youth. How can we sit calmly with folded hands? Behold, men of great knowledge have arisen among us. They wish to lead us in the paths of Torah and wisdom—and shall we turn away from them and not follow their words of truth? Arise, our brethren. Close your ranks. With firm steps set out to seek the treasures that are more precious than the greatest wealth, and faithful watchmen, men of truth and knowledge, will illuminate our way.

57. The author of *Naḥal Ha-Besor* was Isaac Euchel.

At the end of *Naḥal Ha-Besor* there follows a German *Nach-schrift* in which it is reported that in a special supplement of the journal German articles, "especially regarding education," will also be printed. In the month of Tishri 5544 (September, 1783) the first number of *Ha-Meassef,* which had an enormous influence on the first two generations of the era of Haskalah, appeared.[58] *Ha-Meassef* was so loved that when it became rare and hard to obtain, the *maskilim* lovingly copied the major articles, and the editors of *Bikkurei Ha-Ittim* deemed it necessary to reprint for their readers *Mivḥar Ha-Meassef,* the "best of *Ha-Meassef.*" Thereby the journal obtains for the scholar of literature a special cultural-historical significance, notwithstanding the fact that its literary value is very slight. Precisely the weakest is the section in which the editors of *Ha-Meassef* took special pride—the section of poetry and belles-lettres.

Naftali Herz Wessely laments in his *Divrei Shalom Ve-Emet* (I, end of paragraph 7) that in German-Polish Jewry not a single significant poet has appeared for "many generations." He explains this by the fact that the youth study with teachers who are "stammerers," incapable of arousing among their pupils love for the poetic beauties of the Bible. When, however, the children will thoroughly study the Hebrew language in the schools and become familiar with the Torah through the aid of Mendelssohn's poetic translation, it is to be hoped that there will again appear among us "poets and speakers of elegant things."

The founders of *Ha-Meassef* were members of the *Hevrat Doreshei Leshon Ever.* They not only thoroughly studied Mendelssohn's translation of the Pentateuch but some of them continued Mendelssohn's work; they, too, translated Biblical books and accompanied the text with a new *biur,* or commentary. Nevertheless, Wessely's hope was not, for the time being, fulfilled. Among these "speakers of elegant things" not a single poet appeared. The "lion in the society," Naftali Herz Wessely himself, published in *Ha-Meassef* "occasional poems," laudations in honor of the "righteous kings"—the Prussian Frederick, the Austrian Joseph, and the French Louis XVI—or poems and praises for his friends David Friedländer, Isaac Euchel, and others. But in all these pieces there is not a spark of true poetry. Only in his elegy on the tragic death of the young Duke

58. Under the title-page: *Ha-Meassef Li-Shenat 5544, Kolel Shirim U-Michtavim Asher Ne'esfu Ve-Nikbetzu Yaḥad Al Yedei Anshei Hevrat Doreshei Leshon Ever Be-Kenigsberg.*

Leopold[59] are there a few verses that make a certain impression. Nevertheless, Wessely's weak poetic compositions are at an incomparably higher level than the other poems that flood the pages of *Ha-Meassef*.

One must take into consideration in this connection that these puerile, clumsy, woodenly stiff verses, which are very often totally inconsistent with the elementary demands of caesura and meter, were written by battlers for beauty and fine taste almost fifty years after the appearance of Moses Ḥayyim Luzzatto's *La-Yesharim Tehillah*. Only then does one obtain a clear notion of the low level to which the literary creativity and poetic taste of the Judeo-German community had sunk in the eighteenth century.[60] The only poems published in *Ha-Meassef* which have a certain significance belong either to older poets of earlier generations, for example, Solomon Ibn Gabirol's well-known poem "Kichlot Yeini"[61] and a couple of poems of Moses Abudiente of the seventeenth century, or are reprinted from the collections of poems *Eleh Venei Ha-Ne'urim* that was published by a contemporary of the Meassefim, the Italian Ephraim Luzzatto.

Born in San Daniele in the Italian province of Friuli into a wealthy and prominent family in 1729, Ephraim Luzzatto spent a happy youth and obtained a comprehensive education. He considered Italian literature his own, and it aroused in him the drive toward poetic creativity. His favorite verse form was the sonnet. Intoxicated by the splendor of nature and filled with youthful joy, he pours out his feelings in ringing verses (see his sonnet "Mi Anochi U-Mi Veiti"). He also celebrates love and feminine beauty in such artistic sonnets as "Ḥannah Ayelet Ḥen," "Nafshi Asher Ad Koh," "Im Ha-Adon Tzahuv," "Mi Zot Ha-Me'unegah," and "Yaldah Yafah Aḥat." The young poet, however, also understands how to connect the purely Italian forms harmoniously with deep national feelings and

---

59. *Ha-Meassef*, 5545, p. 143.
60. In the *Ha-Meassef* of the later years (5550, p. 95), when the tendencies of the journal changed markedly, one of its contributors complains: "My soul is poured out within me when I remember the evil custom which the children of Israel followed in our days, constantly composing innumerable poems and verses, and not one of them knows anything about the poetic art. What is there between you, my brethren and my friends, and poetry? Do you all wish to be poets?" In this connection the editorship itself makes use of the opportunity and complains in a special note that they are assailed everyday with whole packs "of verses and poems of little value." They therefore request their friends and supporters not to burden them so greatly with poems but rather to send scholarly and informative articles and reviews.
61. See our *History*, Vol. I, pp. 40–41.

motifs, and he creates such tender songs as "Ḥag He-Asif," "Ad An Elohim," and "Al Har Tziyyon She-Shomem." Luzzatto sang his poems only in his youthful years. After he became a practicing physician (he studied medicine in Padua), the Muses, as he himself notes, abandoned him. When he was already in his middle years, he published in 1768 in London, where he was employed as a physician in a Jewish hospital, the abovementioned collection of poems of his youth, *Eleh Venei Ha-Ne'urim.* [62]

It is characteristic that the Meassefim reprinted in their journal no love poems or national poems from Luzzatto's collection but only didactic ones. Didactic poems in general were greatly favored by the editors of *Ha-Meassef,* who devoted a special section of their journal to *mishlei musar,* fables and proverbs. This literary genre, which had been so loved among Jews for centuries, was the only realm in which the Meassefim permitted themselves, albeit in a rather weak fashion, to issue forth with the arrow of satire against their ideological opponents. In the fable "Ha-Kochav, He-Avim, Veha-Ruaḥ" (The Star, the Clouds, and the Wind) the story is told of a brilliant star which lit up from the north. The clouds could not bear its radiance and decided to cover it, so that the world should not see its bright light. But a storm wind broke out, dispersed the dark clouds, and the star reappeared once again in all its splendor. [63] The fable "Ha-Ishah Veha-Devorah" (The Woman and the Bee, *idem.,* 5548, p. 95) is directed against those who admonish men not to occupy themselves with the sciences. Another fable concludes with the following pessimistic moral: "Whoever increases wisdom increases hatred, whoever increases knowledge increases jealousy; only the fool and the boor dwell serenely in the darkness of ignorance like a blooming onion." [64]

The Meassefim also devoted much attention to poetic prose. "Speakers of elegant things" were, after all, their ideal, and the task they set themselves was to revive the Hebrew language, to create a new, genuinely literary style. The representatives

---

62. The edition appeared in only one hundred copies and is now extremely rare. Hence we give the full title (in translation): "These are the children of youth *(Eleh Venei Ha-Ne'urim),* given birth to by the physician Ephraim Luzzatto, when the spirit of poetry rested upon him in the days of his youth when he was still in the land of Italy, and their father mocked them and threw them away to another land as of this day, and they weep and wander about in the streets of London and have made no provision for themselves." Ephraim Luzzatto died in Lausanne in 1792.
63. *Ha-Meassef,* 5544, 150.
64. *Ibid.,* 5548, 335.

of Haskalah in their time marvelled greatly at the successes of *Ha-Meassef* in this realm. The objective literary historian, however, cannot altogether agree with this. To be sure, at first glance it may appear that, with their enthusiasm for the Hebrew language, the Meassefim are reminiscent of the intense interest in the language of the Bible that the Jewish intelligentsia manifested in the first heyday of Arabic culture. The riotous flowering of Arabic, the holy tongue of Islam, had the effect that Jews became jealous and endeavored to bring their own holy language, that of the Bible, to the same high level. Under the influence of the rich and beautiful Arabic tongue and its literature, the Spanish Jews also began especially to interest themselves in the classic poetic treasures of the Bible and its language, and among them was born the desire to attempt to create in this language not only religious poetry but also secular poetic works and, indeed, to employ Arabic forms and principles of meter and verse construction in their efforts.

We also know that the brilliant zenith of Hebrew poetry and belles-lettres was preceded in Spanish Jewry by classical, scientific philology. To be sure, the Hebrew philologists, led by Jonah Ibn Jannaḥ, regarded their scholarly work as a means to a firmly established goal: to explore the language of their *national sanctuary*, the Holy Writings, to understand and explain better the meaning of the Torah.[65] However, they not only helped achieve a more accurate understanding of the meaning of the "Holy Writings, revealed by God" but also, incidentally, laid the foundation of the splendid flowering of Hebrew poetry. The Meassefim devoted themselves much to philological investigations and published in their journal scores of articles on Biblical exegesis and philology. And even if a quite superficial dilettantism is not rarely discernible in these articles, it must, after all, be remembered that among the editors of *Ha-Meassef* several did, indeed, acquire renown[66] as authors of important handbooks and textbooks.

As "Biurists," the Meassefim, like Ibn Jannaḥ's contemporaries in their time, devoted themselves much to the explication of the text of the "Holy Writings revealed by God." The editor of the journal, Isaac Euchel, wrote a *biur*, or commentary, to the Book of Proverbs. The other editor, Aaron Wolfsohn, translated into German the Books of Job and Kings and supplied them with a *biur*. Joel Brill (Loewe) published Men-

65. See our *History*, Vol. I, pp. 23ff.
66. Of this in the later chapters.

delssohn's translation of the Psalms with his own *biur* and with an extensive introduction on Hebrew poetry. He also translated the Book of Jonah and wrote a commentary to it. In *Ha-Meassef* itself he published a commentary to the "Song of Deborah"[67] and, together with Wolfsohn, wrote a commentary to the Five Scrolls.

With this, however, the analogy ends. The Jewish intelligentsia of Arabic Spain, finding themselves under the powerful influence of Arabic culture, endeavored—and, indeed, with great success—to bring the alien treasures of culture and science under the supervision and rule of Jewish religious thought, to bind these organically with their own national cultural creativity. The men of that era regarded the Hebrew language as an organically integral thing throughout the long course of its development. They endeavored to adapt it to the new, highly complicated demands of their day, employing in this connection the verbal material of the later Talmudic and Midrashic literature. They were also not afraid of coining new word-images in their effort to find the capacity for expressing new concepts and ideas. But the Meassefim, who always argued that their chief purpose was to raise the Hebrew language which "rolls about in the dust of neglect and the filth of shame,"[68] in fact endeavored to return, in an artificial, anti-historical fashion, to the pure, ancient language of the Bible that would be free of all later alterations and enrichments in regard to word-construction and word-material. Discernible here is a clear tendency violently to tear through the intensely despised "jargon" and the tasteless barbarism of the rabbinic style of that era.

It must also be taken into consideration that even though *Ha-Meassef*, as long as it appeared in Koenigsberg, did not permit itself any sharp expressions against the orthodox and the old way of life, a rather cool attitude on the part of the Meassefim to Talmudic literature is nevertheless detectable. *Ha-Meassef* designated a special rubric for *Toledot Gedolei Yisrael*, in which were printed biographies of great men who possessed, aside from Jewish knowledge, European culture in broad measure—e.g., Maimonides, Isaac Abravanel, Joseph Delmedigo, Menasseh ben Israel. In it was also published a

---

67. *Ha-Meassef*, 5548, pp. 322–324.
68. See the announcement at the close of the first year's issue. "All our aim is to raise the horn of the language of Judah which lies in the dust of oblivion and in the dung-heaps of shame" (*Ha-Meassef*, 5544, p. 192).

special article on "Der Nutzen von Geschichte und mit ihr verbundene Wissenschaften" (The Use of History and the Sciences Assocated with It, *Ibid.*, 5544, pp. 9–14, 25–30). But when someone applied to the editors of *Ha-Meassef* with a question about the real identity of the emperor Antoninus who, according to the Talmud, studied from "the mouth of Rabbenu Ha-Kadosh," they replied: We can say to this: What has been has been. Of what concern is this to us? Why should we occupy ourselves with such inquiries of ancient times?[69]— The Meassefim had no desire to interest themselves in the Talmudic era.

The Meassefim themselves, however, also grew up in the old-fashioned *yeshivot*, breathed the atmosphere of pilpul and scholasticism, and, as enlighteners and *maskilim*, were permeated with the arid spirit of utilitarian rationalism. In fact, the classic freshness and child-like simplicity of the Biblical narrative-style were alien to them, as was also the emotive pathos of the prophets. Out of the rich verbal material of the Book of Books they were able to produce only a mosaic web, not a living, organic tapestry. Without geniune poetic feeling, the Meassefim mechanically collected Biblical metaphors and expressions in heaps, and in this way created the pretentious, florid, diffuse style that is so typical of their generation.

It is highly characteristic that, even in the battle the Meassefim carried on for the revival of the Hebrew language, there was heard quite sharply the well known leifmotif that resounds in all the social pronouncements of the Jewish "enlighteners": "What will the Gentiles say?" Mordecai Schnaber,[70] when considering in *Ha-Meassef* the question of the systematic study of Hebrew, comes forth, first of all, with the following argument: What will the peoples among whom we dwell say when they become convinced that they are more competent in the Hebrew language than we Jews are?[71]

Enthusiasm for "enlightened absolutism" manifests itself even more prominently in *Ha-Meassef* than in Wessely's *Divrei Shalom Vè-Emet*. The humanitarianism and graciousness not only of the "kind king" who issued the Edict of Toleration, but also of Louis XVI and of the Prussian Frederick who, with his anti-Jewish statutes, reminds one—in the expression of the English historian William Prescott—of the darkest times

69. *Ha-Meassef*, 5546, 183.
70. See above, Chapter Two.
71. *Ha-Meassef*, 5544, 185. "And what will the nations about us say when we converse or debate with them in a language with which they are more familiar than we?"

of the Visigothic regime, are here sung in emotive poems of praise.[72] In talentless, limping verses Frederick's birthday is especially celebrated (*Ha-Meassef*, 5544, pp. 65–69), as well as the great deeds that he manifested in the war (*ibid.*, 5545, pp. 17–20). And when this "gracious king" died, *Ha-Meassef* broke into bitter weeping and mourned for the "orphaned people of Israel." "We are not able," we read in the essay of lament, "to relate Frederick's great deeds. We shall only mention the vast kindnesses with which he favored us Jews, so that you, my people, should know and understand whom you have today lost."

To be sure, no matter how strongly the Meassefim endeavored in their patriotic enthusiasm to discover the "benefits and favors" that the deceased king had done for Jews, they managed only to mention that in the capital city of "old Fritz" there lived and worked such great Jewish figures as Mendelssohn and Marcus Herz, and that numerous wealthy Jews dwell in Berlin in splendid palaces and have the right freely to carry on their trade and business.[73]

This exaggerated patriotic tone is strongly heard in all the articles in *Ha-Meassef* that treat the question of schools and education.

The task of the school is to raise citizens and patriots. Morality and ethics also obtain in the programs of the schools a prominent utilitarian-civic coloration. The idea that Jews ought as much as possible to demonstrate that they are worthy and *deserve* the graciousness of the government is quite strongly emphasized. "Now, in our days," we read in an article on the education of children,

the sun of righteousness and liberation has risen over the depressed and unfortunate people, for God has aroused the hearts of the rulers and their counsellors to be gracious to us. Therefore the first duty of the elders is to give their children a proper education, to implant in them the seeds of virtue and sociableness, so that they should merit

---

72. See H. Jolowicz, *Geschichte der Juden in Königsberg* (1867).

73. With no lesser emotion did *Ha-Meassef* lament the death of Joseph II: "He raised the beauty of Israel from the dustheap and brought him into the chambers of knowledge and happiness to take part in them, like the men of his own people. He set his pure heart towards the children of Israel and gave orders to lead them to school in order that the way to find good and greatness in the land might be cleared before them" (*ibid.*, 1790, pp. 88–89). Even four years after the Austrian emperor's death, a contributor to *Ha-Meassef* laments the premature death of this "gracious king who did so much "good" for the Jewish populace in emotive, rhetorical lines of poetry. "My tongue cleaves to the roof of my mouth," he exclaims feelingly, "and my throat burns. Many are the tears of my eye, and the sighings of my heart are strengthened when I remember your demise" (*ibid.*, 1794, 70).

the grace of the princes and nobles and be worthy, deserving, and fit to enjoy this grace."[74]

No less interesting in this respect is the rather long article "Divrei Ḥochmah U-Musar" (Words of Wisdom and Moral Instruction) that is written in the form of twelve conversations between a teacher and his pupils.[75] The author of the article, Elijah Morpurgo of Italy, declares himself an ardent admirer of Maimonides and at the end admonishes his pupils "to believe in everything that the last of Geonim in time and the first in importance, Rabbi Moses ben Maimon, may his memory be for a blessing, believed." This strongly Maimunistically-minded teacher descants in a sentimental, patriotic tone about the duties of subjects to their king, who is, after all, to his people "like a father to his sons and like the soul to the body." And since all the king's thoughts are "for the good of his people," the subjects must do only his will, blindly follow all his commands, and not depart from them by a single step.

It is characteristic that among "contemporary issues" virtually no less attention is devoted in *Ha-Meassef* to the question of the burial of the dead than to the issue of the education of children. We noted previously[76] how this question arose in 1772, after the edict which the duke of Mecklenburg-Schwerin issued prohibiting the burial of deceased persons earlier than the third day after death. Because the orthodox perceived in this a grievous "decree" or persecution, the question of the burial of the dead became a real battle—issue for many years among the enlighteners. The editors of *Ha-Meassef* published in their journal the entire exchange of correspondence that Mendelssohn had with Rabbi Jacob Emden on this issue. They also published an open letter to Dr. Marcus Herz requesting him, as an expert, to express his competent view on the matter.

Dr. Herz replied in a special brochure "An die Herausgeber des hebräischen Sammlers über die frühe Beerdigung der Juden" (To the Editors of the Hebrew Collection on the Early

---

74. *Ibid.*, 5544, pp. 133–134. A more literal translation would read: "Now has the time come when the sun of righteousness and healing has arisen for the oppressed of heart and the miserable people. For the Lord has made his spirit shine in the heart of kings and the counselors of the land to do good to them and be favorable to them. Therefore, the first duty of fathers is to lead and conduct their children in the right way, to plant in them the sprouts of good deeds and behavior, so that they may merit the grace of the rulers and be fit, worthy, and suited to receive it."

75. *Ha-Meassef,* 5546, pp. 131–137, 147–156, 164–176.

76. Above, p. 37.

Burial of Jews, 1787).[77] The Meassefim, however, were not content with this. Several years later Joel Brill published a special "Schreiben an die würdigen Mitglieder sämtlicher löblichen und wohltätigen Ḥevrot Gemilut Ḥasadim" (Writ to the Worthy Members of all Commendable and Charitable Burial Societies)[78] on this question. Immediately after him, Isaac Euchel also appeared with his brochure "Ist nach dem jüdischen Gesetze das Übernachten der Toten wirklich verboten?" (Is the Allowing of a Corpse to Remain Unburied Overnight Actually Prohibited According to Jewish Law?).[79] And a third editor of *Ha-Meassef,* Aaron Wolfsohn, employed the traditional Purim-play form in treating this controversial issue.[80]

It seems paradoxical that this question about burying the dead became a burning issue of *life.*[81] This, however, is characteristic not so much of *Ha-Meassef* as of the backward and old-fashioned Jewish way of life in that era, with its blind fear of everything that did not bear the stamp of tradition, of long-accepted custom. Typical in this respect is also the following. In the 1770's inoculation, recommended by many doctors as a protection and remedy against the dreaded smallpox disease, spread ever more widely throughout western Europe. This procedure consisted of injecting the healthy person with the pox virus taken from someone infected with the disease who had lived through it relatively easily. In Jewish circles there was also an interest in the procedure. Here, however, no question was asked about the utility and degree of effectiveness of

77. Printed as a supplement to *Ha-Meassef,* 1788; reprinted in 1789 with several additions.
78. Berlin, at the press of the society *Hinnuch Ne'arim,* 1794. Printed at the expense of several members of *Die Gessellschaft der Freunde* and distributed gratis (see *Ha-Meassef,* VII, p. 160).
79. Printed as a supplement to *Ha-Meassef,* 1797; also published separately.
80. In Breslau a prominent man of wealth died on Friday, several days before Purim. His family, therefore, hastened to bury him before the Sabbath arrived. This annoyed the local *maskilim,* and at the Purim banquet, when a company of disguised Purim-players came to the rabbi, among them appeared Aaron Wolfsohn wrapped in shrouds with an inscription on his back: "I am so-and-so who lay in a faint and the burial society people interred me alive, but, with God's help, I managed to free myself from the grave, and now I stand before you so that you should take a lesson from me" (see S. Bernfeld, *Dor Tahapuchot,* p. 93). Also in his polemic work *Siḥah Be-Eretz Ha-Ḥayyim* Wolfsohn deals with the question of allowing the dead to remain unburied overnight (*Ha-Meassef,* VII, 132, 357–360).
81. Even the Kurland doctor Abraham Bernhard (born in 1760) found it necessary to publish two brochures on the burial of the dead among Jews: (1) "Observation sur l'enterrement prématuré de Juifs" (1799), and (2) "Bemerkungen über das Beerdigen der jüdischen Leichen" (1802). See P. Kon's notice in *YIVO-Bleter,* V, 54.

innoculation. First of all, the question had to be answered whether the procedure was not inconsistent with some paragraph of the *Shulḥan Aruch*. Moses Mendelssohn himself deemed it necessary to send to the editors of *Ha-Meassef* a rather long responsum from one Abraham ben Solomon of Hamburg, in which it is demonstrated with great scholarship that, according to the law, it is permissible to employ this medical remedy. The Meassefim promptly printed the responsum.[82]

The literary value of *Ha-Meassef* for the three years that it appeared in Koenigsberg is, as we see, rather slight. Nevertheless it forms a whole epoch in neo-Hebrew literature. The very fact that there had appeared in the Jewish quarter a periodical of secular content in which are treated not questions of ritual cleanness and uncleanness, but the sun and the spring are celebrated, worldly issues are discussed, and newly published books are reviewed—this alone was a great event that stirred up the congealed way of life and brought a bit of fresh air into the stifling environment.

Even though not with an altogether expert hand, a window had been broken through in the melancholy ghetto wall and people managed to see, albeit merely from a distance and not quite clearly, new horizons of European scope. Despite the fact that many scientific articles in *Ha-Meassef* smack of dilettantism and that the examples of belles-lettres given there are quite often childishly clumsy, the journal awakened in its readers love for beauty and interest in the ancient world of the Bible with its cultural treasures. Indeed, in this lay the secret of its immense popularity in the later centers of Haskalah. The Galician maskilim were not content, as we noted earlier, with reprinting the "best of *Ha-Meassef*" in the 1820's in their journal *Bikkurei Ha-Ittim*, but even considerably later, in the 1860's, their most revered poet Meir Halevi Letteris undertook to reprint the entire *Ha-Meassef* "so that not a single line should be missing."[83]

The year 1786 was the last in which *Ha-Meassef* appeared in

---

82. *Ha-Meassef,* 5545, pp. 5–15.

83. Letteris managed to reprint (1862) merely the first volume of *Ha-Meassef.* In the preface it is noted: "And the volumes of *Ha-Meassef* will be printed by me, God willing, in their fulness . . . Nothing will be missing from them, not a single line . . . For even little things whose value is small at the present time, I will not withhold from readers whose soul longs to have in hand the complete *Ha-Meassef* with all its parts and in the perfection of its splendor, as it was published originally, without taking away from it a word or half a word."

Koenigsberg. That year saw two deaths of great significance for the intellectual currents in the progressive Jewish circles of the Prussian provinces. On January 4 Moses Mendelssohn, whom the Meassefim literally idolized, died. While he was still alive they declared that "from Moses unto Moses there arose none like Moses,"[84] and at the end of the third year's issue they asserted that they would follow his ways and faithfully preserve his doctrine and the ideas he had expressed "on Torah and on worship in the true religion."[85] As a loyal adherent of Jewish tradition, Mendelssohn with his authority undoubtedly exercised a restraining influence on the more radically-minded "enlighteners" and kept them from taking extreme steps. In the same year "old Fritz," the Prussian King Frederick II, whose discriminatory laws against Jews were termed by the renowned Mirabeau (who visited Berlin at that time) "cannabilist laws," also died.

As soon as Frederick's nephew ascended the throne of Prussia, there arose in Prussian Jewry the hope that the new king would ameliorate their civic condition. A "reform movement" began, and the Jewish leaders of Berlin and other large communities submitted petitions to the government, requesting alleviation of the burden imposed by the harshly discriminatory laws. At the same time the wealthy and intellectual circles endeavored as much as possible to demonstrate that in their conduct and mode of life they were certainly worthy of being favored by the "righteous kings" and that they fully deserved endowment with full human rights. Hence it is not surprising that the Koenigsberg *Hevrat Doreshei Leshon Ever* at the end of 1786 decided to extend its program, and that in the final issue of the journal it is reported that the association is being transformed into a new, larger society called *Shoharei Ha-Tov Veha-Tushiyyah* (Seekers of the Good and of Understanding). The publishers of *Ha-Meassef* interrupted the appearance of the journal for a year's time, having decided to transfer it to a new center—the major focus of the Jewish enlighteners, Berlin. The battle for Haskalah now enters a new phase.

84. See above, p. 10, Note 16.
85. *Ha-Meassef,* 5546, p. 212.

CHAPTER FOUR

Mendelssohn's Disciples;
THE PERIOD AFTER HIS DEATH

[Haskalah and assimilation—All troubles derive from "religious prejudices"—The world view of the Meassefim—Their battle against the rabbis—Mendel Bresselau's "summons" and Wolfsohn's brochure *Siḥah Be-Eretz Ha-Hayyim*—The protests against *Ha-Meassef*—The demise of *Ha-Meassef*—Aaron Wolfsohn-Halle, and his *Jeschurun*—The slogan "What will the gentiles say?"—The "Mendelssohnian Haskalah"—Mendelssohn's disciples—Herz Homberg as a man and "enlightener"—David Friedländer as a battler for "common sense"—His struggle for equal rights—Friedländer's attitude toward traditional Judaism; his hatred of "mysticism" and "ceremonial laws"—The "epidemic of apostasy"—The Jewish women in the salons of Berlin—The victory of reason and the illumination of hearts—The influence of Jean Jacques Rousseau and of the Romantics.]

LREADY IN 1770 a pedigreed young Christian traveler, after visiting Koenigsberg, marvelled with great enthusiasm at the women, literally overwhelming with their culture and elegant taste, that he encountered in wealthy Jewish homes.[1] Prominent foreigners were even more impressed

1. See Jolowicz, *Geschichte der Juden in Königsberg*, 1867, 92–93.

when in the 1780's they visited the capital city of Prussia and there made acquaintance with the rich Jewish families. We noted above that the wealthy Jewish merchants and manufacturing families were not only the harbingers of the capitalist–bourgeois development in Prussia; they were also the "cream" of Berlin society, the splendor and ornament of the local intelligentsia. The old-fashioned Christian bourgeoisie of Berlin, with its rather small stratum of largescale merchants, still lived in the old-fashioned way and their homes could hardly be compared with the luxurious homes of the Jewish bankers and financiers who carried on largescale business affairs with foreign countries and were in intimate relationships with the French colony in Berlin.[2]

The young of the middle and higher Christian nobility, who at first had associations with the Jewish bankers only on financial matters, later began eagerly to spend their free time in the salons of the latter's wives and daughters. Mendelssohn facilitated and strengthened the process of rapprochement which gave young Jews the possibility of becoming familiar with the Christian world and European culture. Proudly the Koenigsberg *Ha-Meassef* declares[3] that "the Jewish daughters all speak the European languages [German and French] fluently, and Yiddish is entirely foreign to them." The contrast between life-loving Berlin in Frederick the Great's time, and even more especially in the permissive and profligate years of Frederick William II's regime, and medievally ascetic Judaism was enormous. And from the other side of the Rhine, the thunder of the approaching storm was heard ever more clearly and loudly.

The ideas of the French Encyclopedists and enlighteners became increasingly popular among the Jewish intellectuals in Berlin. Especially fashionable was Voltaire. His sharply pointed epigrams found immense favor among the Jewish youth who were raised on the subtleties of the Talmudic commentators and pilpulists. "Voltaire," notes the historian Heinrich Graetz, "had far more followers in Jewish homes than in German." But the influence and consequences of the ideas imported from France were quite different in Jewish society than in Christian. The humanitarian ideas brought over from the banks of the Seine to the banks of the Spree aroused in the progressive strata of German society a thirst for culture and enlightenment. However, by the fact that the German ob-

---

2. See J. Fürst, *Henriette Herz, Ihr Leben und Ihre Errinerungen*, 1858, pp. 126, 128.
3. *Ha-Meassef*, 5546, p. 139.

tained European culture, he did not change from a German into a Frenchman; he did not thereby have to renounce his national past or forfeit the uniqueness of his individuality. On the contrary, the awakened spiritual and intellectual consciousness and the enthusiasm for the ideas of enlightenment stimulated national cultural forces and contributed not a little to the powerful growth of the new German literature. To be sure, the rationalist ideas of the French Encyclopedists and Voltaire's bilious sarcasms evoked hostile sentiments toward traditional religious customs and at times even to religion itself in certain German intellectual circles. Thanks to the freethinking critic, the rationalistically-minded intellectuals began to perceive in religion only a pernicious and obsolete memorial of former dark generations. But the German rationalist and freethinker, in adopting an attitude of contempt for the traditional religion, naturally did not thereby cease to be German, a conscious representative of German culture.

Quite different, however, was the situation among Jews. Religion at that time was regarded as the only factor that distinguished the Jews from the entire milieu and placed a characteristic stamp on them. But if the Jew wipes away this stamp and no longer wishes to recognize the power and authority of the religious factor, then the threads that have bound him to Jewry are, as it were, severed, and he remains on the other side of the fence. The one-sided rationalism of that era did, after all, compel the Jewish freethinker to cast off the religious tradition and everything that cannot be justified through logical argumentation or is not confirmed through common sense.

Moreover, in this connection the following fact must be taken into consideration. The ideas of liberation which, in France, brought men to the new Decalogue, the "Declaration of Human Rights," were a logical result of the demands and requirements experienced there by the young, economically maturing "third estate." The French urban bourgeoisie found the old-fashioned feudal order too narrow and restrictive; hence, instinctively, with all its youthful, accumulated forces, it endeavored to destroy the obsolete forms of life and to win political power. But the Jewish representatives of the youthful bourgeoisie, the harbingers of capitalist development in Prussia, were quite far from these demands. The liberating ideas of France did, indeed, find a certain resonance among them, but they did not dream of a new order, of attaining political might. They merely dreamed of obtaining—and this as a gift from the "gracious kings"—the most elementary human rights. In complete contrast to their economic power, the Jews of Berlin lived under the heavy burden of degrading, literally medieval discriminations. Mendelssohn's children, who were used to observing the reverence with which the most brilliant representatives of European culture regarded their father in their home, found, as soon as they appeared on the streets of Berlin, that they were pursued by the street boys with stones and the epithet "Jüdischkes, Jüdischkes!" was hurled after them.[4]

It is therefore quite understandable that upon penetrating into the Jewish ghetto, the enlightenment ideas, the heretical spirit, and the protest against the spiritual chains that Europe obtained as a legacy from the Middle Ages assumed quite unique forms. In addition, it must be remembered that the French notions of liberation in general could penetrate the capital city of Prussia only in a special elucidation. Frederick II was, indeed, reputed to be a freethinker, but it was precisely under his regime that the principle of "enlightened absolutism" or "benevolent despotism" was especially strengthened. Under the regime of this "freethinker," critical thought was not permitted to raise its analytic scalpel against the social order; it could employ it only in the realm of religious matters. "Do not tell me," Lessing writes indignantly to Nicolai,

about the freedom of the press and of thought in Berlin. The entire freedom consists merely in the fact that you can freely insult religion as much as you wish and in the most foolish manner. It will soon come to the point that a decent man will simply be ashamed to use this kind of liberty . . . Should anyone, however, attempt to come forth in Berlin as a champion of civic rights, should he undertake to raise his voice against despotic oppression, as happens, for instance, in France and Denmark, he would promptly be persuaded which land in all of Europe is most strongly enslaved.

This unique "freedom" that prevailed in Frederick's capital city contributed not a little to the fact that the Jewish "enlighteners" assumed a rather hostile position in regard to matters of faith and the tradition of their fathers. Given the onesided rationalism of that era, it is quite understandable that they perceived in their traditional life and in religious "prejudices" enslavement and degradation. Voltaire's well-known phrase "*Écrasez l'infamie,*" "Crush the infamy" (of superstition), found a particularly sharp resonance in Jewish intellectual circles.

4. Mendelssohn, *Gesammelte Schriften*, 1844, Vol. V, p. 567.

Moreover, it must be taken in consideration that, generally, in every spiritual and intellectual crisis, men experience first of all, at the onset, when self-consciousness and critical thought begin to awaken, the pressure of the closest environment. The narrow restraints of the old-fashioned family and the ancient way of life are felt in the beginning as far more painful than social and political oppression. For this reason, indeed, in the primary stage of intellectual awakening, the entire impetus of protest and battle is poured out, first of all, on the obsolete ways of life, on the tradition of the fathers, on what the grandfathers and grandmothers commanded. It should therefore occasion no suprise that even such a profound thinker and keen observer as Solomon Maimon declares, along with the other Jewish "enlighteners," that "the grievous political and moral condition of the Jewish people has been brought about by religious prejudices." Children of the ghetto with its lack of rights, men who experienced intellectual enslavement, who grew up under the oppressive yoke of rigid rabbinism, they were very little suited to independent, critical-historical evaluation. The entire ancient tradition—except for the Bible, which was, after all, highly regarded in the Christian world— was declared outmoded and reactionary, and the enlighteners were prepared magnanimously to sacrifice on the altar of "enlightenment" all the traditions of the Jewish people.

This was the credo of the circles among which the group of literati who, at the end of 1787, re-commenced to issue *Ha-Meassef* lived and worked: Isaac Euchel, Aaron Wolfsohn, David Friedländer, Joel Brill, and others. Naturally, they refrained from seizing the opportunity to issue forth publicly with their credo, so as not to frighten off the readership and not arouse the wrath of the leaders of the community who still belonged to the old generation. In the summons to the "young people of the sons of Israel" which the editors of *Ha-Meassef* published as a preface to the renewed journal they relate how strongly they were attacked merely because of the fact that one editor permitted himself to speak ironically about the preachers who wish to terrify the public with such "exaggerations" as "torments of the grave" and angels of wrath who lash the bodies of the wicked "with iron combs and pointed rods."[5] To assuage the wrath of the orthodox, they had to print Naftali Herz Wessely's long and diffuse article "Ḥikkur Din"[6] in which he demonstrates with

5. *Ha-Meassef*, 5546, p. 124.
6. *Ha-Meassef*, 5548, pp. 97–111, 145–165. Wessely asserts in this connection, as is his fashion, that he does all this briefly, and he believes that he writes a rather short article.

quotations from Menassah ben Israel's *Nishmat Ḥayyim* and similar sources that what the sages of the Talmud relate "about hell and the torments of Sheol" have their foundations in man's reason (*ibid*, p. 165).

Nevertheless, the editors of the Berlin *Ha-Meassef* issue forth quite decisively in their summons[7] under the banner of the modern world view and general knowledge, and set for themselves as their major goal "to enlighten the eyes of the young people of the nation." "Knowledge and science"—this motto is constantly repeated by *Ha-Meassef*. "Science is the soul of the world." Without science the world can have no endurance, *Ha-Meassef* insists.[8] Natural science, declares one of the founders of *Ha-Meassef*, Mendel Bresselau, is the ladder standing on earth whose peak reaches to the heavens.[9] Whereas in the *Ha-Meassef* of the Koenigsberg years the most important place in the scientific section was occupied by exegesis, commentaries on difficult verses in the Biblical text, in the *Ha-Meassef* of the later years the dominant place is taken by the natural sciences. The capable physicist Baruch Linda (Lindau)[10] published in *Ha-Meassef* a whole series of natural science articles (on physics and geography), which appeared in an enlarged scope, and along with several new chapters, in a special work *Reshit Limmudim* (1789) that was extremely popular among readers.[11] Aaron Wolfsohn-Halle also published a number of articles on zoology and treated, in the form of a discussion between two colleagues Eldad and Medad, various questions about physics.

The tone of *Ha-Meassef* became ever bolder. The Meassefim were no longer willing to fulfill Wessely's wish—not to print wine and love poems. Aaron Wolfsohn-Halle wrote a wine song for Purim in which the guests are told:

Drink, friends, drink—
Here is wine and liquor!
Drink and be intoxicated, comrades,
From evening until dawn.[12]

7. The author of the summons was Isaac Euchel.
8. *Ha-Meassef*, 5549, p. 24.
9. *Ha-Meassef*, 5550, p. 312.
10. Born in Hannover in 1759; died in Berlin in 1849.
11. *Reshit Limmudim* went through four editions. In 1830 the second part (*Ḥamishah She'arim Be-Ḥochmat Ha-Teva*) was published. Both parts were published together in 1869. There was also a plagiarist, a certain Simeon of Cremona(?) who stole Linda's popular work, made a book out of it, and published it under the title *Ammud Ha-Shaḥar, Kolel Ḥochmot Atzumot* (see *Ha-Meassef*, 1790, pp. 285–288).
12. *Ha-Meassef*, 5549, pp. 161–164.

Another editor Joel Brill (Loewe) celebrates in some lusty verses the sweet tumult of the joys of love, "What have we in life," asks the leader of the song, "without love and without wine?" And the choir responds:

Only love and only wine
Are all our joy.

Typical also is the poem "Peti Yaamin Le-Chol Davar" of Jehudah Jeiteles in which those who believe in fantastic legends that contradict sober common sense are mocked. "You believe in every foolishness and in old wives tales; you believe in miracles and wonders that men have fabricated but that no one has seen with his own eyes. You believe everything because—the fool believes everything."[13]

A tale is sarcastically told about a little worm that burrowed into a piece of cheese. This petty little worm was quite certain that the whole world was created only for its sake. The rain falls, the sun shines, grasses and plants grow—all in order that the cow should have pasture and be able to give milk. Man worries about it, milks it, in order to achieve the supreme goal —to produce the cheese in which little worms find housing and nourishment. "We are the choicest of the creatures," exclaims the little worm. "We are the final goal and consummate will of the creator." The worm, however, was not destined to finish its speech. A man came up to the table, cut off a piece of cheese with a knife, put it into his mouth, and with it swallowed the little worm, the choicest of the creatures.[14]

In poetry and prose a planned campaign was carried on in *Ha-Meassef* against blind reverence and self-deprecation before acknowledged authorities. One of the editors of *Ha-Meassef* asks an apparently naive question. Is it, indeed, a duty to hold blindly to the ancient principle that the sages of the Talmud put forth: that we ought to incline after the majority? We know quite well, after all, that only individuals know the truth, and the mob, the majority, roams about lost on false paths.[15] Wolfsohn-Halle, in a special article,[16] confirms that the person who raised that naive question is, indeed, correct. The truth can be found only in a few select individuals. The majority, the masses, however, are quite remote from it.

13. *Ha-Meassef,* 5550, p. 320; reprinted in Jeiteles' *Benei Ha-Ne'urim,* 145.
14. *Ha-Meassef,* 5549, pp. 321–323.
15. *Ibid.,* p. 65.
16. *Ibid.,* 303–312.

With increasing sharpness one hears in *Ha-Meassef* restrained wrath and covert hostility toward the orthodox rabbis, to the "company of hypocrites and company of flatterers." With bitter sarcasm the malicious question is raised: "If the shepherds roam about lost, grope like blind men in the middle of the bright day and cannot find the right way, what shall the poor flocks do?"[17] The tone of the journal became ever more militant the more the historical events on the other side of the Rhine in France, the nation agitated by the thunders of revolution, unrolled.

The occurrences in France made a tremendous impression not only on the French Jews but also on those of Germany. The passionate speeches delivered in the National Assembly on liberty and fraternity awakened the loveliest hopes in the intellectual circles of the Jewish populace. An inhabitant of Metz, Abraham Speyer, in the fall of 1789 published in Judeo-German a special "Bashraybung Fun Der Ferenderung Oder Oifrur In Frankraych Waz Man Nent Revolusion" (Description of the Change and Tumult in France That is Called Revolution). To provide the Jewish reader with an opportunity to gain familiarity with the revolutionary events in France, the same Abraham Speyer undertook a new work immediately after this "Bashraybung" came off the press; during the course of less than six months (November, 1789 to April, 1790) he issued a weekly "newspaper" *(Tsaytung)*, or, more accurately, a bulletin in which he gave reports on the important events occurring in revolutionary Paris.[18]

Ha-Meassef also tells in an emotive tone[19] about what was taking place in the National Assembly, how the revolutionaries destroyed the Bastille, and how "our brethren the Jews who live in the royal city of Paris" have seen "the mighty hand that holds the scale of righteousness and justice and does good to all men equally." The Meassefim translated into Hebrew the petition for equal rights that the Jews of Paris submitted and added: Let this be a sign for the children of Israel that the time of beautiful hopes has arrived, hopes that promise us that perhaps in the near future we may expect better and happier days for "the community of Israel that is scattered and dispersed

17. *Ha-Meassef,* 5549, p. 266.
18. Speyer's *Bashraybung* as well as his *Tsaytung* are extremely rare. Only one copy, located in the library of the Jewish Theological Seminary in New York, is known to have been preserved. We have employed Dr. J. Shatzky's detailed report about this edition in *YIVO-Bleter*, 1931, II, pp. 49–71.
19. *Ha-Meassef,* 5549, pp. 368–372.

among the peoples." A report is given of the Abbé Gregoire's humanitarian oration of friendship for the Jews, and this report is also concluded by *Ha-Meassef* with the words: "And we stand and hope for God's help."

At the beginning of 1790 Moses Ensheim, a resident of Alsace, celebrated the advent of freedom and religious tolerance in the pages of *Ha-Meassef.* The poet asserts that "the flame of hatred has been extinguished, and everyone whose behavior is just is secure and peaceful." In emotive verses he expresses his enthusiasm for the National Assembly in which sit "just legislators who have established for themselves an eternal memorial, and with whom future generations will bless themselves."

With great joy *Ha-Meassef* reports that the National Assembly has decreed equal rights for the Jews residing in Bordeaux, and the report that fifty young Jews arrived with cockades on their hats ready to do battle for the National Assembly and the fatherland is accompanied in *Ha-Meassef* with the following words:

How vast, O God, is Your graciousness . . . The children of Your people Israel will no longer be as aliens in their eyes. They will be accounted among them as brothers and will have equal rights with them. Understand this, all you our brethren in all lands where you dwell, *that only with the increase of knowledge will you also be raised up and your condition be improved. You will be liberated and helped only when the whole earth will be covered with understanding and knowledge.*[20]

The spiritual shepherds, the orthodox rabbis, however, were afraid of reforms, of everything inconsistent with the tradition of the fathers. It is therefore quite understandable that the tone in which *Ha-Meassef* speaks of the "shepherds of Israel" became ever sharper and more hostile. Mendel Bresselau of Koenigsberg,[21] one of the founders of the *Hevrat Doreshei Leshon Ever* and *Ha-Meassef* and also the author of the allegorical-dramatic poem "Yaldut U-Vaharut" (1786), issued forth with a long summons, which bears the motto "O house of Jacob, come, let us walk in the light of the Lord," to the "rabbis and scholars of the land who sit on the seat of judgment." He declares that only the blind can now not perceive how very quickly knowledge and science will be the foundation-stone of the world and

20. *Ha-Meassef*, p. 188 (italicized in the original text).
21. Born around 1760; died in 1829.

the best support of our time. All the sages of the peoples, after all, now declare peace and friendship toward Jews. Therefore we also, "the believers in the religion of Moses and of Israel," must also remove every stumbling-block and hindrance that lie in our path. Be not angered, Bresselau addresses the "shepherds of Israel," that I have the presumption to declare the truth to you publicly. The peoples of the world, after all, also say that the sages of Israel regard with mockery and contempt everyone who longs and seeks for truth.

And so I turn to you, leaders of the congregation of Jeshurun. Consider attentively the marvelous events taking place at the present time . . . You may not stand at a distance. On you lies the obligation to support and strengthen the best representatives of our people who think about the general good and strive to lead our people on the path of knowledge, in order thereby to improve our condition.

Though the point is somewhat disguised, it is nevertheless quite easy to recognize that Bresselau demands of the rabbis that they aid the Jewish communal leaders who were then fighting for reform and for alleviating the civic disabilities of the Jews. He also proposed to the "heads of the house of Jacob" that they assemble and earnestly consider how to lighten the yoke of ritual rules among the people. We must, Bresselau stresses, investigate everything according to human reason; this is the way, after all, that the sages of the Talmud themselves followed. They elucidated everything critically with the sharp light of reason, and it never even entered their minds to place Rabbi Simeon under the ban because he permitted the flesh of a bird to be cooked in milk. The *Gemara*, after all, relates that a heavenly voice called out over the house of Hillel and Shammai: "These *and* these are the words of the living God." This is to show that on all questions we must follow our own reason and freely explore and illuminate everything, not like blind oxen bound to the plow, following the leader without understanding.

First of all, Bresselau stresses, we must reform the order of educating children "that has been until now so barbaric and ugly." Especially we must disseminate natural sciences, which are the foundation-stone of all knowledge, among our people. He realizes that the rabbis fear that if the young obtain modern education, "they will become corrupted," and that the rabbis, indeed, point in this connection to former students of the *yeshivah* who used to spend day and night over the Talmud and rabbinic codes but who, as soon as they became familiar with modern science, entirely cast off the yoke of the Torah and set out on crooked ways. But the rabbis should know that the chief responsibility for this lies, in fact, in the bad education these *yeshivah* students enjoyed in their youth. They were brought up and educated in wild superstition. They were told the most foolish legends, things that never happened, and assured that these were pure truth. They were threatened with the assurance that hell is already prepared for anyone who occupies himself with the sciences, and that he is lost forever. Indeed, for this reason, when they became familiar with modern science, their eyes were opened. When they realized how foolish and benighted they had previously been, they poured out all their wrath on their teachers and educators. They could not forgive them for the vainly lost best years of their youth. They came to the conclusion that their guides had misled them. Thereupon they threw off with hatred and contempt everything that they learned in their youth and set out on new, strange paths.

See, Bresselau calls out bitterly, the people around us follow the right ways. They attempt to separate falsehood from truth as rapidly as possible, preach humanitarianism and love of mankind. Even with us Jews, who were previously so despised by them, they now make peace. As for us, we ought to be ashamed and hide ourselves in embarrassment! Among us one hears only of persecutions and controversies. Our leaders hurl the arrows of excommunication for every little cause. There are not among our preachers understanding men who would be able to show the people the right way and teach them what is useful and necessary.

Shortly after Bresselau's summons there appeared in *Ha-Meassef* a sharp critique[22] of the morality-book *Marpe Lashon* composed by the well known rabbi of Hamburg, Raphael Kohen. The reviewer was not satisfied with sharply attacking the author of *Marpe Lashon* in a malicious tone but also exclaimed angrily: "And such a person, who does not even understand the exact meaning of the words, has the impudence to be a leader of the people. What will the nations among whom we live say thereto?" In this connection he also incidentally utilizes the opportunity generally to attack the "Talmudic scholars" for whom grammar is an "abomination," and he deplores

22. *Ha-Meassef*, 1790, pp. 362–380. This review appeared anonymously. However, we conjecture that it was written by Saul Berlin, of whom we shall speak later.

the contemporary "heads of the people" who despise all secular sciences and charges that it is, in fact, through these "leaders" that the Jewish people have become a mockery and a shame among all peoples. With contempt and ridicule they say of us: "A base and unwise people."

The chief editor of *Ha-Meassef*, Aaron Wolfsohn,[23] however, was not content with all this and came forth with a lampoon *Siḥah Be-Eretz Ha-Ḥayyim*[24] filled with hatred and mockery for the "misleading guides," for the obscurantist "rebels against the light" who despise culture and science.

Wolfsohn relates how in the "land of life," in the "other world," Moses Maimonides is met by one of the recently deceased German rabbis. Wolfsohn does not name him specifically but indicates that in his life he passed as "a great scholar in Israel" and in his day hurled fire and brimstone at Mendelssohn's *Biur* and translation of the Pentateuch. Maimonides greets the Ashkenazic rabbi contemptuously: "I know your countrymen, I know how badly educated they are and how wild and crude their deeds are. They cannot even speak a pure, correct language such as men ought to speak."[25] A long dialogue develops between the two rabbis, the author of *Yad Ha-Ḥazakah* and the "great scholar of the generation," the "mighty hammer" of the end of the eighteenth century who even attempted to write a commentary on Maimonides' work.

With acid irony Wolfsohn portrays how degraded, how ridiculously petty the Ashkenazic rabbi is in comparison with the highly cultured Sephardi. When the latter speaks of logic and philosophical problems, the Ashkenazic rabbi replies with foolish subtleties and wild *pilpul* or cites a statement from the *Zohar*, a work of which Wolfsohn says emotively in a special note: "Who of us would not be ashamed and his face not flush with embarrassment on reading such a statement, and many others besides, with which the *Zohar* is filled."[26] And wrathfully Maimonides exclaims: "Yes, I see he [the Ashkenazic rabbi] is still not cleansed from his filth, closes his eyes from seeing, and stops up his heart from understanding." He admonishes the rabbi: "Remove false opinions from your midst; learn to know the Lord in truth."

The dialogue is further accompanied with notes by Wolf-

---

23. From the end of 1790 Aaron ben Wolf Halle began to sign his articles with the name Wolfsohn.

24. *Ha-Meassef*, Vol. VII, pp. 54–67, 120–158, 203–227, 279–360.

25. *Ibid.*, p. 55. This "sin" is also reiterated later, p. 324.

26. *Ha-Meassef*, Vol. VII, p. 149.

sohn himself, some of them written in Hebrew and others in German in Hebrew letters. With piercing mockery he points out the "mode of thinking of some rabbis of our time" for whom the greatest insult is to be reminded of grammar. Their hatred and disgust for grammar, Wolfsohn relates, is so great that one of them even preached a sermon on the Great Sabbath on the subject, noting that "every wicked man is a grammarian," and boasted in this connection that he himself never studied any grammar. Further on Wolfsohn relates how he personally once witnessed a large carp buried with great pomp and ceremony in consecrated ground. This fish had been bought by a good housewife in honor of the Sabbath. On cutting open the carp, certain tones were heard from under the knife, and the pious housewife believed she heard a voice that sounded in her ears like *Shema Yisrael*, "Hear, O Israel." Beside herself, she ran to the rabbi, who at once realized that this fish was obviously a transmigrated soul. He therefore ordered that the carp be brought to Jewish burial with great honor.[27]

The dialogue between Maimonides and the Ashkenazic rabbi is suddenly broken off. With great parade and in the company of a radiant angel, the author of *Phaedon* and *Morgenstunden*, Moses Mendelssohn, appears. Maimonides is exceedingly glad and embraces and kisses his new comrade. Mendelssohn immediately recognizes the Ashkenazic rabbi; the latter, after all, had persecuted him in his lifetime. "Like a bear robbed of its cubs he came to swallow me up," he complains. And when Maimonides indicates that he intends as much as possible to work on this opponent of his, so that he will change his mind and free himself from his views, Mendelssohn exclaims bitterly:

Will an Ethiopian change his skin and the leopard his spots? Just as the Negro cannot alter his pigmentation and the leopard his spotted coat, even less can it be conceived that this man should change himself. You waste your speech for nothing. Your words will be of no avail, for foolishness and ignorance are deeply inscribed in his heart as with an iron chisel and a pen of sharpest stone. They cannot be erased from there except through a divine miracle.[28]

Mendelssohn further complains to Maimonides: This is their foolish manner; they avoid right paths and wander lost over crooked ways. They are not interested in grasping each

27. *Ha-Meassef,* Vol. VII, p. 153.
28. *Ibid.,* Vol. VII, p. 213.

thing according to its proper essence. Their entire wish and desire is simply to manifest their mental acuity, their skill in building and destroying, in planting and rooting out. Out of spider webs they build whole towers that hang in the air and are blown away by the lightest breath.

As a "Biurist" and translator of books of the Bible,[29] Wolfsohn devotes much space in his lampoon to the battle against Mendelssohn's translation of the Pentateuch. Characteristic in this connection is the following point. Wolfsohn indicates in a note that the rabbis are obliged to issue an edict that everyone ought to pray "in the language of his country that he knows and comprehends," i.e., in the language of the country which he commands and understands. But one ought to have no mistake about this. What is involved here is not that everyone ought to *pray* in the language that he speaks and understands; the chief thing is praying in the *language of the country*.

When the Ashkenazic rabbi explains to Mendelssohn that the earlier translators of the Bible made use, in their translation, "of the language that is customary among the children of Israel in Germany, and therefore the reader finds it easily comprehensible," Mendelssohn rejoins with anger: "I have never seen such an erroneous language as that of the German translation that the Jews had before I issued my translation."[30] Wolfsohn himself indicates in a special note that in general one can say that in regard to all the German translations which Jews employed before "the translation of our master Rabbi Moses Mendelssohn" appeared, the ancient comment of the sages of the Talmud is appropriate: "Great shame on you, for they have neither writing nor speech." Indeed, these translations, Wolfsohn exclaims feelingly, have ruined us and brought the house of Jacob to shame, because from them we have accustomed ourselves from childhood on to speak barbarically and incorrectly.

At the close Mendelssohn turns to Maimonides, pointing to the Ashkenazic rabbi:

You see now how right I was when I indicated that foolishness and ignorance are deeply inscribed in his heart . . . They roam about lost in the dark, they do not know and understand in what they will stumble, and they refuse to listen to the voice of understanding, whose only desire is to open the eyes of the blind and to fill their darkness with light.[31]

29. On this, in the following chapter.
30. *Ha-Meassef*, Vol. VII, pp. 287–288.
31. *Ibid.*, p. 290.

With its sharp tone, Wolfsohn's lampoon made a certain impression.[32] Against the radical tendency of *Ha-Meassef* issued forth not only such pietists as the Vienna supervisor of ritual slaughterers, Dov Baer,[33] but also Mendelssohn's ardent disciple the young Naḥman ben Simḥah Barash,[34] a former editor of *Ha-Meassef* itself. Already in 1791 the well-known exponent of Haskalah Mendel Levin (Lefin) sharply attacked *Ha-Meassef* in his French brochure.[35] Bitterly Levin exclaims: "Those who have led it *(Ha-Meassef)* further, thinking that they are more enlightened, have personally conducted themselves badly and publicly attacked the weak sides of the rabbis in their journal; thereby they have called forth the universal contempt of the people and finally become no more tolerant than the orthodox fanatics whom they ridiculed."[36] No less sharply did the cultured physician Baruch ben Jonah Jeiteles, who served on the editorial board of the first year's issue of *Ha-Meassef*, come forth against it. In his pamphlet "Ha-Orev" which appeared in 1795 in Vienna under the synonym Pineḥas Ḥananiahu Argosy da Silva, Jeiteles emphasizes that the *Ha-Meassef* of the last years is in no ideological affinity whatever with the previous journal of the same title. Praising the first years' issues of *Ha-Meassef* to the skies, the author asserts that this journal has long since been silent. Now a company of quite different men have come forward. They give themselves out to be members of the *Ḥevrat Shoḥarei Ha-Tov Veha-Tushiyyah* (Society of Seekers of the Good and Knowledge) and use the popular firm *Ha-Meassef* for their journal which, with its impudent tone, is completely alien to the *Ha-Meassef* of the 1780's. "Let it no longer be called *Ha-Meassef* (The Gatherer)," Jeiteles angrily exclaims, "but *Ha-Asafsuf* (The Rabble)."[37]

I will battle against them until they fall, Baruch Jeiteles declared. In fact, however, they were already finished. The same political and social events that compelled *Ha-Meassef* to become ever bolder and more militant also, to a certain degree, brought it about that it had to fall. First, and most important,

32. Wolfsohn at first kept it secret that he was the author of the tract and pretended that an acquaintance of his ostensibly obtained it from one who was about to die, and the latter expressed the wish that his work be published posthumously. Only after the tract was attacked from various sides did Wolfsohn admit that he had written it and publicly declare: "I, I am the author of it from the beginning to the end" (*ibid.*, p. 300).
33. For Wolfsohn's reply to Dov Baer's attacks, see *Ha-Meassef*, Vol. VII.
34. On him, see one of the later chapters.
35. See our *History*, Vol. VI, p. 276.
36. M. Erik, *Etiudn Tsu Der Geshikhte Fun Der Haskole*, pp. 142–143.
37. "Ha-Orev," p. 5.

it remained without readership. Already at the end of the sixth year's issue (Fall, 1790), the editors complained that the "number of subscribers has declined markedly." They were therefore compelled to transform *Ha-Meassef* from a monthly into an irregular publication. From time to time they would issue a number consisting of six printers sheets, and four such numbers would constitute a volume. As soon as the number of subscribers reached no less than two hundred, the editors promised "promptly to continue" the journal, "according to our best possible powers."

However, all of four years passed before the first number of the irregular journal appeared. The editors were already a new group, no longer Euchel and Berlin but Aaron Wolfsohn and Joel Brill (Loewe) both of whom were in the leadership of the Wilhelm-Schule in Breslau.[38] Each year only one number appeared, so that the seventh volume extended through all of four years (1794–1797). At the end of this volume, the tidings are given in a letter from Amsterdam[39] that, on September 2, 1796 at the Hague, a decree granting equal civic rights to the Jews was adopted in the Batavian Republic. It is extremely symptomatic that immediately after the decree about the emancipation of Jews in the Batavian Republic, which was published in German translation, follows the statement of the editors that the number of subscribers has declined recently from 150 to 120. Given such a small number, the journal cannot survive. The editors, however, hope "that our journal will be supported and properly received by the better part of the nation," and that there will be 200 persons who will annually contribute two thalers to it. "The sequel must show," we read at the close of the statement, "whether we have been over-optimistic or not."[40]

The two hundred persons were *not* found, and *Ha-Meassef* had to succumb. For the moderate elements the *Ha-Meassef* of

38. The Wilhelm-Schule was founded in 1791.
39. It is virtually beyond doubt that the correspondence was sent in by Tzevi Hirsch of Ilfeld who, two years later, in 1799, published in Hebrew translation under the title *Divrei Negidim* all the debates that took place in the Batavian National Assembly before the decree regarding equal rights for Jews was issued. Characteristic is the long introduction *(petiḥah)* of the translator. He feels delighted that the great maxim "And thou shalt love thy neighbor as thyself" is presently realized through the motto "Liberty, Equality, Fraternity." Now that we have been granted all rights, we also must behave towards the people in whose midst we live with love and friendship. As citizens with full rights, we must, above all, no longer be isolated and ignorant. We are obliged to obtain as much knowledge and secular culture as possible.
40. *Ha-Meassef*, VII, p. 401.

the 1790's was already too radical, and those who were in agreement with Wolfsohn considered a Hebrew journal quite superfluous. It must be taken into consideration in this connection that the "Declaration of Human Rights," proclaimed under the thunder of the French Revolution, was reflected in the Jewish ghetto in a rather extraordinary way. The motto "Liberty, Equality, Fraternity" logically led to the demand for equal rights for Jews also, but for Jews simply as men, as members of the universal human family, not as representatives of a separate community, adherents of a religion which is, after all, "filled with prejudices."

It seemed self-evident that, if the Jew wished to participate in the new order and become a member of the universal human family with equal rights, he must cast off the old, obsolete, and irrational, i.e., renounce the tradition of the fathers and place himself under the radiant wings of all-human reason. One must also consider, in this connection, the following highly important fact. In that era of cosmopolitanism and extreme rationalism, the concept of the nation was completely merged with the concept of the state, the kingdom. The French Encyclopedists, for instance, explain the word "nation" as follows: "a collective word denoting a significant number of people who live in a territory with firmly established boundaries and are under the sovereignty of the same government."[41] It was therefore obvious that, if the Jew wished to enter into fraternal relations with the new world and desired to become a member of civic society with equal rights, he must cast off the old and obsolete, everything that distinguishes him from the community. And, of course, his faith, the Jewish religion, by which was actually understood at that time the whole national culture of historic Jewry, did separate the Jew. Of an objective, critical examination of the historical development of the Jewish religion, of its role and significance in the growth of the national culture, there could be no discussion in that anti-historical age.

It is therefore quite understandable that the "enlightening" movement in the intellectual Jewish circles of Berlin soon assumed sharply assimilatory forms. Under these circumstances an organ such as *Ha-Meassef*, which propagandized for enlightenment in the traditional language of the Bible, became quite superfluous. It was drowned by the stormy waves of assimila-

41. *Encyclopédie* etc., tom. XI, Neufchatel, 1765: *Nation . . . mot collectif dont on fait usage pour exprimer une certaine etendue de pays renfermée donc de certaines limites et qui obéit au même gouvernement.*

tion.[42] A very unique mixture of naive assimilation and servile self-deprecation, of thirst for knowledge and impetuous pursuit of pleasure and the joys of life, is prominently discernible in the tumultuous initial period of the assimilation movement. With the ardor of newly converted disciples the Jewish enlighteners displayed their self-deprecation before Christian society and its world-view and uncritically assumed everything as revelation—even the notions this society had concerning historical Judaism and Jewry. Very typical in this respect is the German brochure *Jeschurun* that was published by Aaron Wolfsohn, the editor of *Ha-Meassef.*

In this work, planned as an *apology* against anti-Semitic attacks, the author concedes that persons raised and educated on the Gospels must be men of ideal virtue, for the Gospels are filled to overflowing with maxims that preach pure love of mankind; those, however, raised on the Talmud have to be morally degraded persons. Wolfsohn therefore concludes that the government should establish a special commission that would carefully investigate the Talmud and the Midrashic literature, and that it be granted authority to eliminate all passages that it finds harmful and improper.[43]

Having grown up in intellectual serfdom in the ghetto with its disabilities, the Jewish enlighteners were unable freely and independently to undertake a critical analysis of the values of their historical past and to appreciate them properly. Voltaire's slightest sarcastic remark in regard to religion in general and the Jewish religion in particular used to be accepted among the Jewish enlighteners of Berlin as divine revelation. Everything associated with tradition and traditional Judaism was *ipso facto* considered by them old-fashioned and obsolete, and only on "the other side," in the Christian world, did the goddess of enlightenment shine before them in all her magical splendor.

"What do the Gentiles say?" "Why should the Gentiles

42. Only twelve years later, under different conditions, was *Ha-Meassef* revived for a short time.

43. In his *Siḥah Be-Eretz Ha-Ḥayyim,* in which Wolfsohn issues forth very sharply against the *Zohar,* despite the fact that he recognizes that there are in it also "many very good and proper things," he expresses the wish: "It would be very good for us if some person whom God has filled with wisdom and understanding would labor to extract from this book the precious from the worthless and to distinguish between the holy and the profane, so that we might receive from it only the good and not the bad. And it would be accounted to him for righteousness from the Lord, for he would have lifted up a stumbling-block from the way of his people" (*Ha-Meassef,* Vol. VII, p. 346).

say . . . ?" This was the basic motif among the Jewish enlighteners of the "Berlin school." To obtain favor among the peoples
of the world and to be accepted in Christian society, they did
everything—only to be similar to "others," to be like "all." The
historian Heinrich Graetz remarks of this era:

They set themselves the task of rooting out from Jewish life and the
Jewish customs everything that could offend elegant taste, everything that renders the Jew ridiculous. But, along with this, they also
rejected everything inexplicable through reason, everything that has
a national stamp and was associated with memories of great events
of the historical past. They endeavored especially to eliminate everything that could make the Jews appear a separate community in the
eyes of Christians. The greatest compliment one could pay to a representative of this tendency was to tell him that it was literally impossible to distinguish him from a Christian, either by his external appearance or his entire demeanor.

The most characteristic thing in this connection is the fact
that this movement came to be known in history as the "Mendelssohnian Enlightenment." These representatives of assimilation and spiritual mimicry passed as Mendelssohn's disciples
and adherents, and they themselves praised the "Jewish Socrates" to the skies as their guide and spiritual leader. At first
blush this seems paradoxical—so diametrically different were
Mendelssohn's philosophy and world view and his entire behavior from the ideas expressed in Wolfsohn's *Jeschurun*.
Nevertheless, this is not at all an accident, a caprice of history.
It is a logical and just decree of Providence, an instructive
illustration of the ancient notion of "reward and punishment."

Mendelssohn concludes his *Jerusalem* with inspired lines in
which he speaks with high enthusiasm about "our loveliest
treasure *(unser edelstes Kleinod)*"—freedom of thought. In literature and in life Mendelssohn was the noble knight who faithfully served the ideal—freedom of thought, speech, and persuasion. His contemporaries enthusiastically note how tactfully
and sagely he manifested his tolerance for ideological antagonists and persons whose philosophy was alien and inimical to
him. Given Mendelssohn's pliable character, however, tolerance not infrequently passed beyond desirable bounds and became—lack of principle. His yielding nature at times made him
forget the well-known principle that tolerance must not wipe
out the distance between varying philosophies and world
views, must not pass over into opportunism. Lessing, the mili-

tant battler for tolerance and freedom of thought, indeed, notes, albeit in rather soft words, that his friend's weakness was that he "endeavors to see in everything also the good side."[44]

Mendelssohn not only associated with persons of opposed philosophies and world views; he also found it proper to entrust to these persons, who were quite alien to him in their tendencies and strivings, the realization in life of the ideals that were precious and beloved to him. He used to say frequently that men can be judged only for their "acts of commission and omission," but that one cannot take away from them the capacity freely to "think and speak." However, in this connection he not infrequently forgot that principles and convictions also obligate one to certain acts. Hence it is extremely interesting, in this context, to consider carefully Mendelssohn's friendly relationships with his two closest "disciples and followers," who played a rather significant role in the first period of the "Berlin enlightenment." These two men were Herz Homberg and David Friedländer.

Educated in a *yeshivah* in Pressburg, Naftali Herz Homberg remained throughout his long life[45] a bitter enemy of rabbinic Judaism and its official representatives. His was a rather averagely endowed nature, with a one-sided and short-sighted intellect of rather small scope. In addition, he had a heart dry as last year's palm-branch, without a spark of the "holy spirit" and lofty emotions. Everything beyond the narrow boundaries of practical, sober utilitarianism was dismissed by him as vain and pernicious. It is difficult to explain wherewith the young Homberg obtained favor with Mendelssohn and became a frequent visitor in his home. After Solomon Dubno broke with Mendelssohn and left Berlin, Mendelssohn entrusted Homberg with writing the *Biur* to the Book of Deuteronomy.[46] The author of *Jerusalem*, as we see quite clearly from his letters,[47] knew very well that, in regard to the question of how one ought to evaluate the significance of the cultus and the observance of the commandments in Jewish life, his own position was

---

44. It is interesting that Solomon Maimon also says in praise of Mendelssohn that the latter "understood the art of finding the good side of each person and of each event" (*Lebensgeschichte*, p. 379, quoted according to the Yiddish translation).

45. Homberg was born in Lieben (near Prague) in 1749, and died as a very old man in Prague in 1841.

46. Many years later (1817) Homberg published his commentary to the entire Pentateuch, and also to Jeremiah and Job (under the title *Ha-Kerem*).

47. *Gesammelte Schriften*, 1844, Vol. V, pp. 669ff.

diametrically opposed to that of his young friend. Neverthe-less, he did not perceive in this any reason for not entrusting Homberg with the education of his son Joseph, in whom he desired to implant piety and love for the traditional faith and the customs of the fathers.

In 1782, shortly after the publication of Joseph II's Edict of Toleration, Homberg left Mendelssohn's home in the expecta-tion that he would manage to obtain some government post. On parting, Mendelssohn gave him his portrait with the in-scription: "My friend, my son, the second father of my own son." After spending a year as a teacher in Trieste, Homberg returned to Vienna and was soon appointed inspector of the Jewish normal schools. In a short time he gained universal hatred among the orthodox Jews by his conduct.

Taking the position that traditional Judaism consists only of "prejudices" and that the government is the radiant bearer of progress and culture,[48] Homberg considered it necessary to carry through "enlightenment" among Jews by coercive meth-ods. In 1778, a couple of years after the issuance of the notorious "Judenordnung," which so thoroughly ruined the economic existence of the Jewish community in Galicia and threw more than a hundred thousand Jews into the abyss of hunger and distress, Homberg published in Lemberg "by sovereign de-cree" a summons to the rabbis *Iggeret El Ro'ei Seh Pezurah Yisrael* (A letter to the Shepherds of the Scattered Sheep Israel).[49]

Praising to the skies the great mercies which the "enlight-ened" emperor Joseph shows to the Jews, Homberg explains, incidentally, that he applies to the leaders of the people and not

48. To provide some notion of Homberg's exaggerated patriotism, we present here several quotations from his textbook *Imrei Shefer:* "The king is not impetuous in words and deeds but first takes counsel with his advisors and sages and weighs their counsel well in the spirit of his very deep understanding (there is no fathoming of the heart of kings). And afterwards he decrees and gives laws . . . and, lo, Scripture says: 'The heart of kings . . . is in the hand of the Lord; He inclines it withersoever He wishes' (Proverbs 21:1). If it be so, then all the orders of the king are the will of God Himself Blessed be He . . . The wisdom of the king is very great, for the will and desire of the king is none other than to do good and benefit the people of his land, and the command-ment of the king is [issued] with the counsel of the Lord . . . and it is not permitted to search and inquire if the order that goes out from the ruler is good or not. . . . Every citizen faithful of spirit and clean in hands trusts, in the innocence of his heart, in the righteousness and graciousness of his king, that the latter will not decree anything that is not good and beneficial to the people of his land . . . the Holy One Blessed be He, in His holy will, seats kings upon the throne, and they are the agents of his sovereignty to do justice in the land and to lead the nations in righteousness."
49. Published also in *Ha-Meassef* (5548, pp. 222–236).

to the people itself, the "multitude," because the multitude consists, after all, entirely of men who grope in the dark and "who are not worth having the slightest moment spent on them." He adds that "a certain sage long ago said of this, 'Whoever wishes to persuade fools and to make the skin of a Negro white expends his effort in vain.' "[50] Homberg also turns to the rabbis simply because he is modest and wishes to give them the choice of fulfilling with good will the commandments of the gracious emperor. But if they will not do so, he warns them beforehand that he will at once inform the officials, those who are close to the throne, and "as the latter will decree, so shall it be."[51]

The shepherds of Israel understood Homberg's "hint" and carried on an obdurate battle against him as an informer and "troubler of Israel." Six years later, after Homberg had become persuaded how slight and insignificant was the success of the new Jewish normal schools, he addressed to the Austrian government a "memorial" on how to carry through religious reform in the most rigorous fashion among the Jewish populace. In the "memorial" it is indignantly noted that the Jews especially distinguish themselves by such defects as enormous national and religious arrogance. All this must be rooted out. Among the other Jewish national defects, their profligacy in sexual intercourse is particularly stressed ("They yield more to the sexual drive than Christians"). The government has the obligation to purify Judaism and Jewry from the filth with which they are covered.

Joseph II's "mild measures," Homberg asserts, have not obtained their goal. To make an end of Jewish isolation and separateness, it is necessary, first of all, he is fully convinced, to nullify the spiritual power of the rabbis. The rabbinic office is not merely superfluous; it is harmful. The rabbis are responsible for the moral barbarization of the Jewish populace. On the Days of Penitence, as well as on Sabbaths and festival days, they address God with the prayer that He avenge Himself for the blood of His faithful servants that has been shed. The leaders of the people should be appointed by the government. All the *yeshivot* or rabbinic schools in the land should be closed,

---

50. *Ha-Meassef*, 1788, p. 236: "To you, the sages of Israel and the understanding of my people, not to them, have I given my word. And they are not worth wasting one minute upon them, for the sage has already said: he who argues with fools and wishes to whiten the skin of a Negro—both have lost their labor."
51. *Ibid.*, p. 236.

and only one higher Jewish academy should remain in Prague; the Hebrew language should be left entirely "outside use." The teachers in this academy ought to be appointed, according to Homberg's proposal, through the *normal school teachers*, i.e. by Homberg and his assistants,[52] under whose supervision all the instructors of the academy *ought constantly to be*. The Yiddish language must also be prohibited in the school. Furthermore, a special committee should be selected that would re-examine all the Hebrew and Yiddish books and immediately eliminate every expression that may arouse religious fanaticism or superstition and prejudices.

Homberg himself found it necessary to come to the aid of the censors and revisers, "so that they might deal with the numerous Jewish books that are filled with prejudices and partisan spirit," and assembled for them a roster of Jewish religious works which, in his view, are full of superstition and rabid hatred for other peoples. "Let an *auto-da-fé* be made over the Jewish books," the aggressive inspector of the Jewish normal schools declares.[53]

It is this "enlightener" to whom the Jewish masses are indebted for the fact that at the end of the eighteenth century (in 1795) the intensely hated "candle tax" was imposed upon them, to cover the expenses of maintaining the normal schools and their teachers.

In the militant activity of Herz Homberg are revealed most prominently the characteristic notes that later also were not infrequently discernible among a certain class of "enlighteners"—their argument that the "dark" masses must be forcibly educated, and their servile enthusiasm for the "enlightened government." All this did not flow simply from ideological sources, from pure "enlightening principles," but was closely associated with financial motives: prospects for a teaching position in the schools, or for other means of livelihood. To provide the schools with textbooks and proper catechisms that would be free of "prejudices" was also not a bad side-income. The higher academy projected by Homberg was, indeed, to use his

52. *Die Lehrer dieser hoher Schule werden von den Normalschullehrern gewählt, unter deren Aufsicht sie stehen.*

53. For a discussion of Homberg's activity, see the work of G. Wolf "Die Versuche zur Errichtung einer Rabbinerschule in Österreich" (*Zeitschrift für die Geschichte der Juden*, 1890, V), written on the basis of archival sources; M. Balaban, in *Yohrbukh Far Yidish; Herz Homberg i szkoly Josefinskie dla zydów w Galicyi; Geschichte und Literatur*, 1916, pp. 189–221; also A.H. Weiss, *Zichronotai*, 33–36.

own religious-ethical textbooks and catechisms: the Hebrew *Imrei Shefer* (1802) and the German *Bnei Zion*.[54]

The latter work was especially despised by the Jews in Bohemia and Galicia. For decades the Jewish youth suffered from the unique "oppressive decree" that the right of a young Jewish man and woman to marry was obtained only on the condition that they had well studied Homberg's *Bnei Zion;* only the thorough mastery of the principles of this catechism could guarantee that the young bridal pair were quite familiar with the principles of morality and religion. It should therefore occasion no surprise that Homberg's name was inscribed in the memory of the common people as "a seducer and misleader," and that there circulated in Galicia numerous legends that portrayed the author of *Bnei Zion*[55] as "an apostate out of spite" who used publicly to ridicule the customs hallowed by the people.

Of a different type was Mendelssohn's other disciple, David Friedländer. He had no need, as did Homberg, to exert any efforts to obtain a well-paid position. As a son of a wealthy Koenigsberg family and the son-in-law of a well known Berlin banker, he was free of concerns about a livelihood. After his marriage (1771) Friedländer took up residence in Berlin and there became friendly with Mendelssohn, would frequently accompany him on his travels, and considered himself his loyal follower. After Mendelssohn's death Friedländer was universally acknowledged as the chief leader of progressive Jewry in Prussia. His fellow editors on *Ha-Meassef,* when mourning their great loss in Mendelssohn's death, immediately pointed to the "deceased's friend" as his worthy successor.[56]

However, the distance between this new Joshua and his deceased master Moses was enormous. To be sure, one must concede that Heinrich Graetz's judgment of Friedländer, whom he declared a "flathead" and "Mendelssohn's ape," is

---

54. *Bnei Zion, ein religiös moralisches Lehrbuch fur die Jugend israelit. Nation* (1812). Also in the case of the candle-tax which the government introduced at Homberg's initiative, the "enlightener" enjoyed quite a profit. The Jewish businessmen who farmed this tax obliged themselves to pay him two percent of the income.

55. An irony of history is to be seen in the following fact. Precisely on the title-page of his *Bnei Zion* Homberg considered it necessary to note that he is "a pupil of Mendelssohn's."

56. One of the most involved contributors to *Ha-Meassef,* Joel Loewe (Brill) notes in the introduction to his *Biur,* or commentary, to the Psalms: "And now, alas, for the light of our glory! It is quenched and gone. The chosen of the treasured people lift their eyes to his friend."

overly harsh and not altogether justified. Nevertheless, there is a certain historical irony in the fact that precisely such a person as Friedländer was recognized by everyone as Mendelssohn's fellow-battler and the fulfiller of his will and spiritual testament. Friedländer was certainly much more a merchant than a writer and thinker. He considered himself a convinced freethinker and recognized only one authority before which he bowed humbly throughout his life—sober human understanding. "Healthy human understanding," "healthy reason," "common, straightforward human sense,"—this was Friedländer's idol. On it he bestows his best incenses. He enthusiastically declares it the sole assessor of all values, the "true pillar of fire with which Providence has endowed mankind, so that it would be its leader through the night of life."[57]

In this smug conviction lay Friedländer's power but also his one-sidedness and the narrow range of his world view. In the name of "healthy human understanding" he courageously and indefatigably struggled for equality of civil rights for the Jews of Prussia. When, after Frederick II's death, the throne was ascended by his nephew Frederick William II (1786), the representatives of the Jewish community submitted, as a result of Friedländer's initiative, a petition to the new king requesting amelioration of the condition of the Jews in Prussia. Indeed, Friedländer himself, who, together with his father-in-law Daniel Itzig, led the specially chosen "general deputies," particularly stressed—basing himself on "the fundamental theses of healthy reason"—that if it be desired to make useful citizens of the Jews, "it is very clear" that one must, first of all, remove all discriminations and grant them equal rights with the rest of the populace.[58]

When the government, however, promised only insignificant ameliorations, Friedländer prevailed on the "general deputies" to reject completely such petty concessions.[59] To propagandize the idea that Jews ought to obtain equal rights with the remainder of the population, Friedländer published in the *Berlinische Monatsschrift* (1791) the reply that the Jews of Lotharingia (Lorraine) sent to the National Assembly. It was also through him that all the material was assembled for the

---

57. *Aktenstücke*, 4: *Die gesunde Vernunft, diese wahre Feuersäule, welche die Vorsehung dem Menschen zu Führerin durch die Nacht dieses Lebens beschieden.*

58. See Friedlander's *Aktenstücke*, 1793, 27–28; *ibidem,* "Über die Verbesserung der Israeliten im Königreich Polen," p. 49.

59. All the documents pertaining thereto were published by Friedländer in 1793 in his *Aktenstücke zur Reform der jüdischen Kolonien.*

Sammlung der Schriften an die Nationalversammlung, die Juden und ihre bürgerliche Verhältnisse betreffend that appeared in Berlin (1789). Battling stubbornly for the emancipation of his brethren, Friedländer at the same time agitated strongly within the Jewish milieu for religious reforms according to "the spirit of the time." And it is here that the utter one-sidedness of his philosophy first reveals itself most clearly. An ardent adherent of the rationalist ideas of that era, Friedländer saw in the millennial traditions and the religious cult nothing more than an "intoxicating cup of mysticism" and an obsolete memorial of former generations which must presently be regarded as pernicious and hindering ballast for the purified deistic religion and its moral foundations.[60]

The basic cause of all the troubles of the Jews was perceived by Friedländer in the "ritual and ceremonial laws" that burden life, are completely inconsistent with common sense, and represent nothing more than the "offspring of an inflamed brain." Friedländer was therefore decisively opposed to the name "Jews." We ought, he asserts, to be called "Deists," "Mosaists," or "Israelites,"[61] for "Judaism," after all, places the emphasis on "ceremonial laws" that are obviously, in the light of the present enlightened era, "ridiculous and senseless."[62] And for this "ridiculous absurdity," Friedländer affirms, the Talmud and the rabbis are solely responsible. "Only from the Talmud and the later rabbis," he declares, "did this absurdity come upon us." For him it is beyond doubt that in all "the Talmudic regulations, there is no reasonable sense underlying them."

Hence, Maimonides is a genuine enigma to Friedländer. He can in no way understand how it is conceivable that such a rationalist and freethinker as the author of *A Guide for the Perplexed* should be a codifier of "ceremonial and ritual laws" which are obviously contrary to "healthy reason," and that in this connection he should have so seriously investigated the theories and conclusions of the authors of the Talmud, men so filled to overflowing with the most pernicious mysticism.[63] In

---

60. Especially typical in this respect are Friedländer's letters to Meir Eger which are published in *Zeitschrift für die Geschichte der Juden*, I, 258–272. These letters are interesting not only for the character of their author, but also for that of the whole contemporary period.

61. For this reason, indeed, Friedländer's memorandum on the amelioration of the Jewish condition in Poland bears the title "Über die Verbesserung der *Israeliten* in Königreich Polen."

62. *Ibid.*, 41.

63. See Friedländer's letter to Meir Eger, *op. cit.*, I, pp. 269–270.

the great author of the philosophical *Guide for the Perplexed*, Friedländer sees with terror the image—so despised by him— of a rabbinist and recognizes in him the representative of the institution "under whose tyranny the Jews unfortunately sigh in an incredible manner."[64] Like Homberg, Friedländer was firmly persuaded that it is no longer possible to correct the rabbis. One must therefore free himself from their heavy yoke as quickly as possible.

Friedländer endeavors especially to persuade Christian society that it is gravely mistaken in believing that the rabbis play in Jewish life the same role of spiritual representative as the priests and pastors do among the Christians. The rabbis, he asserts, are merely experts in the tortuous ceremonial laws of the Jews; hence, people apply to them especially with questions regarding what is permitted and prohibited in the matter of food, or what is *kasher* and what is *taref*.[65] Friedländer's hatred for the rabbis goes so far that he even refuses to take account of well known historical facts. When, for instance,[66] he discusses the question of the relationships between the rabbis and the communities, he boldly asserts: "In general, communities were *never*[67] in association with each other." It is absolutely necessary, he maintains, to return to "the pure sources of holy religion." The Jewish faith must be freed from the crude Talmudic-rabbinic husk, and we must go back to the pure religion of Moses, the psalmist King David, and the prophets—a religion that is, according to his firm conviction, constructed on the foundations of healthy rationalism and pure Deism.

Friedländer also concludes that three-fourths of the prayers Jews recite in the synagogue are "complete blasphemy and idolatry."[68] During worship there ought to be as little pomp as possible, without dazzling ornamentations that affect only man's feelings; everything must be calculated to illuminate the mind and warm the heart.[69] The preachers must speak clearly

---

64. *Aktenstucke*, p. 19: *Seufzen die Juden unter der Tyrannay ihres Rabbiners auf eine unglaubliche Weise.*
65. "Über die Vebesserung . . . ," pp. 28–34; *Aktenstücke*, p. 24.
66. *Ibid.*, XXXII.
67. Italicized by Friedländer himself.
68. *Zeitschrift für die Geschichte der Juden*, I, 259. Proceeding from the point of view that a Jew ought to pray in the "language of the country," Friedländer translated the Jewish prayers into German (*Gebete der Juden auf das ganze Jahr*, 1786) and printed the work in Hebrew letters. The arid rationalist Friedländer, lacking the slightest poetic spark, was very little suited to this work. His translation is pallid and colorless. In the same year there appeared in Koenigsberg Isaac Euchel's German translation of the prayerbook (*Gebete für deutsche und polnische Juden aus dem Hebräischen übergesetzt*).
69. "Über die Verbesserung . . .", L.

and in an easily comprehensible fashion, without parables and metaphors, and, "most important of all, avoid mysticism and revery as much as possible."[70]

When Friedländer became convinced that the Prussian government would not, in its stubbornness, listen to the voice of "healthy human understanding" and that the Prussian Jews had no reason to hope for speedy emancipation, he and his followers applied (1799) to the head of the Consistory of Berlin, Probst Teller, with a *Sendschreiben*[71] or open letter that is highly characteristic of the world view of certain progressive Jewish circles of that era. It is beyond doubt that the author as well as initiator of this *Sendschreiben* was Friedländer himself, and it is not without reason that he refers to it so frequently in his work cited above, *Über die Verbesserung . . . etc.*"

In dry, sonorous fashion Friedländer here again repeats his attacks on the "ceremonial laws" in which he perceives the major cause of all the political and social troubles of the Jews. In complete antithesis to "the mystical book" the Talmud, Friedländer sets forth a "religion of reason" with the following major dogmas: "There is one God, there is one soul, and men were created to become happy." Friedländer and his associates were capable merchants and bankers, and therefore thought highly of the principle set forth in the *Sendschreiben:* "It is an indispensable duty to promote every person's welfare." Thus, they applied to Probst Teller with the following proposal: They, as well as others in agreement with them, are prepared to assume the Christian faith, but on condition that they be exempt from fulfilling certain ritual customs; further, that they be permitted not to recognize the divine birth of Jesus, or at least be allowed to interpret the Christian dogmas according to their own understanding.

Teller, however, was not enchanted by Friedländer's "religion of reason." He was a plain Protestant pastor, not a rationalist "enlightener," and so decisively rejected the entire proposal. His response was: Let the authors of the *Sendschreiben* remain where they have been up until now; Christianity does not need such "converts." Teller does not find it possible to bargain in religious questions and cannot relinquish a single Christian dogma. If they have made up their minds, let them accept the Christian faith in its full compass, without any conditions or reservations. Whether the government will then

---

70. *Ibid.*
71. *Sendschreiben an Teller von einigen Hausvätern jüdischer Religion.*

find that they are deserving of having equal rights granted to him is beyond his competence; in this matter the government alone must decide.

The *Sendschreiben* in its time called forth a great sensation. In the course of one year scores of lampoons[72] appeared. A novel entitled *Charlotta Sampson,* in which the questions that are put forth in the *Sendschreiben* are treated, was even written (1800).[73]

The one-sided but principled Friedländer who gloried so in the "rational" foundations of the Torah of Moses did not consider it possible to go over to Christianity, which is so unfree of "mysticism." He remained faithful throughout his life to the principles of "enlightened rationalism" and with indefatigable energy fought for the civic rights of Prussian Jewry. When in 1812 the long awaited edict on equal rights for Jews finally came, Friedländer promptly issued an anonymous brochure which may be considered the first modern manifesto of religious reform among Jews. In this brochure, which he also circulated among many prominent officials, he issues forth especially against all messianic hopes as well as against the custom of prayer in Hebrew in the synagogue. "Previously," writes Friedländer,

when Jews were considered strangers and aliens, they saw in Palestine their fatherland and waited impatiently for the day when an end would come to their exile and they would return to their land. Now, however, the situation has changed radically. The Jews have no home other than the land which has recognized them as citizens with equal rights. The Prussian Jews love their fatherland, and the German language is their mother tongue. Only in it do they wish to pray; they require no other language.

It is therefore easily understandable that Friedländer had to regard "Judeo-German" with hatred and contempt. In his *Sendschreiben an meine Mitbrüder,* which he published as a supplement to *Ha-Meassef* (5548), he notes:

Healthy reason, experience, and particularly the example of our Italian and Portuguese brethren teach that the first step to the improvement of education must take place through the institution of *a correct and precise speech.* This is the first essential condition, without which all other improvement is in vain and ought to have no place. *The Judeo-German customary among us, a tongue that is without rules, mutilated,*

72. See *Zeitschrift für die Geschichte der Juden,* IV, 57–64.
73. *Ibid.,* III, 224–225. Here the content of this romance is given.

*and incomprehensible outside our circles, must be completely eliminated . . .
If the child, as everyone agrees, cannot attain in the so-called Judeo-German
language any proper conceptions of anything whatever in the world, how can
there be any question of right principles in ripe age?*

We noted earlier that Friedländer remained faithfully at his
post. He did not "exchange the coin" and fought courageously
for the rights of his brethren. Not all, however, were as principled as he. After it became clear that there was nothing to be
hoped for from the petition submitted to Frederick II's successor on the throne in the matter of ameliorating the condition
of the Jews of Prussia, many educated and half-educated Jews
in Berlin, Breslau, Koenigsberg, and other Prussian cities
found another road that might lead to equal rights. Is it worthwhile for "enlightened" men living in the contemporary world
to continue to take account of the "prejudices" of their ancestors? Does it pay to languish in the shame of slavery for the sake
of the "superstitious" legacy of the backward and dark past?
The rationalist foundations of all faiths are, after all, the same.

The logical conclusion was clear and self-evident. The Jewish "enlightened rationalists" by the thousands found the equal
rights for which they longed so ardently in the bosom of Christianity. Friedländer himself, the standard-bearer of "sober
common sense," was greatly saddened when he saw the forms
that the movement of enlightenment assumed in the progressive Jewish circles. He deplores the "abuses of enlightenment
and culture," the frivolous chase after petty and worthless
glamour and after sensual pleasure,[74] and in his letter to the
minister Hardenberg (1811) he speaks of the epidemic of conversion as of a "great moral sin."[75]

It would, however, be a serious mistake to think that all those
who betrayed the religion of their fathers were motivated only
by material considerations. The epidemic of conversion which
rose so enormously at the end of the eighteenth century in the
bourgeois and cultured Jewish circles was a rather complicated
phenomenon, as some of our historians of culture note. This
must be especially stressed in regard to the feminine half of the
Jewish youth of that age in the larger Prussian cities. Ludwig
Geiger writes: "Among the women and men who played a
prominent role in Berlin society in the eighteenth century a
very important distinction is discernible: the women in all
their behavior and thought aimed to illuminate hearts, while

74. *Aktenstücke*, p. 36.
75. *Zeitschrift für die Geschichte der Juden*, III, pp. 232–233.

the men were striving for the definitive victory of reason." Among the Jewish young people who had been raised on *pilpul* and intellectual subtleties, the rationalist ideas of the "enlighteners" were extremely popular. The intellectual Jewish women, however, were more inclined to emotional strivings and dreamy romanticism. But the Jewish national culture in this respect could give them nothing, simply because these women of the Jewish salons had no conception whatever of it.

Their grandmothers and great-grandmothers had, like Glückel of Hameln, enriched their mental world through the folk literature; from the old Yiddish morality books and story books they generously drew nourishment for their loving hearts. Through these works they became familiar with the treasures of the national culture, with the moral teaching of Judaism, with the rich, colorful world of legends and traditions. The enlightened daughters of the wealthy Jewish merchants and bankers, however, already saw in Judaism only a frozen, monotonous, ritualistic cult that no longer said anything to their imagination and heart.

Mendelssohn's daughters, who inherited from their father sensitive and deeply believing hearts, for instance, had as their tutor the sober, arid, and grim Herz Homberg who hated, no less than Friedländer, everything that had any affinity whatsoever with "mysticism." And now such talented women, who grew up in the strict, old-fashioned traditions of the Jewish family, occupied, as a result of their rare beauty, clever understanding, and high culture, the leading roles in the salons established according to the French pattern. Thanks to them, these salons became the gathering place for the leading representatives of literature and science. Should it occasion surprise that these queens of the salon turned away from Judaism as from something old-fashioned and monotonously congealed, which darkens brightness and love of life with its melancholy? Even Rahel Levin, that marvelous and profound woman, on her deathbed acknowledged that her Jewish descent "had for many years been for her the greatest misfortune, the deepest shame, and the most painful suffering."

The enlightened men looked with contempt on Judaism in the name of "sovereign reason," the women in the name of sentiment and beauty. The men bowed before the authority of Voltaire; the idol of the women was Rousseau[76] and the Romantics. Among the men the logical, clear, intellectual

76. It is worth noting that Heine's mother was also an ardent adherent of Rousseau and her favorite book was *Émile.*

ideas of the French enlighteners and rationalists were especially popular. However, it is beyond doubt that not Voltaire's malicious sarcasm, not Montesquieu's cold logic, and not the atheism of Holbach and the other materialists could become the credo of the profoundly sensitive and believing hearts of the women. Their *sancta* became the thundering, ardent preachments of the stormy, unrestrained Jean Jacques Rousseau. Like the blind Samson in the Bible who destroyed the pillars of the hated temple of his enemies, so this brilliant maniac blinded by hatred wished to destroy the pillars of the obsolete feudal world, to destroy it not because this world was inconsistent with the demands of "healthy reason" but because it leads, with its falsehood and baseness, to moral barbarization. This was a protest not in the name of reason but in the name of the offended conscience. The bearer of social justice is not the man of polished reason, but the man of the earth who stands closest to nature and who, thanks to his naturalness and simplicity, has still preserved under his crude outward garment the goodness and frankness of the primal instincts.

It must not, however, be forgotten in this connection that, like the ideas of the rationalists, Rousseau's ideas were also reflected on the banks of the Spree in a rather unique fashion. Not the social, revolutionary content of Rousseau's doctrine, not his protest against social inequality, interested the German progressive circles, but the humanitarian spirit of this doctrine which found such a living resonance in the works of Schiller, Herder, and others. "Rousseau," the young Schiller exclaims emotively, "in the Christian searches for the human being."[77] In fact, however, he sought not the real, suffering, and struggling man, but the sweetly sentimental figure, the hero of pastorales and garden idylls that were sated with the perfumed atmosphere of "tender hearts" and "beautiful spirits" with which the contemporary salons, where, as noted previously, the cultured and splendid young Jewish women played such a prominent role, literally swarmed. Rousseau's doctrine that the golden era, the paradise of the children of men, is to be sought in long-gone, ancient times greatly strengthened interest in dreamy, romantic tendencies.

In opposition to the rationalist enlighteners, who wished to take account only of what is clear and prominent and recognized only what is in full consonance with sober reason, the Romantics, who especially stressed the high value of mystical

77. *"Rousseau—der aus Christen Menschen wirbt."*

experiences in the realm of morality and cognition, issued forth. The rationalists strove to reject everything associated with anthropomorphism, but in the Romantics living feeling, the recognition of the infinite in the finite and limited, was awake. Before their enchanted gaze the whole universe, all of nature, revealed itself in a divine vesture. Everything in the world, everything that is dear and precious, is holy and divine. "Man was born for happiness." But the thirst for happiness, according to the philosophy of the Romantics, is assuaged not through scientific investigation, but through receiving and experiencing the whole abundance of being.

The Romantics lost faith in reason as the sole guide through the labyrinths of life. They came to the conclusion that with reason alone it is impossible to know the world in its full scope. Hence they sought new ways, sought wherever their aroused and finely developed sentiment led them. With feeling, not with reason—the Romantics teach—do we receive the divinity of the world which surrounds us. In complete opposition to the rationalists, who saw in every religion, above all else, superstition, the Romantics, in the person of their talented theoretician August von Schlegel, declared that religion in general is free of all superstition whatever; every religious idea is true, because it is grounded, after all, on true experiences.[78]

Historians of Romanticism frequently underscore the exclusive role that women played in the romantic culture, and not the least role among these was played by Jewesses such as Henriette Herz and Dorothea Mendelssohn.

Indeed, Henriette Herz relates in her memoirs the ardent discussions that took place between her and her husband, the well known "enlightener" Dr. Marcus Herz, on the significance of Romantic literature. Marcus Herz, a prominent physician and natural scientist, a talented disciple of Kant and an ardent admirer of Maimonides,[79] was firmly persuaded that

78. August von Schlegel, *Vorlesungen über schöne Literatur und Kunst*, I, 332–333 (we quote according to Zhirmunski, *German Romanticism* (Russian), 1914, 160.

79. In his above-mentioned work "Über die frühe Beerdigung der Juden" Herz bestows upon Maimonides such panegyrics as the following: *Der Mann, der zuverlässig einer der scharfsinnigsten philosophischen Köpfe war; der Mann, dessen allgemeines, weitumfassendes, aus sich selbst gebildetes Genie die Bewunderung seiner und jeder anderen Nation, die ihn so ganz kennt, sein muss; der Mann, der in den Systemen der griechischen Weltweisen so ganz lebte und webte, dass er überal Gelegenheit mühsam aufsuchte, die Lehren seiner heiligen Religion mit diesen in Übereinstimmung zu bringen; der Mann, der mit so stiller Weisheit den Saamen zur ächtesten Aufklärung unter sein Volk streute, dass die shönsten Früchte, die es unter sich hat, reifen sehen und in der Folge nach häufiger sehen wird, im Grunde sein Werk sind; der Mann, dem miemand, der ihn so recht kennt und fasst, weder in dem Gebiete irgend einer Wissenschaft das Bürgerrecht absprechen kann.*

"only in knowledge is man's happiness," and that "without the sciences there is no good in the world."[80] He regarded the works of Novalis[81] and his colleagues as a senseless and fantastic chaos of dreams, while his wife, the renowned beauty Henriette, was an ardent admirer of the Romantic school.[82]

The arid, sober David Friedländer and his colleagues argued that worship ought to be as simple as possible, without superfluous splendor and luxury that affects only the feelings. Dorothea Mendelssohn, however, declares with firm conviction that everything the human heart has created ought to ornament and beautify worship; to the wellspring from which every art derives, it ought to return. To utilize it for petty, transient, boastful purposes—this is simply a blasphemy, and in complete contradiction with the divine source of art. Music and painting, architecture and the finest tapestries—everything ought to express a single idea, ought to belong to the entire community, in order to arouse the sentiment of religious enthusiasm.[83]

Should it, then occasion surprise that this uncommon and talented woman rejected the arid Deism of the Friedländers and Hombergs and, together with her sister Henriette, departed for the lofty vaults of the Catholic church? How great, however, would have been the wonder of Dorothea von Schlegel[84] if it had been revealed to her that the most intimate thoughts and feelings that she, along with her husband, expressed in their jointly written novel *Lucinda*—on mystical eroticism, on the holiness of sexual intercourse, on the union of the spiritual and the corporeal, on the *Shechinah* which hovers over the bed of man and wife, and that "God is love"—that all this is closely interwoven with the world view of the medieval Jewish mystics and is incorporated in their work in colorful images breathing the pathos of fervent conviction and ardent belief.

But for Mendelssohn's daughters, and for others like them, the wells of Jewish faith were sealed with seven locks.

These wells, however, were not dried out and exhausted— and suddenly, unexpectedly, they disclosed themselves with

---

80. In his letter, printed as a *haskamah* to the first part of Baruch Linda's *Reshit Limmudim* (1788), Herz writes: "Without the sciences there is no good. Without the sciences happiness is inconceivable. And without the sciences knowledge of the glory of God is not possible."

81. An important representative of the German romantic school.

82. See *Henriette Herz*, 1859, 99.

83. *Romantische Briefe*, 422.

84. Dorothea left her first husband Veit and married Schlegel.

extraordinary power before the free world, calling forth hatred and indignation among some, and joyous wonderment and enthusiastic enchantment among others. Of this in subsequent chapters.

CHAPTER FIVE

Solomon Maimon, Isaac Euchel, and Aaron Wolfsohn-Halle

[Rousseau's ideas and their influence on the Meassefim—Idylls in the Biblical style—Back to productive labor and reforming the system of education—The spiritual and intellectual crisis—Rahel Levin and her "reckoning of the soul"—Solomon Maimon and his *Autobiography*—Maimon's world view—Isaac Euchel and his romantic love for the Biblical language—Euchel's literary activity—The significance of his comedy *Reb Chenech, Oder Vos Tut Men Damit*—Aaron Wolfsohn-Halle and his comedy *Leichtsinn und Frömmelei*.]

E NOTED earlier that the journal *Ha-Meassef*, with all its defects, must be considered an important stage in the developmental history of neo-Hebrew literature. In this connection, however, an interesting point to which the majority of Jewish literary historians devote very little attention and in fact frequently leave completely undiscussed, must be especially noted. The founders of *Ha-Meassef* and their close associates were convinced rationalists. Among them the greatest authority was the sarcastic, mocking Voltaire whose Deism and "natural religion" were based solely on logical arguments established through reason. At the same time, the style of the Meassefim, as well as their program, was under the strong, albeit indirect and unconscious, influence of Voltaire's opponent and antithesis, the author of *Émile* and *La Nouvelle Héloïse*, Jean Jacques Rousseau.

Not education and knowledge, but virtue and good deeds, not reason, but sentiment, are the sources of man's happiness —in this consisted Rousseau's motto.[1]

"The best person is the one who feels most deeply and most strongly." Back to nature! There is only one sound and healthy way of life—on the bosom of nature, amidst the green fields, without any coercion, without the slightest luxury, drawing sustenance from Mother Earth, living from her gifts and beneficences, finding oneself amidst good neighbors, all of whom are equal. Of all social classes, the most honorable is that which consists of the persons who toil with their own hands —the only class that is really useful. And because these people, as a result of their occupation, are closest to the natural condition, among them are still perfectly preserved, under the appearance which externally looks so severe and crude, the kindliness, goodness, and frankness of the primordial instincts.

Rousseau's ideas were extremely popular in Germany. The most eminent figures were enchanted by them. Lessing gave Rousseau the title "Wise Man of the World." Schiller compared him to Socrates, and in inspired verses celebrated the basic thesis with which the French author's *Émile* begins.[2] Most beloved in the German literature of that time was the type of "beautiful spirits" and "tender, feeling hearts" that are literally awash in sentimental sighs and tears, and in all their activity and behavior follow the imperative command of their only recognized guide—feeling. The poet Gessner acquired a reputation with his saccharine-sweet idylls in which calm and carefree village life on the bosom of nature is portrayed as a true paradise.

The influence of Rousseau's ideas was also discernible in Jewish circles. We spoke in the previous chapter about the effect of the author of *Émile* on the educated Jewish women, but his ideas also penetrated, on their triumphant march, into the camp of the Jewish rationalists and enlighteners. These sons of the ghetto with their lack of rights could not be indifferent to the humanitarian motto proclaimed in *Émile:*

1. In opposition to Descartes' motto, *Cogito, ergo sum* (I think, therefore I am), which was a harbinger of the fact that the religious era was being displaced by the generation of rationalism, Rousseau came forth with his motto: *Exister pour nous est sentir.*
2. *Tout est bien, sortant des mains de l'auteur des choses; tout dégénere entre les mains de l'homme.* Well known are Schiller's verses:
   Die Welt ist volkommen überall
   Wohin der Mensch nicht hinkommt mit seiner Qual.

Teach the child under your supervision to love all men, even those who regard you with contempt. Give him an education such that he will not perceive himself as a member of a definite class but feel his closeness to all classes. Speak to him about the human race with love, even with sympathy, not with contempt. No man may degrade another man.

Persons so isolated from nature and productive labor, who grew up in the stifling atmosphere of the *yeshivot* and spent their youthful years with *pilpul* and overly subtle scholasticism, had to be impressed by Rousseau's thesis: "Man's natural condition is to till the soil and to live from its fruits; this condition is the only essential and useful one" (*La Nouvelle Héloïse*, V, Second Letter). Of all the occupations that can provide man with a livelihood, manual labor is best suited to bring him close to the natural condition. Of all vocations, the most appropriate and the one least dependent on Providence and other persons is the calling of the artisan (*Émile*, Book Three).

A return to productive labor and a reform of the system of education were, as we know, the major points in the program of the Meassefim. The Meassefim were hostile to the Talmud and the later rabbinic literature. On the other hand, they regarded the Bible, in which the earth and agriculture play such an important role, with high reverence. In the Bible men still feel very strongly their closeness to the earth; in it are preserved imperishable examples of genuine idylls. This contributed not a little to the fact that the Biblical world, the Biblical style, became among the Meassefim the supreme ideal, the classical model from which one ought to learn and which ought to be copied.

The sagacious Lessing, however, is right: *Es sind nicht alle frei, die ihrer Ketten spotten!* "Not all who mock their chains are free." The transition that took place in the generation of the Meassefim was overly sharp and precipitate. Having torn themselves away from their own soil, they remained suspended in the air without any ground under their feet. It is not so easy to cast off the old world view in which one has grown up and spent his youth. In the name of rationalism the Meassefim endeavored to free themselves from the traditional and old-fashioned; in the depths of their souls, however, nostalgia for the bygone past unconsciously resounded. It expressed itself in romantic love for the Bible. As we know, the Meassefim set themselves the task "of showing to the other peoples the beauties of the Bible." But, having been raised in the arid, overly subtle environment of pilpulist scholasticism, they themselves were not suited to receive and feel this beauty. They could only copy and imitate the Biblical style, but the classical world of that ancient era remained alien and incomprehensible to them. In pseudo-Biblical style they translated the mediocre idylls of Gessner and Ramler's odes. Even the arid David Friedländer indited idylls. In the sentimental effusiveness of these works, however, there was mellifluous rhetoric only, without a spark of artistic creativity. In the poems of the Meassefim the breath of life is basically felt as little as in the pilpulist subtleties of the old-fashioned rabbis whom they so ridiculed.

Among the Meassefim and their colleagues there were men of keen minds and great knowledge. However, there was not among them one person of integral character, a single original personality. The rupture with the past occurred too precipitately. Overly abrupt was the leap from the old-fashioned medieval Jewish way of life to the new, alien world of ideas with its abstract metaphysical-rationalist conceptions in which the dominant place was occupied not by the real, living person brought up in a special social-historical environment with his complex psyche and unique world of experiences, innate sympathies, and moods, but by the abstract concept "man," without a past, without traditions, without "inherited superstitions," beyond time and space.

In the twilight era of penitential moods, after the ideals of Haskalah were so ruthlessly shattered, Jewish authors fell with special indignation on the representatives of the Berlin Haskalah and branded them as assimilationists, persons who denied their past and rejected their national heritage. Their errors and failings were wrathfully mocked, and there was a refusal to note the *tragedy* of these men, to take account of the fact that in their spiritual crisis, in the rapid and not altogether justified transvaluation of national values, the major role was played not so much by the ill will or bad faith of these men as by the abnormal circumstances in which they were fated to live and work.

Very characteristic in this respect are the moving words one of the most remarkable women of that time, Rahel Levin, uttered with such candor. "It seems to me," she wrote in her youth to David Veit, "that when I appeared in the world, a heavenly being inscribed in my heart, at my first steps on life's way, the following words as with pointed arrows: 'Have deep feelings, see the world as few in your generation do, be great and noble. Also I cannot prohibit you from thinking about eternal problems.' But one thing they forgot to announce: Be a Jewess. And now my whole life is a perpetual bleeding." But lying on her deathbed, this "apostate" who "betrayed" her faith and the heritage of her fathers exclaimed with a trembling heart:

How marvelous it is! I, an exile from Egypt and Palestine, and you surround me with so much care and love. With a feeling of enchantment I think of my origin and of my wondrous fate that unites the oldest memories of mankind, the longest past, and the most distant lands with our present. This, which for so long a time was the greatest shame to me, the most painful suffering, and the deepest misfortune—that I was born a Jewess—is now so precious to me that I would not be willing to part with it for anything in the world.

Another representative of this generation, the "generation of deceitfulness," as it is called by the historian of culture Simon Bernfeld, disclosed to all with marvelous candor the tragedy of his life's way and that of others in his generation similar to him. With bated breath the civilized European world read his sad *Autobiography*,[3] and reverently included it in its treasures of culture. Solomon Maimon[4] was the name of its author.

Maimon wrote numerous works in Hebrew.[5] However, had he not managed, despite all hindrances and obstacles, to break out into the broader world and inscribe himself in the history of German philosophy, his name and work would probably have been as forgotten as that of Abba Glusk and others like him. To the Jewish grandees of Berlin, the rich financiers and bankers who wished to play the role of "enlightened" Euro-

---

3. *Lebensgeschichte*, Berlin, 1792–93.
4. See our *History*, Vol. VI, pp. 244ff.
5. Maimon wrote the following works in Hebrew: (1) *Givat Ha-Moreh*, a commentary to Maimonides' *Guide for the Perplexed;* (2) *Biur Pilosofi Al Perush Ha-Mishnayyot;* (3) *Heshek Shelomoh*, in five parts; philosophical commentaries to Ibn Ezra, Rabbenu Bahya, Rabbenu Nissim, and philosophical speculations about creation and algebra (mentioned in Geiger's *Zeitschrift für Wissenschaft und Leben*, 1866); (4) *Ta'alumot Hochmah*, on mathematics and physics (mentioned by Geiger); (5) *Torat Ha-Matematikah* (mentioned in his *Lebensgeschichte*, p. 417); (6) *Torat Ha-Teva*, natural science, according to Newton's system (*ibid.*, p. 433); (7) *Korot Ha-Yehudim*, according to Jacques-Chrétien de Beuval Basnage, translated from French (ibid., p. 424); (8) *Mo'adei Boker*, a translation of Mendelssohn's *Morgenstunden* (*ibid.*, p. 433); (9) a critical treatise on Wolff's *Metaphysics* (*ibid.*, p. 366); (10) a metaphysical investigation of natural and divinely revealed theology. Of Maimon's Hebrew works only the first part of his *Givat Ha-Moreh* was published. His *Biur Pilosofi* is printed in *Ha-Meassef* (5549, pp. 131–136). Maimon signs this article "Solomon the son of Joshua from the land of Lithuania." The rest of his Hebrew works remained in manuscript.

peans, however, the brilliant Lithuanian Maimon was quite repugnant with his figure, his walk, his speech. He shocked them with his Polish-Lithuanian manners, and they coldbloodedly let him die of hunger, perish in poverty and want. He himself reports with naive simplicity that in his "sad condition he decided to turn to Christian scholars in the hope that their recommendation would have the proper effect on the wealthy men of his own people."[6] And indeed, it was a German nobleman Count Hans (Adolph) von Kalkreuth who took pity on the poor, homeless Jewish thinker. Generously the count gave him rest and shelter on his estate in Silesia, and with great patience endured the bizarre behavior and caprices of the mentally and physically broken philosopher. When Maimon died in his forty-sixth year and his body was brought to Glogau to be interred in the Jewish cemetery, the fanatical leaders of the community avenged themselves on the "heretic," and the brilliant Jewish thinker who had suffered so much was mockingly and contemptuously laid in the ground with the "burial of an ass" behind the fence of the Jewish cemetery.

Solomon Maimon wrote his *Autobiography* in German. He realized quite well that such a work in Hebrew would be like a voice crying in the wilderness; it would have no readers. Indeed more than a hundred years passed before his masterpiece was translated into Hebrew.[7] Nevertheless, the *Autobiography* must be noted in the history of Jewish culture. No historian of Jewish civilization dealing with the second half of the eighteenth century can overlook this remarkable work in which an objective portrayal of Jewish life in Lithuanian Poland in the eighteenth century is given.

With disengaged calmness and with a sure hand, the most melancholy pictures of Jewish poverty and lack of rights under the rule of barbaric, crazy landowners and fanatical priests are unrolled before our eyes. As in a kaleidoscope, there hovers before us the most marvelous panorama, with the colorful figures of Kabbalists, ascetics, landowners, and scholars—remarkably beautiful personalities, such as the rabbi of Posen, Rabbi Hirsch Ḥarif, and base hypocrites; crude villagers who do not even know a word of Yiddish and brilliant Torah schol-

---

6. *Lebensgeschichte*, 430 (we quote according to Goldschmidt's Yiddish translation).
7. Translated with abbreviations by Y.H. Tavyov under the title *Toledot Shelomoh Maimon*, 1898–99. In 1871 David Kahana published an abbreviated reworking in Yiddish of the autobiographical part of *Lebensgeschichte*. A complete translation by A.J. Goldschmidt appeared in Vilna, published by Tomor in 1927.

ars; the Maggid of Mezhirech and Moses Mendelssohn; the first Hasidim and the *maskilim* of Berlin; poor, ignorant beggars and renowned philosophers and thinkers. In the midst of it all is the remarkable figure of the author himself, with his extraordinary life-path that is portrayed with such brilliant simplicity and modesty.

Not without reason did Maimon's *Autobiography* make such an enormous impression on Goethe, Schiller, and other celebrated personalities. "Solomon Maimon," correctly remarks his translator into Yiddish Goldschmidt,

was a phenomenal event as a person, as a Jew, and as a philosopher. Like a young tree in a wasteland, without dew and without rain, he appeared unexpectedly and astonishingly in a dark, miserable land without any means and rose extremely high—to the loftiest heavens of thought. A malicious fate, however, accompanied him and did not leave him from his birth till his last breath . . . Not a single event in his life aided the normal development of his intellectual powers; on the contrary, many events retarded the course of his development and hindered him from finding his way in life.

In the earlier volumes of our work we spoke of the remarkable type of "seekers" *(mevakkeshim)*[8] who wished to explore all the ways on which men seek the supreme degree of perfection, who look everywhere for the pure, bright truth, search after God's living, burning word. With none of these "seekers" was the path of search and wandering so terribly filled with poverty, hunger, want, and inhuman degradation as in the case of Solomon Maimon. And remarkable is the tone in which Maimon's *Autobiography* relates the painful, wandering way traversed by the poor, brilliantly endowed village teacher[9] in a castaway and darkened corner of Lithuania until he was transformed into a competent German philosopher, one of the profoundest and keenest exponents of Kant's philosophy. The terrible distress and poverty in which he spent his years stained his noble soul thirsting after truth, corrupted his character, and broke his health and powers to such an extent that he died at forty-six of malnutrition and emaciation. All this he relates with marvelous simplicity and genuinely philosophic calmness.

It suffices to mention the sad episode when the "seeker,"

8. See Vol. III, pp. 6ff.
9. At the age of eleven, Maimon already received ordination to the rabbinate (*Lebensgeschichte*, p. 87).

wearied unto death by hunger and misery, finally arrived at the door of his goal, the Rosenthaler Gate, leading to the source of culture and science, the capital city Berlin. The pious leaders of the Jewish community closed the gate in his face and strictly ordered him to depart as quickly as possible. The spiritually and physically broken wanderer threw himself down on the ground behind the city and broke into bitter weeping.[10] Maimon, relating all this, manifests no feeling of bitterness toward the pious community leaders or toward the severe supervisor of the *hekdesh*, the paupers' hostel, at the Rosenthaler Gate. On the contrary, he even argues in their favor and notes that "in part the pious Jews of Berlin were really justified."[11]

With great philosophical objectivity Maimon portrays the impression he made the first time with his figure, movements, and strange way of speech on the European Dr. Marcus Herz:

At first this Herr H. (Herz) considered me a *speaking animal* and amused himself with me as one amuses himself with a dog or with a bird one has taught to speak a few words. The strange mixture of something bestial in my mien, expressions, and external demeanor, and the mental acuity in my expressed thoughts worked more on his imaginative power than the content of my words worked on his reason.[12]

It is worthwhile to note another characteristic point, because it is closely associated with the world view of the Berlin *maskilim* and the collaborators of the Meassefim. Solomon Maimon was, in many respects, considerably more sharp-sighted than his contemporaries and had a better feeling for historical phenomena than the representatives of the Berlin Haskalah. He finds it necessary to note, for instance, "how closely bound up the Jewish religion is with national existence, so that the abolition of the Jewish theocracy must necessarily entail the annihilation of the Jewish nation."[13] He concludes that the Men of the Great Synagogue, in adding new ordinances, did so "according to the demands of the time and according to the circumstances."[14] He also endeavors to demonstrate how "positive" is "the method of the sages of the Talmud," and

10. *Lebensgeschichte*, I, pp. 208–10.
11. *Ibid.*, p. 209.
12. *Ibid.*, II, p. 269.
13. *Ibid.*, II, p. 425.
14. *Ibid.*, I, p. 119.

believes that everyone "who has penetrated into the *true spirit of the Talmud*"[15] will agree with this. And he repeats once more that "all the new laws which the sages of the Talmud and the Geonim after them initiated" came "according to the requirements and needs of the time."[16]

In regard to the moral doctrine of the sages of the Talmud, Maimon notes "that it is quite similar to Stoicism and, in many important points, even superior to it."[17] In the chapter in which he speaks of Hasidism, Maimon incidentally points to the "useful activity" of the rabbis.[18] He was also the only one among the Berlin *maskilim* of that generation who came forth with a concrete, matter-of-fact critique[19] of the theses presented by Mendelssohn in his *Jerusalem* and declared openly:

When I see Jews who identify themselves with the *Jewish religion because of family ties or on account of certain interests,*[20] and who thereafter violate the commandments where the factors mentioned do not, in their view, prevent them from doing so, then I assert that such Jews behave unjustly and commit illegal deeds. Hence, I do not understand how, when the chief rabbi of Hamburg excommunicated a Jew from his community because the latter publicly violated the laws of the religion, Mendelssohn wished to release the man from the ban for the reason that the religious community has no rights in civic matters, seeing that he himself asserts that the *state of the Jewish religion is eternal* and will never be altered and nullified. What kind of a state is it that has no rights? In what, then, do the rights of this religious state consist?[21]

However, Solomon Maimon was an ardent disciple of Maimonides, saturated himself in Berlin with the rationalist ideas of that age, was enchanted by the European educated "enlighteners" of the Prussian capital, and considered David Friedländer the "great *maskil* with fine taste."[22] Hence, it is not surprising that he also arrives at the conclusion that "Judaism is based on clear, absolutely necessary laws of reason."[23] He forgets what he himself wrote earlier about the sages of the

15. *Ibid.,* p. 129. Italicized by the author.
16. *Ibid.,* p. 243.
17. *Ibid.,* p. 131.
18. *Ibid.,* p. 185.
19. *Ibid.,* pp. 384–387.
20. Italicized by the author.
21. *Ibid.,* p. 386.
22. *Ibid.,* p. 364.
23. *Ibid.,* pp. 188–189.

Talmud and the laws they innovated, and points out bitterly and quite in the fashion of the Berlin *maskilim:*

Finally the Talmudists came and introduced into Judaism a mass of regulations and laws which have no real purpose and thereby transformed Judaism into an arid and embalmed religion and distorted it even more. The result of this was a melancholy one: instead of this religion making the people of Israel a "wiser and more understanding people than all the other nations," as was the intention of the first lawgiver of Judaism (Moses), it made them—by reason of the fact that it was used without sense and without purpose—into the most ignorant and non-understanding of all peoples.[24]

Maimon understands very well that *"various* (italics mine— I.Z.) factors have brought about the unfortunate political situation of the Jews, and the common masses of the people became, because of this, extremely ignorant not only in all useful knowledge and sciences but even in the laws of religion."[25] But he was under the influence of the Berlin *maskilim* who, as he himself relates, firmly asserted that if Jews were better acquainted with their history, they would "realize and understand that *only their ignorance and stubborn opposition to all rational institutions* (italicized by the author) are responsible for all the misfortunes and catastrophes that have happened to them."[26] Maimon nullifies himself before the enlightened *maskilim*, forgets his own point of view, and notes that the founders of the *Ḥevrat Doreshei Leshon Ever* and of *Ha-Meassef* "*rightly* (italics mine—I.Z.) recognized that the cause of the bad situation, *moral as well as political,*[27] of the Jewish people lies in religious prejudices, in the lack of a rational commentary to the Bible, and in the distorted translation of the text which comes from not knowing the Hebrew language."[28]

It is natural that Maimon, like the Berlin *maskilim*, also regarded the Yiddish "jargon" with contempt. He concludes that the "Yiddish mother tongue" is poor and filled with grammatical errors and defects,[29] that it is a language which is "a mixture of Hebrew, Judeo-German, Polish, and Russian, with the specific grammatical defects of all these languages."[30]

24. *Ibid.*, pp. 190–191.
25. *Ibid.*, p. 456.
26. *Ibid.*, p. 424.
27. Italicized by the author.
28. *Ibid.*, p. 454.
29. *Ibid.*, p. 35.
30. *Ibid.*, p. 203.

The logic of life, however, is very frequently stronger than rational theories and fine, subtle hypotheses, and this iron logic produced the paradox that the grim opponents of the "despised jargon" who set themselves the goal of "revealing before the peoples the beauty of the language of the Bible" unwillingly laid the first stones for the mighty structure of the new secular literature in Yiddish.

Especially interesting in this respect are the two comedies or, more accurately, *Familiengemälde* (family portraits), written by the prominent "Biurists" and editors of *Ha-Meassef*, Isaac Euchel and Aaron Wolfsohn-Halle.[31]

Born in Copenhagen, the capital city of Denmark, Isaac Euchel,[32] while still quite young (in 1773), came to Koenigsberg,[33] which was already then a center of culture. As a teacher of Hebrew he found entry into the wealthy and enlightened banking family of the Friedländers. Thanks to this family, the talented young man acquired European education, attended Immanuel Kant's lectures on philosophy at the University of Koenigsberg, and soon occupied an honored place in the left-wing group of the local *maskilim*.[34] This freethinking rationalist, however, remained throughout his life loyal to his first romantic love—the language of the Bible. Following the pattern of the modern school *Hinnuch Ne'arim* that had been established in Berlin, the *maskilim* of Koenigsberg also ventured to establish such a school in their city, and Euchel published (in 1782) a Hebrew appeal to the members of the community under the title *Sefat Emet* in which he propagandizes for the projected "free school." Nothing came of the project because the orthodox were decisively opposed to it. Euchel, however, was more successful in another undertaking. At the beginning of the following year there was established at his initiative the *Hevrat Doreshei Leshon Ever*, already known to us, and in the fall of the same year (September, 1783) *Ha-Meassef* began to appear under his editorship.

31. On Wolfsohn's attitude toward Yiddish, see above.
32. Born in 1756; died in Berlin, 1804.
33. In his well known letter to his comrade Joel Brill, which is dated 1788, and was published as the introduction to Euchel's biography of Mendelssohn, Euchel writes: "It is now fifteen years, and I was seventeen years old when I departed from here to wander abroad."
34. On Euchel's free conduct and his refusal to acknowledge Jewish ritual, testimony is provided by the following witty statement related in the name of the rabbi of Berlin, Tzevi Hirsch Levin: "Indeed, truly a world turned upside down. Once pigs used to eat acorns *(Eichel)*, and now Euchel eats pig."

In 1784 Euchel traveled to Copenhagen to visit his family. At that time such a journey was a major undertaking and took a long time. Hence the *Ḥevrat Doreshei Leshon Ever* presented him with a farewell poem in Hebrew expressing its best wishes before his departure from Koenigsberg. In the cities through which he passed, especially Berlin, the local *maskilim* wrote in his album *(Stammbuch)* poems of praise and greetings. Naftali Herz Wessely asserts in his poem to Euchel:

Everywhere you come, they will rejoice to welcome you.
Many will come to greet you with peace,
And *Ha-Meassef* goes before you to declare your praise in
    the land,
But what will my praise give and add to you?[35]

En route Euchel himself sent numerous letters (also written in Hebrew) to his fifteen-year-old pupil Michael Friedländer in Koenigsberg, and some of these he published after his return to Koenigsberg in *Ha-Meassef*, to show "that in our holy tongue one can find sufficient expressions to describe everything in the world."[36] These letters,[37] especially the one to his friend and colleague Joel Loewe (Brill) published at the beginning of his monograph on Mendelssohn, obtained great favor in the circles of the *maskilim*. All were enchanted by Euchel's brilliant epistolary style. In more recent times, the historian of culture Ludwig Geiger also bestowed on Euchel the title "the renewer of Hebrew prose." We believe, however, that a certain correction must be made here. He was the renewer of the *artificial* and *rhetorical* prose that was regarded as a model by the *maskilim* of the generation of the Meassefim. Euchel attempts to imitate the style of Biblical narrative prose, the style of the Book of Judges or the Book of Ruth. However, he lacks fine artistic taste and the sensitivity for strict measure that is closely associated with what is called in Hebrew *sod ha-tzimtzum*, "the secret of concentration," or brevity.

In 1786 Euchel suffered a grievous disappointment. After he had studied for five years at the University of Koenigsberg, he

---

35. On Euchel's *Stammbuch* that has been preserved, see H. Vogelstein's article in the *Philippson-Festschrift*, 1916.

36. *Ha-Meassef*, 5545, p. 117.

37. The poet Letteris indicates in his *Zikkaron Ba-Sefer* (p. 94), that the interesting letters that are printed in *Ha-Meassef* (5550, pp. 38–50, 80–85, 171–176, 285–289) under the name of the Sephardi Meshullam ben Uriah Ha-Eshtamo'i and his associates also derive from Euchel's hand.

submitted an application for a lectureship in Hebrew which was just then vacant. Immanuel Kant, who knew Euchel as a capable and diligent auditor of his, warmly supported his candidacy. The administration, however, rejected Euchel's application, because every *Dozent* had to belong to the evangelical faith.

A year later (in 1787) Euchel moved to Berlin where he became manager of the printery in the school *Hinnuch Ne'arim.* With Euchel *Ha-Meassef,* in which he published many critical and journalistic articles, as well as his comprehensive monograph on Mendelssohn that was subsequently reprinted several times, also moved to Berlin. In the same period (1789) he published his translation of, and commentary to, the Book of Proverbs. A great admirer of Maimonides, Euchel also intended to issue *A Guide for the Perplexed* with two commentaries —the old commentary of Moses Narboni[38] and a new one by Solomon Maimon. He even published a prospectus-extract of this edition in *Ha-Meassef.*[39] However, Euchel managed to realize his project only partially. He succeeded in printing (in 1791) merely the first part of *A Guide for the Perplexed,* and this with only one commentary, Maimon's *Givat Ha-Moreh.* His translation of Avicenna's *Sefer Ha-Refuot* also remained unpublished; only a small fragment of it was printed in *Ha-Meassef* (5554, pp. 93–95).

Euchel sadly observed how his beloved, the language of the Bible, became ever more forsaken by the new generation. The enlightened and educated no longer needed it; they drew from other sources and even regarded him, the faithful knight of his youthful love, with a smile of contempt. He felt solitary and abandoned. His platform *Ha-Meassef* was closed; it no longer had any readers. Euchel translated Mendelssohn's *Jerusalem* into Hebrew, but the translation remained in manuscript, for it had no purchasers who were interested in it. The enlightened read the original, and the orthodox refused even to take the heretical work of the "man of Dessau" in hand.

Euchel had to suffer another disappointment. Life demonstrated to him very clearly how much bitter truth there is in Leibniz's maxim that superficial enlightenment and a smattering of education are far worse than strict orthodoxy. He saw that many Jewish women who were devoid of true knowledge, whose entire "enlightenment" consisted in the ability to carry

38. See our *History,* Vol. III, pp. 125–28.
39. *Ha-Meassef,* 5548, pp. 241–262.

on a salon conversation in German and French, and to whom their parents' wealth gave the opportunity to live in luxury and to lead a carefree existence, were carried away by the most insignificant military uniform and considered it the supreme joy and honor to obtain a smile or an ambiguous compliment from any "noble" clod. This distressed him deeply and he became embittered. Unfortunately—he writes to his friend Joel Brill—the spirit of our nation after the death of our teacher (Mendelssohn) has assumed an extremely undesirable form. In place of the erstwhile ignorance, malice now rules. "Something may be brought into emptiness, but arrogance appears to be overflowing."[40]

Euchel witnessed with bitterness how the epidemic of apostasy was magnified in the circles of the "enlightened" from day to day. The feeling of solitariness continued to grow in him and he sought a remedy for it in a new society which he founded in 1792, together with Mendelssohn's son Joseph and his friend and colleague on *Ha-Meassef*, Aaron Wolfsohn-Halle. *Die Gesellschaft der Freunde* (The Society of Friends) was the name of this association, established with philanthropic purposes especially for lonely young *maskilim* without families who were struggling against the old, rigid manner of life but did not allow themselves to be carried along by the stream and refused frivolously "to exchange the coin," i.e., to convert.

In 1794 an attempt was made to revive *Ha-Meassef*. Euchel, however, declined to be the editor. He did not believe in the resurrection of the dead and when, several years later (1799), the young poet Shalom Cohen[41] addressed him on the subject of a new attempt to establish a Hebrew journal, Euchel replied in a letter filled with despair and bitterness. This letter is an interesting *document humain* and we therefore present a rather long extract from it:

. . . . You are precious to me with your splendid style and, indeed, because of this, my heart grieves for you. I know your pain, and my heart is no less fearful than yours that your words will be in vain and that nothing will come of your undertaking. I have sympathy with you, my friend; I grieve that you have brought with you a precious gem and no one has need of it. You have brought balm of Gilead, a healing and a remedy for all who seek morality, and no one pays any attention. Why were you so late in your coming? Why did you tarry so long, so that now, when you call, no one answers? To me also, who

40. *Ha-Meassef*, 5557, p. 363.
41. We shall speak of him in a later part of our work.

am in agreement with you, you call in vain. Who am I that I should be able to help you? In what does my power consist that you should be able to find protection and support from me? . . . I also have tasted the cup of poison that has been poured out on the Jewish people and on its enlightened. Gone are the precious days, departed are the days of my covenant with the sons of Israel when the shoots of wisdom appeared and the Hebrew language bloomed in glory and splendor. The Jewish youth would come forth daily to gather the fruits of its knowledge. Now they have fled and are no more. Woe, they will no longer return! Since they have decided in their hearts to say, "The whole earth is filled with science and knowledge," the language of their ancestors has become despicable to them and they have rejected it. They have also forgotten me and have abandoned me as a solitary in the wilderness. To whom, then, should I turn and seek support for your unhappy soul? Go through the streets, wander over the market-places, open both eyes, and see. Will you find even one in a city and two in a family who will listen to you, as soon as they realize that you bear Hebrew on your lips? So have the times altered in their courses. So have men changed in their views . . .

Euchel, however, was too much of a fighter by nature to remain merely a silent witness and not respond to everything that was taking place before his eyes. He wished to throw the bitter truth into the face of his generation with mocking laughter, and he came forth from his hiding-place with a mordant satire—not, however, in the language of the Bible that the young generation had "rejected." He knew, after all, that this would be useless, but he also considered it impossible to write his satire in German, for the reason "Tell it not in Gath," i.e., the truth should not be published abroad so that the "gentile quarter" would know of it.

In the introduction to the previously mentioned essay *Ist nach dem jüdischen Gesetze das Übernachten der Todten wirklich verboten?*, Euchel thanks his colleague and fellow-battler, Professor Loewe (Joel Brill), for having treated the same question in a Judeo-German *Sendschreiben*, i.e., as Euchel himself explains, in a brochure that is written in German but printed in the script of *Weiber-Deutsch* (Old Yiddish type-face). For, he further explains, if Loewe as a Jewish scholar had written in Hebrew, the purpose of his brochure "would mainly have failed," because those who understand Hebrew refuse to read books that the enlightened write, and those to whom such works might indeed be congenial would not have understood them. On the other hand, if Loewe had issued his work as a German writer in the German language and script, it would have been accessible outside the "Jewish school," i.e., beyond the Jewish milieu, and it could then have provided the "enemies of the Jews," who unfortunately were so numerous at the end of the eighteenth century, "opportunity for mockery and contempt."[42]

The question of language was therefore entirely set aside by Euchel. He wrote a comedy in which every character speaks his own tongue—the old-fashioned Jew, his typical Yiddish dialect; the enlightened man, literary German; the Englishman, English or mutilated German; and the French *émigré*, a mixture of German and French. But all the stage directions, both for the enlightened and for the old-fashioned characters, are written down and printed in Old-Yiddish type-face. Since the most successful and substantial figures in the comedy are the representatives of the older generation and since the author further endeavored—in order to represent these figures in their full comicality—to report faithfully and correctly all their movements, their demeanor, and the slightest nuances of their old-fashioned Yiddish speech that was so despised and mocked by the enlightened, Euchel's comedy unexpectedly, and contrary to the will of its author, became an important event for Yiddish literature—one of its two first modern secular comedies whose influence is distinctly discernible in the historical development of Yiddish comedy. *Reb Chenech Oder Vos Tut Men Damit* is the title of Euchel's comedy. Its motto is the characteristic quotation from Horace's satires: *Ridentem dicere verum quid vetat?*, "What can prevent one from laughingly speaking the truth?"

The year in which Euchel wrote his comedy has not been determined. Of the first printed editions of the eighteenth century not a single copy has been preserved, but Steinschneider indicates that in his youth he saw a copy of Euchel's play from the year 1797. The historian Isaac Marcus Jost, however, relates that Euchel's comedy was already widely disseminated while still in manuscript, and he notes, incidentally, that the printed editions do not contain the original in its complete, authentic form.[43] Apparently Euchel's *Reb Chenech* was known to the public even before 1797 in manuscript. In any case he began his comedy no earlier than the beginning of 1793, for in a scene of the first act the French king Louis XVI "who will soon be

---

42. *Ha-Meassef*, 5557, pp. 361–362.
43. On the texts of Euchel's comedy that have been preserved, see M. Erik in *Filologishe Shriftn*, III, pp. 573–576, and in *Tsaytshrift*, VI, pp. 285–294; Zalman Rejzen in *Arkhiv Far Di Geshikte Fun Yidishn Teater Un Drame*, I, pp. 85–93. We employ the older text that Rejzen published in the just mentioned *Arkhiv*.

handed over to the guillotine" is mentioned, and this, as is known, occurred on January 21, 1793.

This play, which was so popular at the end of the eighteenth century, was completely forgotten in the course of the nineteenth century. Like a fantastic legend, its title wandered about from one literary historian to another, because not a single one of them had ever seen it himself and all relied on the meager and not altogether accurate information of Steinschneider and Jost. Eleazer Schulmann was the first of the more recent literary historians who had opportunity to become familiar with Euchel's *Reb Chenech*. Unfortunately, however, he provided, as was his fashion, overly brief and dry information about the play.[44] Nahum Shtif[45] and, after him, Max Erik[46] were the first to provide a full account of the content of Euchel's play and also to provide a literary-historical appreciation. The complete text of *Reb Chenech* was published by Zalman Rejzen.[47] From the structure of the play, with its numerous characters and frequent change of the scene of action in the middle of an act, it is easy to perceive that Euchel devised his comedy not for the stage but for reading.

In the final act, the enlightened Nathan addresses his relative Reb Chenech with the words: "Unfortunately, we become more corrupt morally from one generation to another. You are not alone in being an unfortunate father; there are many such. And it will not be long before you see the sad consequences." In fact, it is not the "provincial deputy" Nathan who says these words, but the author himself. This was the painful truth to which melancholy reality had brought him. In the milieu he knew, in the wealthy merchant classes of the *haute bourgeoisie,* Euchel witnessed the decay of the traditional Jewish family. The parents with their backward, medieval outlook were incapable of grasping the demands of the new era. With fanatical stubbornness they clung to everything they had obtained as a legacy from their fathers. So they were abandoned by their own children, and the children themselves, abruptly torn away from the old, firmly established way of life were carried like splinters of wood over the stormy waves of the new life, without any solid moral support, without any clearly defined goal. It is this decay that Euchel portrays in his comedy.

According to the manuscript that was in the Jüdisches

---

44. *Sefat Yehudit-Ashkenazit,* pp. 175–176.
45. *Di Royte Velt,* Kharkov, 1926, Nos. 7–8 and 10.
46. *Filologishe Shriftn,* III, pp. 555–584.
47. In *Arkhiv Far Di Geshikhte Fun Yidishn Teater,* I, 1930.

Theologisches Seminar in Breslau, Euchel's play was called *Ein Familien Gemälde,* "A Family Portrait." In deeply somber colors Euchel portrays family life in the house of the wealthy money-changer Reb Chenech Katzenellenbogen of Halberstadt. It is beyond doubt that Reb Chenech is not an imaginary figure. Euchel had the original before his own eyes, saw a living Reb Chenech, and painted a faithful picture of him. It must be conceded that the picture is highly successful. One sees before him a living, old-fashioned, wealthy Jewish money-changer with his entire demeanor and movements—how he scratches his head under his head-covering and blows his nose, with his little proverbs, with his refrain "What's to be done with it?," with his ardent pursuit of profit and his self-deprecation before the silver dollar, with his grim hatred for everything that smacks of secularity and contemporaneity and is not hallowed by the tradition of the fathers. He is exceedingly fond of himself, takes great delight in his own jests and proverbs, considers himself as belonging to a very distinguished family, and thinks he is a great expert in worldly matters. "Fifteen years I sat, praise God, at the table of the community council; will you tell me what is just and unjust?," he exclaims indignantly.

Reb Chenech loves to quote a saying from the *Gemara,* and Friday evening when the gentile woman comes in with her snuffer to trim the candles, he does not utter any profane words but speaks in a special Sabbath style: "So! Let the bad odor be gotten rid of." He holds fast to the principle obtained from his grandfather to the effect that "whoever wishes to innovate anything, prepares a grievous loss for himself." "Our fathers' fathers did not learn any grammar; so we also can get along without it . . . Of those who praised grammar in their time, it is said: 'All who come to her will not return.' " And he drives away the poor student Marcus who takes his meals at his home because his wife saw him eating "wormy, rotten plums when he thought he was unobserved." "May his name and memory be blotted out. Mother is right; let him no more cross the threshold!" Reb Chenech regards with extreme hostility the "new reform" for which the *maskilim,* led by David Friedländer,[48] battled so obdurately. He consoles himself: "Let my enemies have a headache as long a time as before anything will come of this." He fears, and rightly so, that reform would destroy the old way of life. He, Reb Chenech, however, wishes

48. See above, pp. 114ff.

everything to remain the same and to continue sitting at the "community council table."

Life, however, was stronger than he, and he was compelled to see this in his own family. We noted earlier that the Jewish merchants and largescale business men, even those of the old type like Reb Chenech Katzenellenbogen, were not opposed to having their daughters obtain a certain measure of European culture. A daughter is, after all, exempt from the obligation to study Torah, and her knowledge of languages may be a bit of an advantage in business; she will receive customers, be able to read a ticket or a business letter. Hence, it does not trouble Reb Chenech that his older daughter Elka is transformed into Elizabeth, reads "gentile" books, and can even speak English. The younger daughter, the not overly clever Hadass-Hedwig, has obtained a smattering of education. It appears that tutors were especially engaged for her. Hence, when it comes to reading over a German letter, Yitl, Reb Chenech's wife, complains to the younger daughter: "You have cost enough money; you should be able to read Latin."

Reb Chenech marries his daughter Elka to an inept merchant named Model, who is pious and God-fearing like himself and, like himself also, prepared to forget honor and his own self-respect for the sake of a livelihood and a little side-income. A conflict between the ill-matched couple is therefore inevitable. Isaac Euchel witnessed many such conflicts in the Jewish families known to him. Elka-Elizabeth despises her husband and the entire old-fashioned way of life in which she grew up. Her ideal, the hero of her dreams, is the Prussian officer von Horn with his ringing spurs and richly decorated uniform. The officer himself, with whom Reb Chenech's daughter, the mother of children, carries on a love affair, cynically boasts to his comrade: "Do you know what magic power the little word *von* has among these creatures? . . . Conceit, disgust for their own people, and a quasi-culture which they imagine they find among us make up the entire existence of these beings. Love is no more important to her than to me."

It is even worse with the education of Reb Chenech's son Herzche (Hartwig). The father's educational program is quite simple: "Herzche should go to school morning and evening; Herzche should study a section of the Gemara; he should fast on Monday and Thursday and become a businessman." Herzche-Hartwig relates how until he was sixteen he studied with "a Polish rabbi" who taught him "things of which he himself had no conception;" hence, he "rarely listened to what the man babbled in his jargon." His sister Elka-Elizabeth took pity on him and secretly, so that their father should not know, studied German and French with him and gave him good books to read.

The father finally learns that his older son has become a heretic and denier. They begin to persecute Herzche strongly; they do not let him out of their sight for a minute. The son begs his father to "let him learn a manual trade." "What do you wish to become?," the father asks. Herzche wishes to study architecture. "A builder?" exclaims Reb Chenech; "and what will you do on the Sabbath? Will you desecrate the Sabbath?" Herzche then proposes to become a sculptor. "Of course," the father cries; "to carve idols? Unfortunately, nothing will come of you. If you had wanted to, you could already have been a fine householder."

The end of the matter is that Herzche falls into the company of some frivolous Christian youths with whom he became acquainted through his sister and is corrupted. "We," Herzche relates, "hold folly to be enlightenment and luxury freedom. I forgot all bonds of family and mocked my parents and my whole people." He roams about with his new friends among the taverns, becomes a cardplayer, incurs debts, and—having no money to play—cheats at cards. He is caught, flogged, and put in jail.

The author has, to a certain degree, a positive attitude toward Herzche. In his mouth he places many of his own thoughts, for instance: "Unfortunately, among us they call religion what is really nothing other than observance, wherein neither the head nor the heart can take part." Herzche becomes a penitent, and the author hopes that he will still become a true representative of culture and enlightenment. Here, however, Euchel stands at the limit of his power of portrayal. For his observing eye to be able to obtain a correct and faithful living image, a certain distance was required. An author must be spiritually and intellectually superior to the characters he portrays; only then is he capable of giving a clear picture. For this reason the old-fashioned characters in Euchel—Reb Chenech, his wife Yitl, their younger son, the base hypocrite Samuel, who on Friday evening steals the beaker with the silver coins (he is afraid to desecrate the Sabbath, but, having no alternative, extinguishes the candle and sighs with a pious mien: "Woe! I have sinned, I have transgressed, I have done perversely")—come out vividly. Vivid also are the supposedly cultured daughters of Reb Chenech, Elka-Elizabeth and

Hadassah-Hedwig, "a foolish creature but one who is good-heartedness itself," as her brother Herzche testifies. Typical also is the idle pedant, the student Breitenbauch, formerly a teacher's assistant. Breitenbauch undoubtedly was not an imaginary figure; Euchel saw many such persons among the young Jewish students. Only yesterday a flatheaded *yeshivah* student, he suddenly becomes a "Kantian," a "critical philosopher." Abstract, badly digested philosophical notions completely confuse the weak mind of the self-satisfied fool. "He has studied," exclaims the enlightened doctor with disgust, "how one must not be a decent person, learned how to adorn absurdity and inhumanity with big words."

As soon, however, as Euchel attempts to portray "positive" figures—the just-mentioned doctor, the provincial deputy Nathan, the studious Marcus, or Herzche as a penitent—his inspiration at once departs. These, after all, are his ideal; in their mouth he places his own thoughts and demands. Nevertheless —and perhaps, indeed, because of this—we do not obtain living persons, but paper mannequins with nine measures of "enlightened" speech. The author himself does not perceive how much irony there is in the words with which the fourth scene of the fifth act ends, where Reb Chenech calls out to Nathan and then to the doctor: "Do you know what? Make a book out of it!" The author's intention was naturally to stress precisely the comical and the backward in the old-fashioned Reb Chenech. However, in time, ideas and taste changed so much that it happens quite frequently in Euchel's comedy that the comic springs out precisely from the side in which the author himself saw only the "positive" and desirable.

We noted earlier that in Euchel's comedy the enlightened speak pure German, the old-fashioned plain Yiddish, and the language of Reb Chenech is rendered faithfully with all its tags, with all its peculiarities of dialect. The author does this not so much for the sake of realism, as in order to make clearer the comical and ridiculous aspects of this "jargon" in which the beautiful "language of the country" becomes so distorted. To render old Reb Chenech funnier, the author emphasizes how he does not understand when he is spoken to in a cultured language. Even the very superficially educated Hedwig, who believes that Breitenbauch comes from the "region of Kant" when the latter introduces himself as a "Kantian," and who considers this fool a tremendously profound philosopher because he spouts Kant's philosophical expressions which he does not even begin to understand—even she considers it absolutely necessary to speak to her father precisely in the "enlightened" language.

When Reb Chenech falls into a faint on hearing that Hedwig spent Friday evening with Englishmen in a gentile restaurant, she gives him a vial of smelling salts and revives him with the words: "Here, smell, *mon cher papa!*" Reb Chenech, however, is an unenlightened orthodox Jew, and so he replies to the loving words of his modern daughter: "To hell with you and all your *cher papa!*" And when the elder daughter Elizabeth, after the scandal with the officer, comes to beg forgiveness from her father, she naturally does this in a purely "cultured" fashion; she begs: "*Verzeihen Sie, lieber Vater* (Forgive me, dear father)." The father pardons her because, according to the law, she, as the mistress of a household, is already outside his authority. But he considers it necessary to note: "Well, yes, but wean yourself away from this nonsensical language."

Reb Chenech's daughters are only half-educated, "falsely enlightened;" but the same thing and, indeed, in still sharper form appears among the truly enlightened in whose mouth the author places his own wishes and demands. So, for instance, the studious Marcus, of whom the enlightened doctor attests that "he will some day bring honor to the nation." Marcus is of "pure olive oil," in fact, completely an angel of God; everything he thinks and does is simply out of love for mankind. From the fact that Reb Chenech's wife Yitl saw Marcus buying "rotten plums" in the marketplace and on the spot commencing to eat them without examining them, one must not think that it was simply for his own pleasure that he bought plums in the marketplace—God forbid! Indeed, the author himself lets Marcus explain how it happened: "Today for the first time in my life I myself bought plums on the street. The sick man whom we are visiting today wishes to have a little pot of them. I saw some in the marketplace and thought to provide the man with some nourishment; it may be that, without thinking of it, I ate some."

When this same Marcus on a Friday evening sees a house burning in the closest vicinity of Reb Chenech's residence, he knocks at the door and urges them, for God's sake, to rise from sleep at once, for the danger is great. But even at this moment the erstwhile *yeshivah*-student deems it impossible to "besmirch" his tongue with the "corrupted jargon" and talks with Reb Chenech in High German. The latter, however, is an ignorant man; he understands very little and sighs: "How this one pains me with his talk!" And the author is certain that in this scene the comical one is not the "highly noble" Marcus with his "enlightened" speech but the orthodox Reb Chenech. The same thing happens again in the scene where the enlightened Nathan comes after his conversation with Yitl to Reb Chenech with the report: "Now, Reb Chenech, from your wife I have *plein pouvoir*. But the ignorant Reb Chenech does not understand what *plein pouvoir* means. So he asks his wife: "What is he talking about? What has he from you? This one always speaks such big words!" And he begs Nathan: "Why don't you speak Yiddish? I am a Jew!" Only then, having no alternative, Nathan "breaks his tongue" and explains to Reb Chenech: "I have *koaḥ harsha'ah* (power of attorney) from your wife to do with Herzche what I wish!" *Koaḥ harsha'ah*—this a Jew like Reb Chenech understands clearly and precisely.

A twin to Euchel's play is the comedy *Leichtsinn und Frömmelei* by his colleague and fellow contributor to *Ha-Meassef*, Aaron Wolfsohn-Halle. Aaron Wolfsohn was born in 1754 in the little town of Niederheim in Alsace, where his father Wolf Halle practiced as a physician.[49] Dr. Wolf was a scholar and of a distinguished family, and his son, in fact, frequently stresses this in his signature: "Aaron, the son of the doctor, the rabbinic scholar, our teacher, Wolf Halle." Dr. Wolf had already acquired European education and corresponded with Mendelssohn, and the young Wolfsohn probably became familiar with the new tendencies of the *Aufklärer* while still in his father's house.

In 1785 he settled in Berlin and there entered into close relationships with the *maskilim* who grouped themselves around *Ha-Meassef* and continued Mendelssohn's *Biur*. Wolfsohn became a frequent contributor to *Ha-Meassef*, writing poems, exegetical articles, and popular works on zoology and physics. The seventh volume of *Ha-Meassef* appeared under his editorship,[50] and the outspokenly militant tendency of this volume is to be attributed to the new editor. As a "Biurist," he translated and published, with his commentary, the Biblical Scrolls—Lamentations, Ruth, and Esther (1789). A year later Job came out, and afterward the Book of Kings (1800). Like many other *maskilim* of that era, Wolfsohn also devoted considerable attention to pedagogy. In 1790 he published his Hebrew textbook *Avtalyon* which went through four editions.[51] In the announce-

---

49. See Shatzky's article in *Amerikaner Pinkes*, 1929, p. 16.
50. On Wolfsohn's polemic work *Siḥah Be-Eretz Ha-Ḥayyim*, see above, pp. 100ff.
51. Reprinted in 1800, 1806, and 1814.

ment of this textbook that he published in *Ha-Meassef*,[52] he notes how unpedagogical is the practice of beginning immediately to teach the Pentateuch to small children who still do not know the Hebrew language. "Have you ever," he asks, "seen people beginning to study Latin directly from Virgil or Horace, without any preparation whatever?"

From 1791 on Wolfsohn for many years was head teacher and inspector of the well known, reformed "Königlicher Wilhelm-Schule" in Breslau. We noted previously what a stubborn battler against the orthodox and the old mode of life he was.[53] Graetz calls him a "daring stormer." But life brought him, as it did to his friend Isaac Euchel, not a few disappointments. He also became convinced that the number of the modern youth who, like Herzche-Hartwig, considered "frivolity enlightenment and luxury freedom" was very large. And so he, like his comrade Euchel, also decided "laughingly to tell the truth" and wrote his comedy *Leichtsinn und Frömmelei* (Frivolity and Bigotry).

Undoubtedly a certain affinity between Euchel's and Wolfsohn's plays is discernible. Even the names of some of the characters are identical in both plays. In Euchel the chief character is called Chenech, in Wolfsohn Chanoch. In both plays a young *maskil* named Marcus figures. In Wolfsohn's Chanoch's son is called Samuel, and so also is Reb Chenech's younger son. It is difficult, however, to determine which play is older. Euchel's play was first printed in 1797, but was already known earlier within rather wide circles in manuscript. Wolfsohn's play first appeared in print in 1796; however, it is very possible that it, too, was composed several years before. It is highly probable that the two writers, who were friendly with each other, did, in fact, in their frequent personal intercourse, decide that each of them should bring to their generation a "family portrait" and, in this connection, even discussed certain details of their projected plays.

In the preface that Wolfsohn wrote in 1798 to the second edition of his play,[54] which was published in Amsterdam, he notes that he composed his comedy "for amusement on our Purim festival in the place of the otherwise customary absurd and unsuitable farces." This is not the only attempt that Wolf-

52. *Ha-Meassef*, 5549, pp. 373–376.
53. On his attitude toward the Talmud, see above.
54. In modern times Zalman Rejzen reprinted Wolfsohn's play in his *Fun Mendelssohn Biz Mendele*.

sohn made to displace the "absurd farces." Another play of Wolfsohn's "for amusement on the Purim festival," which he composed with songs in two acts especially for the pupils of the Wilhelm-Schule, has been preserved. This is, indeed, a common Purim play and is called *David der Besieger des Goliath* (David the Conqueror of Goliath).[55] But Wolfsohn set himself quite different tasks in his *Leichtsinn und Frömmelei*, and he actually points to these in the abovementioned preface: "I intend nothing other with this than merely to set before the nation graphically, in vivid colors, the evil consequences that can be called forth by rigorous fanaticism and hypocrisy under the mantle of religion, on the one side, and, on the other side, by the false or inauthentic enlightenment of our present-day fashionable youth, along with the defective education of children."

Precisely this dual goal—to lay bare fanaticism and hypocrisy, on the one side, and superficial, "false" enlightenment, on the other—is noticeable even in the title of the play. The author does not spare black colors in portraying the Jewish Tartuffe, the hypocrite Reb Yosefche, one of those "who do the deeds of Zimri and demand the reward of Pineḥas." The ardent battler against the fanatics here frequently obtains the upper hand over the artist.

But he also does not spare pointed arrows for the "falsely enlightened," for Reb Chanoch's daughter Yettchen who is constantly surrounded on her promenades with a whole company of officers and "each one of these introduces another foolishness in her head, overwhelms her with flattery which she takes for pure truth." In addition, it must be noted that in Wolfsohn the *maskil* Marcus comes out more successfully than Euchel's *Aufgeklärte*. Wolfsohn's Marcus is a living figure, not a "talking machine." Blood is discernible in his veins, and even when he appears in the third act in the house of the marriage brokeress Lemgin with the emotive monologue of a typical *raisonneur*, one must take into consideration the style of that era when the pathetic cries of Schiller's hero Karl Mohr evoked tears of enchantment among the sentimental auditors. It is therefore quite natural that while Euchel's Reb Chenech regards the enlightened with a certain irony and advises them to "make a book out of it," Wolfsohn's Reb Chanoch takes Marcus for his son-in-law, explaining: "The new Jews are a thousand

---

55. Printed in 1802. See Shatzky's notice in *Arkhiv Far Di Geshikhte Fun Yidishn Teater*, I, pp. 148–49. On Wolfsohn's participation in a Purim-play see above, p. 85.

times more precious to me, for they at least disclose what they are doing, but the others (the hypocrites) wish to do everything in secret, and they deceive God and men."

As a scenic work also, Wolfsohn's play is more successful than Euchel's. There is not in it such an abundance of extraneous characters as in *Reb Chenech*. *Leichtsinn und Frömmelei* was, after all, designated "for entertainment on our Purim festival;" hence, the plot is much more compact and not as diffuse as in Euchel. Only eight persons take part in it, and each is in place, each a necessary, organic part of the comedy.[56]

Euchel and Wolfsohn lived through grievous disappointments. They felt themselves abandoned and lonely, as "in the wilderness," and already in the prime of their lives they removed themselves from literary activity. In the last years of his brief life Euchel no longer took part in Hebrew literature. His friend Wolfsohn lived for a long time (he died in 1835 at the age of eighty-one), and in his old age even forgot the Hebrew language. But a third contemporary who, like Euchel, also studied in Königsberg had a different fate.

The name of this man was Moses Marcuse. Of him in the chapter that follows.

56. In the year 1933 both comedies were translated by D. Hofstein into modern Yiddish and published with an introductory article by Max Erik.

CHAPTER SIX

Moses Marcuse;
DOV BER OF BOLECHOW

[Moses Marcuse "the doctor of Koenigsberg"—His life "in the territories of Poland"—The question of language in Marcuse—His *Ezer Yisrael*—The style of Marcuse's work—Dr. Marcuse as a reprover—The cultural-literary importance of *Ezer Yisrael*—Aaron Isaac (Isak) and his wandering life—The significance of his *Autobiography*—Dov Ber Birkenthal of Bolechow and his literary legacy.]

 OSES MARCUSE, the "doctor of Koenigsberg," undoubtedly deserves to have his name occupy an honored place in the history of modern Yiddish literature as one of the first authors who attempted to employ the folk-language, the "jargon" so despised by all the *maskilim* and "enlighteners," as a secular, *literary* language, and who wrote a book which retains, to the present day, considerable ethnographic interest. This work provides many vivid pictures of the former Jewish way of life, and tells us simply and tenderly how our grandfathers and grandmothers in the second half of the eighteenth century in White Russia, Lithuania, and Poland lived and acted.

Yet Marcuse's life-work was so thoroughly forgotten in the course of the nineteenth century that he is not even mentioned by our foremost bibliographers—neither by Steinschneider and Benjacob, nor by Samuel Wiener and Eleazar Schulmann.

Only in the twentieth century was Marcuse resurrected. Noah Prylucki[1] was the first who discovered that there was once a Dr. Marcuse in the world and that he wrote a book entitled *Ezer Yisrael.*[2]

Who was this Dr. Marcuse? For the few biographical details that we have, we are indebted to Marcuse himself. From certain indications he gives in his book, we know that he was a Prussian Jew, born in the 1740's. From his father, a learned Jew, he obtained a religious education, and he was a scholar in Talmudic knowledge.[3] He studied medicine at the University of Koenigsberg and thereafter wandered for a long time throughout Europe. "And further," Marcuse tells of himself, "I was in Holland, England, and other lands in maritime countries." In 1773 he came to the "land of Poland" *(medinat Polin).* At first he lived in Kapust, four miles from Shklov, and later lived for a time in Great Poland, or Major Poland. In the 1780's he settled in Volhynia in the town of Turisk. As a skilled physician he occupied a government post[4] for several years and was highly regarded by the local official Michael Bobrowski.[5] Among the Jewish populace also he apparently acquired a great reputation. "I know," Dr. Marcuse proudly declares," "that when my book appears, they will already know that I, blessed be God's name, have helped thousands of people. My name Marcuse, the doctor of Koenigsberg, is well known, and they will certainly, with God's help, obey me."

While he was still quite young, immediately after becoming a doctor, Marcuse set himself as his life's task "to benefit the

1. See his notice in *Der Moment*, 1914, No. 10, and his longer article in his *Zamlbikher Far Yidishn Folklor*, Vol. II, 1917.
2. *Ezer Yisrael* is extremely rare. Apart from Prylucki's copy there is another in the public library in Frankfurt-am-Main, and a third was found by the writer of these lines in the state library in Leningrad (see *Filologishe Shriftn*, III, 181).
3. The rabbi of Kovel, Jacob Kahana, writes in his *haskamah* to *Ezer Yisrael:* "This is the doctor, and he is called by all Doctor Marcuse. He is the wonderful and distinguished rabbi, the complete and perfected scholar, our master, our teacher, Moses, son of the Torah scholar, our teacher Mordecai of blessed memory, and he is very well versed in Torah, a man of learning and of family distinction, and his heart is open in wisdom, and his hand reaches all books, especially books of remedies." Among the subscribers who undertook to buy Satanow's first part of *Mishlei Asaf* (published in 1788), Mordecai Marcuse is noted. Can this be Moses Marcuse's father?
4. On the title-page and in the *haskamot*, it is noted that Marcuse "was close to the king and the commission, may its majesty be exalted, a government-paid doctor."
5. In one *haskamah* it is noted: "Doctor Marcuse is a permanent resident of the holy community of Turisk, he whom God has given grace and favor in the eyes of the great count, the lord of the holy community mentioned above."

people and write a popular book on hygiene and medicine.
"Dear brethren," he relates,

I have long known and thought how I might benefit the people. It
is already sixteen years since I came into our land of Poland from the
schools of the gentile sages. It was difficult for me to present a book
to you. The great rabbi of the holy community of Hamburg, Rabbi
Raphael[6] (Kohen), advised me against publishing it in Hebrew, for
he said to me: "In the holy tongue wisdom or science is already
written . . . If you write on a difficult science in the holy language,
the result will be that few will understand you." The sage was right,
for the community in Poland, I mean all, can have no use for my book
—only one in a city. I wished many times to write in German; then
the public, neither the scholar nor the common Jew, would have
understood me.

Like all the *maskilim* of the "Berlin School," Marcuse was
firmly persuaded that the language which the Jews speak "in
the lands of Poland" was a "corrupted German" which it is
literally shameful to speak. For him, however, what the *maskilim* of Berlin, the "Marcuses" and the "Nathans,"[7] refused to
understand was clear and plain: since the common people understand only this "corrupted" language, it is precisely in it
that one must write and speak if he wishes to have any effect
on the people and be of use to them.
Marcuse further relates:

I had to wait until I crippled my speech and learned to speak German
badly and falsely as you speak it . . . I am ashamed and must laugh
at myself when I consider how falsely we speak. But I have no
alternative: I must give you to understand. How will you understand
what I mean if I write pure German for you? I am even more ashamed
when I must sometimes corrupt a Hebrew word and write it half
Hebrew and half Yiddish. What can I do? The common people would
not understand me; what use would they have for my book? From the
scholars I beg forgiveness a hundred times for tearing out a word
from Hebrew and mixing it with bad German.[8] If they ever see my
book, they will not understand me and will laugh. God knows my
thoughts and intentions; I wished to benefit our people in Poland, for
my countrymen are very poor in science, and in my generations I

6. Raphael ben Yekutiel Kohen—a prominent rabbi of that time, author of *Torat
Yekutiel* and *Marpe Leshon* (about him in the next chapter).
7. See the previous chapter.
8. Marcuse not infrequently writes Hebrew words according to Yiddish phonetics,
e.g., *bargenen, darshenen,* and the like.

have not seen anyone troubling himself and taking up the cause of people so that they not be cripples and not die before their time.[9]

At the end of the year 1789 (Marḥeshvan, 5550) Marcuse's wish was finally fulfilled. His book appeared under the following title-page:

Sefer Refuot Ha-Nikra Ezer Yisrael (the Book of Remedies that is called *Ezer Yisrael*): For those who dwell in the country of Poland written in Polish *Taytsh* (Yiddish), which Rabbi Moses, who is called Marcuse Doctor and is well known to many, composed, and who was a government-paid doctor appointed by the king and by the commission; he wishes to benefit the people with his book, so that each person might be able to help himself where there is no learned doctor; and whoever holds to the course of conduct that he prescribes need not become sick. Printed here in the holy community of Poritzk in the year 5550.[10]

The book is divided into eighteen chapters and more than two hundred sections. At the end, as a supplement, is a special section entitled *Hanhagat Ha-Refuot* in which it is explained how to put together various remedies.[11]

In the first introduction Marcuse, the contemporary of the Meassefim, deems it necessary to explain why he, the German *maskil* who had studied in universities, writes his book in plain Yiddish. This explanation of his is so characteristic that we present it here virtually *in toto*:

. . . Even more will be found to say or ask: Why did he write his book in *Taytsh* [Yiddish] and not in the holy language [Hebrew]? I must myself reply to these people, and I ask them, in turn, just the opposite: Why do we all speak Yiddish, i.e., bad German? We carry on

9. *Ezer Yisrael*, Chapter Fifteen, No. 87.

10. A characteristic feature: the expenses of printing the book were covered by the local "ruler." The author reports this in Hebrew: "And I am obliged to praise the lord and I will give glory to the honor of his name, Michael Bobrowski, royal master of the castle, who spent money from his pocket to support me in this work of piety; and may He who gives salvation to kings bless him, and pay him his recompense, and send blessing and prosperity on the work of his hands, and may he see the consolations of his children and his children's children forever. Amen." Unfortunately the print is extremely bad. The letters are broken and rubbed off, the paper thick and grey, and in places the text is extremely difficult to read.

11. It is beyond doubt that Marcuse in this connection used as a model the well known book of the doctor of Lausanne, Tissot, which Mendel Levin (Lefin) translated at the proposal of Moses Mendelssohn into Hebrew and published in 1794 (see our *History*, Vol. VI, p. 278). In Tissot's book there is also at the end, as a supplement, a special section which describes how to mix various remedies.

business, we study, we finagle, we tell lies, we flatter—in short, we cook, roast, burn, denounce and inform, make additional summonses to the reading of the Torah, exorcise the evil eye, all in *Taytsh.* Or when we write to one another, do we write just then in Hebrew? Why, I ask you, do you not write *Taytsh* as we speak? If we write Hebrew, let us speak Hebrew. May I not be blamed for saying it, and I exclude scholars: How many thousands write Hebrew—but it is neither *Taytsh* nor Hebrew nor Russian? Until I have an answer to my questions, I beg people to leave me in peace.

But Marcuse knows very well that they will not "leave him in peace," and many *maskilim* will not forgive him for his great sin of "besmirching" his pen with "jargon." Hence, he returns again at the end of his introduction to the same question:

But how does it remain with the question that whole groups will ask: Why did I write my book in Polish *Taytsh* and not in Hebrew? I know there will be very few who will justify me, and so I am inclined to justify myself. I say: I had to write in *Taytsh,* because I wished to benefit many thousands of people with my book each year and to save them from such quacks and defectives as, for instance, old women, bad midwives, exorcisors of the evil eye, bad epidemics, good air(?), evil and dirtied things, ignorant *baalei shemot,* and terribly wicked people; from pourers of wax [for magical purposes], from fortunetellers who magically diagnose all diseases, from inept preachers who carry about remedies to sell for a good supper, for the sake of a small contribution, and from worthless little "doctors" who have made themselves doctors, or have been made such by foolish old women. Tell me, dear people, do all these know Hebrew? Certainly not. They do not even know Polish *Taytsh.* If someone wishes to see himself in a mirror, does he cover the mirror? How will he be able to reflect himself? He will certainly not be able to see himself. But my intention is that all these fools should look into my book and see what sort of face they have. How could I write Hebrew when they would not understand it? For our scholars I need no justification. Who was greater than Rabbi Moses ben Maimon, may his memory be a blessing, most of whose books on philosophy and the natural sciences were written in Arabic so that all his contemporaries should understand and know? Also the Gaon Rabbenu Bahya, may his memory be for a blessing, who composed the book *Hovot Ha-Levavot* and wrote the rest of his books as well in the Arabic language. So I, the humble one, have followed in their footsteps, I, the physician Marcuse, resident of Turisk.

The Berlin *maskilim,* the Euchels and Wolfsohns, had before themselves the youth of the rising Jewish bourgeoisie, the children of the Reb Chenechs and Reb Chanochs. Doctor Marcuse, however, lived in a totally different environment. This Prussian Jew and physician of Koenigsberg spent many years in castaway Jewish towns and townlets in Poland. He saw before himself the poor, suffering, benighted, ignorant Jewish masses. To this foreign doctor, this "German with the shaven beard," as Marcuse portrays himself, it never even occurred to try to "ennoble" the poor "jargon," to write *Daytshmerish*. Granted that "Polish *Taytsh*" is badly corrupted German, but in order "to benefit the people," in order that his book might be more comprehensible for "the brethren in Poland," he endeavors to write in an authentic folk-language. And it is truly touching to see how he takes pains to make his style more popular and comprehensible to everyone. But this does not come to him so easily. In the construction of a sentence or in a casual word, the "German" is occasionally noticeable. Nevertheless, Marcuse attained his goal: his style is, indeed, popular, his Polish *Taytsh* is a pithy Yiddish which does not lose its substance and vitality through the not infrequent "High German" words.

Marcuse addresses his readers: "Dear brethren, gentle brethren, dear people, gentle friends, my beloved masters," etc. This European-educated physician had the sensitivity required to realize that, in order to write a genuine book for the people, one must closely intertwine his life with the mass of the folk, breathe its air, and assume its manner and style. And it is quite remarkable that a German Jew, a contemporary of the Meassefim who regarded Yiddish with hostility and contempt, considered it a duty to learn this language thoroughly in order to write a popular book that might be useful not only for the elect few but for the broad strata—"all the brethren in Poland." It suffices to take the first casually torn-out passage, for instance, page 122. There a few German words do, indeed, come through. Nevertheless, it will not even occur to the reader that he has to do with a European-educated physician and not with a *bet midrash* scholar who has spent all his days among the common folk.

. . . If I would explain the reason whence their "colics" come, I would be able to help them in a trifling matter. It would cost them little, and I would also save more lives. But, unfortunately, I ought to say whether this comes from our ignorance, or whether I could add a third point: Because we in Poland are very stingy in paying a real doctor. We would rather place confidence in a Jewess, or a gentile woman, or other such charlatans for a little glass of brandy—the cheap *baalei shemot*, the fortunetellers who come and "diagnose" and administer some holy drops. But with this they make great misfortunes for you. I have been called many times to patients who are already close to "Ha-Tzur Tamim Pa'alo" ("The Rock Whose Work is Perfect"—a prayer for the dead) and with this Rock [i.e., God] I saved them. In the case of many, however, I came when I already had to say to myself "Baruch Dayan Emet" ["Blessed Be the True Judge" —the benediction spoken at the moment of death] and went away and cursed the class of the mischief-makers. And I say again today: May those who publicly kill people and no one prevents them from doing so have their names wiped out. They are given food, drink, and a few gold coins for expenses, so that they may travel further and again make dead men out of living ones. It is high time, dear people, for you to open your eyes for once and not let killings take place in your house, in your city. Put officers and guards on such rabble or vile persons and transfer them into the hands of another people; let them be killed for all of you. Take a lesson from the whole world. One does not hear there of such wantons dragging themselves about and openly killing people with no one to prevent them. Unfortunately, many clothe themselves in the garments of rabbis and have a bit of learning; these kill even more persons. Punish them so that they may hear and see and not act wickedly. My heart trembles in my body as I write and must recall how many hundreds of people I have had to see who were compelled to die for no reason—not because they were sick. No, they were killed with bad advice, with noxious remedies. Young, middle-aged, male, female, only sons, young wives, scholars, sages themselves. All of these I had to let die; I could not help them. They were burned to death, and unfortunately this was mainly done through these charlatans—may their name be blotted out and may they be condemned to death by burning.[12]

Not only the form, the style of Marcuse's work, but the content as well is of interest. The physician who, in the course of many years, became thoroughly familiar with the life of the Jewish masses in Poland, understood quite well that merely with medical advice or with prescriptions on how to put remedies together, very little help could be made available here. Not without reason did Marcuse give his work a double name—not

---

12. It is worth noting that the well known doctor and physicist, Marcus Herz, also deems it necessary to say in his "Tefillah La-Rofe": "O God of faithfulness, place faith in the heart of the sick to trust me and my work and an ear to listen to my advice. Remove from their bedside every quack doctor and all the honorable host, friends and relatives, who stand around like sages and privy councillors to consult together; also the crowd of care-taking women, wise in their own conceit, who act destructively in presuming to criticize the work of the doctor. For this is a foolish people. In the arrogance of their heart they hinder the good effect of medicine and bring men down from Your health-giving and healing to the chambers of death" (*Ha-Meassef*, 5550, p. 424).

only *Sefer Refuot* (Book of Remedies) but also, indeed, *Ezer Yisrael* (Help of Israel). He realizes that many diseases and sufferings are a consequence of the intellectual and social backwardness of Jewish life "in the territories of Poland" and can therefore be healed and assuaged not with prescriptions but through changing the whole way of life with its abnormal economic foundations.

Therein, indeed, consists the importance of Marcuse's book. In consequence of his broader view, he provides us in his *Ezer Yisrael* with interesting portraits of contemporary Jewish life, and many pages of this work have, to this day, a certain ethnographic and cultural-historical importance.

Here, for instance, is how Marcuse writes in the eighth chapter of his book about such an ordinary sickness as ague:

Dear people, if I knew that you would listen to me, it would be very easy for me to give you advice. But be that as it may, since I already hold pen in hand I shall write further, and though many will not listen to me, perhaps one from a town or a family will. So I will have also repaired what I wished and achieved my desire . . . The first is that I have seen in our country so many vacant taverns, empty granaries, and so many dung-heaps before your doors. You do not realize how many diseases come from the heaps of filth, and the majority of the rotting diseases deriving from uncleanness about which I have begun to write: abscesses, scabies, and still other things. Vacant, abandoned ruins have sometimes killed in a moment. How often have people gone into an abandoned shed or into a granary that has been locked up for a long time and promptly fallen down and died. And the one who comes to call that person because he has tarried also falls down and dies in a moment. This results from the fact that the air has been locked up for a long time. Our rabbles say: A demon injured them. They were injured, but they themselves are the demons and injurers, because of the great filth that always lies near many houses and becomes wet from the rain. Then out comes the sun and, with it, flies—millions of them every minute in the air, and the air becomes fetid. Our dear little children walk about in the filth or play not far from it, and they become sick. People cry and weep. The child has just been playing! The foolish old women say: The evil eye attacked them. How do they prove that this is true? They take embers, utter incantations, bark, and yawn. The children look at them, and so they, too, yawn. The women do like the wicked *baalei shemot*; they also yawn assiduously. The sick children look at them and yawn, too. In short, the mother, the father, the servant—all yawn. The women say: Look, I told you; the child, unfortunately, has an evil eye. Woe, woe! The woman opens her mouth wide like an animal and holds her hand before it so that no one will see that she no longer has any teeth in it. I must inform you that they lie twice. First—when one weeps, the other, looking at him, also weeps. Even the stranger who enters and still does not know what the weeping is all about begins to do so. If one laughs, the other laughs also. So it is with the old women's yawning. But why does this happen? I have no time to write about it; it is a natural thing . . . As for the embers, here again they make their fraudulent deception. Whether the embers rise up or fall below —either way it is the evil eye. This also is false. There are all kinds of woods, hard woods, such as oak, birch, and still others. If the wood is hard, the embers are heavy; but pinewood is lighter, and so the embers are also lighter.

Marcuse, however, is not content with ridiculing the exorcisors of the evil eye. "I say," he declares, "that you should rather make of the evil eye a good eye, I mean that you should make from the rotten, fetid air a garden. Sow onions, beets, radishes, parsley, and you will enjoy a double profit. You will have beautiful, pure air which is very healthy, and you will not have to make the peasant rich by buying everything for the last *groschen* that you still own or have begged."

At once, in this connection, Marcuse gives a vivid and clear portrait of the contemporary taverns, of the whole corruption and poverty of Jewish life "in the territories of Poland." As a typical *maskil* of that generation, he proposes a whole program on how to make useful agriculturalists out of *Luftmenschen* and idlers.[13] All this is written in a very unique style and with genuine publicistic temperament.[14]

Marcuse undoubtedly had the eye of a keen observer. In addition, he possessed a clear literary talent, one that is particularly noticeable when he issues forth against the backwardness and benightedness of Jewish life and carries on war with the "frauds and sinners" who deceive and mislead the common people. His bitter words of reproof are filled with vivid images and healthy humor. Here, for example, is a portrait of the healers of that time and, incidentally, also some interesting details about the author himself and about the conduct of contemporary Jewish doctors:

Dear women, I have already warned you in my book against ignorant *baalei shemot*, Tatars [i.e., soothsayers], wax-pourers, exorcisors

13. Prylucki rightly notes in his above-mentioned work (pp. 18–19) the echoes that are to be found in Marcuse's work of contemporary political events in Poland, which had just lived through the catastrophe of the first partition. The upper strata of the people then became convinced that the solution of the "Jewish question" must become the cornerstone of a reformed Poland.

14. *Ezer Yisrael*, folios 49–52. These interesting pages are reprinted in Prylucki's article, pp. 21–22, 46–49.

of the evil-eye, fortune-tellers, and worthless little doctors—may all
the frauds, the sinners in Israel, who, with their lies, obtain money
through swindlery and make cripples or even kill thousands of people each year, have their names blotted out. I also warned you about
the old midwives who unfortunately do not themselves know how
they harm you—may God forgive them for what they have done until
now in ignorance and without intent. However, I have not yet mentioned our dear doctors or healers, who are called among us in Poland
Rofe'im and *Feldschers.* I call them public, well-known specialists in
killing *(bravitne memitim),*[15] not *Rofe'im.* Of these I will not write a
great deal for you, because it is our good fortune that in every town
they are known, and so cannot do much harm. But, God forbid, if
they travel to some strange place, it is certainly bad for people. If one
of them puts on an elegant professional frock, he is already a *"doctor-
joctor"* among us. You call him: Master, help me! So he goes to some
strange place and scrapes off half his beard. Then you even say that
he is certainly a good, pious Jew because you have seen me and other
doctors besides who wear no beard at all. So these wanton rogues are
already respected by you, and you place your confidence in the little
half-beards. If these transgressors can say "hocus-pocus-triocus pras-
pril," then they already know Latin, as far as you are concerned. If,
moreover, they can drink brandy well and cheat you out of money
expertly, they are even better. About all of these I have already
written you. I do not need to justify myself for never having had a
beard. When we study in academies among the sage doctors, among
so many dukes, counts, and princes, we cannot go with beards; we
cannot obtain any patents to practice medicine, we are close to kings.
But if you require beards, why are you content with half-beards, with
men who drag themselves around with half a beard while the other
half is too hard for them to carry[16] . . . with a barber or even a jester.
The man did this so that he might better deceive you, so that you
would say: This one is still half a Jew, compared to that doctor who
goes around completely like a gentile. If, God forbid, some other
"German" comes dragging about with a full beard and goes around
with a hat like Haman's ears that you make on Purim, this Haman
causes you much more woe than Haman, the ancient enemy of the
Jews. You say: This is an honest Jew; he goes around like a Jew with
a beard—and with a full one. Perhaps the *Gemara* sends your good
healers to hell. I ask you once more, gentlemen: If you need a beard
and not a doctor, why do you accept a "drag-beard" who drags himself around with his beard to deceive you? After all, thank God, you
have enough decent, honest people with beards in your towns. Why
do you need the beards of frauds and transgressors—may their name

15. In Volhynian Yiddish the word *bravitne* is still used to the present day. It means
"quite open," "sharply expressed," "known by all." *Memitim* are killers, specialists in
slaying people.
16. Here apparently several words fell out in print.

be blotted out—when they have acquired no knowledge? They have snatched a little bit, one from *Maaseh Tuviyyah*, another from "the story of comrades." They have snatched something and kill you for your money.[17]

But Doctor Marcuse is not always angry and reproving. At times a good-natured smile appears on his face, and then his style obtains a humorous aspect. As we know, our ancestors were very fond of having themselves bled. This was considered the best remedy for all kinds of diseases. Apparently Marcuse was not particularly fond of the remedy. However, he understood quite well that if he were to express such a heretical idea as that a person can live out his years and not let himself be bled several times a year, he would merely be ridiculed. So he tells a story about something that happened to himself.

So that you may be more certain, my friends, I will give you myself as a proof . . . From my youthful years when I was still studying medicine, I was accustomed each year, two or three and even four times, to be bled. And as soon as the time came and I wanted to be bled and did not have the time to do so, it bothered me greatly. Sixteen years ago—this was the first year that I came to Poland from Prussia and lived in Kopishn four miles from Shklov—I sent for a doctor to bleed me. This doctor, whether he was frightened at a German such as myself or whether he was incompetent—to tell the matter briefly—cut into me three times and did not find a vein. I begged him not to trouble himself a fourth time, lest he not find a vein the fourth time. But soon after midday I traveled four miles to Orshe, a little town, and had myself bled by a German *Feldscher* who had lived among the Muscovites. From then on, thank God, I was finished with blood-letting. Furthermore, to my good fortune, I am a very timorous man. I was afraid of your healers; perhaps I was considered superfluous by them and maybe they did not need me in Poland. And for fear there is no remedy. I confess to you, dear people: Since that time I have not let myself be bled, and I am—thank God—healthy. I wish all people were as healthy as I. I have written for you so that you should listen to me. I cannot teach you to do better than I myself did.[18]

This humorous tone in Marcuse's book reminds one in places of our grandfather Mendele (Mocher Seforim) with his smile and his "Not this do I intend." As illustration, it is worth

17. *Ezer Yisrael*, 81–82.
18. *Ibid.*, 103.

pointing to the thirteenth chapter which discusses children's diseases and begins as follows.

My beloved masters, up until now I have had a labor that is not easy: to destroy the thorns from the vineyard, the vineyard of the house of Israel. And I have come as far as where the roses grow—I mean the little children. These are the proper roses from whom we all have pleasure, and this is the purpose of the owner of the vineyard: to grow in it beautiful, very beautiful, odorous roses. One may not ask the owner of the vineyard: Why do you, great Master, need so many piercing thorns and thistles for the sake of a few roses? That one may not inquire, for all of us Jews are likened to roses . . . I ask people: Do you not know the intention of the great Master—why, for the sake of several roses, thousands of thorns grow? They all gave me the same answer: It must be so. It cannot be otherwise; good must be mixed with bad and bad with good. When I heard this "It must be so!," I was afraid to ask further. But why must it be so? When the explanation is, "It must," one may no longer ask . . . If it must be so, why do I need to cut down thorns and thistles? If God wishes that there be so many murderers in Poland—let them be. Why need I further take up the cause of the people in Poland, if no one before me took it up? And again, perhaps I act—Heaven forbid—against God? . . .[19]

Just like Mendele, the "government-paid doctor" Marcuse becomes kindly and tender when he begins to speak of the poor Jewish women and little children, of the troubles and afflictions they have to suffer, of their dismal, dark fate.

"Dear women," Marcuse begins the chapter that speaks "of birth," i.e., of childbirth,

I come now to your midwives. I will also give you advice in your greatest distress that you have as a legacy from old mother Eve. But not much; to write about everything thoroughly would require a separate book for each thing. First, however, I would ask you: Dear women, why do you have on the High Holy Days in the synagogue two or three or four *zogerkes* (precentresses) who translate the *Maḥzor* for you so that you should know when to weep and when not to weep, and pay them for their service? Why do you weep before your husbands, that they should make for you Sabbath and festival clothes —three, four breastscarves (they are also called *zoleshkes*, heaven and hell breastscarves)? You think about heaven for yourselves, and for some men, unfortunately, it is a hell. And you yourselves bring everything about, for the "bribe and the slaughterer (*ha-shoḥed veha-*

19. *Ibid.*, 103–104.

shohet) are in your bosom."[20] Let me lecture you; perhaps you will have more to weep about. Why do you not persuade your husbands to let the midwives study from learned doctors, so that they should not kill you, make cripples of you. They [the midwives] kill many mothers along with their infants in childbirth, and they destroy many when they have already had their children. I have seen many thousands of women with whom I have spoken; they became weak, sick, and crippled at the hands of the midwives, because of our many sins. How many men have had to divorce their wives, though before their confinement they loved them much? You understand, women, what I mean thereby . . . How many in confinement or thereafter become insane, melancholiac? How many have become ill with epilepsy? How many have gotten tuberculosis, blood-poisoning, growths in the womb? How many became ill with jaundice, swellings, hernia? From how many do the midwives not tear the bladder out of their bodies or make a hole from which afterwards the urine cannot be contained . . . I know three such women but I could not help them. For one of them, her husband wanted to give me a hundred gold pieces to cure her, but I saw that I could not heal her and he had to divorce her. How many hundreds of other things I could tell you . . . Can you imagine, dear women, how many thousands of women and children had to die young at the hands of the midwives? Why do you make so many new weddings for your husbands? Why do you leave us so many orphans in the hands of other women? Why do you not rather beg your husbands for your lives—I mean that they should let the midwives study. It will not cost you much. Let one from each town or townlet study, and twenty will learn and know. These twenty trained midwives will teach a hundred others, and the hundred will in turn teach a thousand others . . . For your sake, let me bring it about that in every town or townlet all should read my book for the sake of their health, that you might have some knowledge—the men what pertains to men and the women what pertains to women—and that there will be people who know my book properly, so that when—God forbid—some disease occurs, the people who are versed in my book will, with God's help, be able to aid you. Through the good deeds which these people will merit I wish to have a portion in the world of truth [the next world]. If they are poor and honest people, give them a subsidy from the community, so that they may be doctors among you with my book; and your own people from your town, being honest people, will certainly not deceive you. Even at every estate-lessee in a village, there will be a teacher, and he or they themselves will be able to read *Taytsh-Yiddish;* they will be capable of helping themselves with God's aid.[21]

20. An untranslatable play on words. The meaning of the words is: "You bribe and, in fact, thereby kill the other."
21. *Ezer Yisrael,* folios 76–77. In the "announcement" which is printed at the beginning of Mendel Levin's Hebrew translation of Tissot's "Book of Remedies," the publishers

No less interesting is the passage in which Marcuse gives a colorful picture of how the women "with their foolish sense make of bad, ignorant *baalei shemot* good *baalei shemot*, and of bad, common peasants, they make good Tatars."[22]

"Dear people," he exclaims at the end,

I mean men and women in our territory in Poland: I ask you why did I not hear of such things in other countries, I mean in the land of Germany *(Ashkenaz)*. This, after all, is one of the oldest countries that is mentioned in our precious Torah *(Ashkenaz, Tzarefat, Ve-Togarmah)*. Moreover, I have been in Holland, England, and other overseas countries, and have not heard what I have constantly heard in our land of Poland. How long will we hold on to such a great transgression and not believe in the wisdom of the Creator, in medicines and medical stratagems, but continue to believe in people who do not know the shape of a letter, cannot read or write. And as you make out of thieves *baalei shemot*, so you make out of common peasants and laborers on the earth wanton Tatars, and give the money of Jews into the hands of gentiles. Only consider and figure out how many years you have already travelled to Tatars, and the foolishness becomes more widespread each year . . .[23]

Marcuse's tone becomes especially tender and gentle when he speaks about the "weak little children." Not without reason does he compare them to the roses "from which we all have pleasure," and it is moving when he addresses his readers as follows:

Dear brethren, I have begged you many times to believe in a man who has acquired knowledge. But there is much to write to enlighten people. Believe only what I shall here beg you for our little babies. You should keep them very clean and not let them lie wet. You should let the rooms where new mothers lie with their weak little children be clean, dry, and disinfected with sulphur. You should not shout near a woman in confinement. It harms her head greatly, her whole body . . . Should an old midwife—the witch—wish to intrude forcibly to harm your women and children with her foolish, stupid sense, throw her out to the devil! Do not believe in old wives. Believe in God, Blessed be He and blessed be His great name, and in His wisdom of which He has given us so much, so that we may be helped

---

also address the community and the rabbis, urging them to disseminate this book as widely as possible in the hospitals and to familiarize special persons with it, so that these should know how to conduct themselves with sick people and how to heal them in case there is no doctor in the place (see our *History*, Vol. VI, p. 278).

22. *Ezer Yisrael*, Chapter Twelve, No. 112.
23. *Ibid.*, folio 72.

with the aid of the Creator. And who are these ignorant women who condemn people to death without mercy and without knowledge?[24]

But Marcuse realizes quite well that it is not only the midwives with their foolishness who injure the "little babies." He recalls that after the little children leave the hands of the midwives, they are soon given over into other, no more competent hands—those of the elementary-school teachers and their assistants. Like all the enlighteners of that generation, Marcuse also "shakes worlds" and argues with intense passion that the whole order of learning among Jews must be changed. But here again the tone, the style in which Marcuse comes forth with his demands, is of chief interest. In places when we read these old, yellowed pages of *Ezer Yisrael* we must again be reminded of Mendele Mocher Seforim; it is, indeed, somewhat akin to his style, his fashion.

The introduction is characteristic: "Let us see the difference between a horse of a peasant and a horse of a ruler. Which is stronger? That of the ruler who leaves his colt running around unburdened four years and does not harness him to work, or that of the peasant who harnesses him to a wagon when the colt is two years old? Which is more beautiful and stronger? Certainly the ruler's. His is stronger and larger and more beautiful. The peasant's is small and looks like a carcass."

After this example Marcuse proceeds to the subject he wishes to illustrate—the Jewish school children:

. . . so also the mothers do with their little children. Also we men, the fathers, have in Poland a lovely custom with our dear little boys. When they attain the age of four, we already send them to prison— the elementary-school teacher. They must sit as prisoners over the alphabet the whole day, and early in the morning, when it is the best time for children to sleep and thereby grow, the assistant teacher comes and drags them to the *ḥeder*, to the synagogue.

And when the child has already been imprisoned for a year with his alphabet teacher, they release him from the *Siddur* (prayerbook) and he must go to prison with the *Gemara* teacher. Here he no longer has time to pray, let alone to study the Pentateuch—but only *Gemara* and more *Gemara*. He must, at the age of five, know the law that in the case of "damage caused by pebbles in a public domain, half the damage is to be paid." It does not befit our wine-sellers and butchers that their children should not know what other men's fine, genius-like children know. Their child, too, must become a scholar, and even

24. *Ibid.*, folio 136.

if he does not know the prayerbook—that is fine as long as he is a scholar. I believe, dear people, that you also drive your children to work a little too early. You do not know that to work with the head is a little more difficult than chopping wood with the hands. You make your children pale, yellow, green. They cannot sleep well. Hence, they do not grow, and many common men are afterwards mistaken about their children: they think they are already scholars because they have pale faces. They forget and perceive only in old age that they have also neglected even what is in the *Siddur* . . . Would it not be better for a father to let his child sleep longer and become a scholar later? At least, even if he did not become a great scholar, I guarantee them that these boys would be strong men and more honest; they would be able to support wife and child rather than be ignorant and weak, sickly and unable to learn or work.[25]

Marcuse was firmly persuaded that his book would live for generations. Proudly he addresses his "dear brethren":

I write for you so that you may listen to me. If you listen to me, you will later see many generations hence: the doctor has not died yet. He wrote, and it is all true. Just as if he were alive, he heals with his book as when he himself lived. I also have learned a great deal from persons who died long ago, and I have perhaps also recited benedictions over vegetables or fruit that have sprung up from the plot of earth in which those learned doctors were interred. And on these plots already grow large fruits that are fit to have a blessing made over them. But their books still live and will never die. People believe they are dead, but their truth shows that they live to the present day.[26]

One can here apply the Talmudic expression: "He prophesied, but did not know what he prophesied." As a *physician*, Doctor Marcuse died long ago; as a book of remedies, his *Ezer Yisrael* has lost its value and meaning for many generations. And yet, there is a certain truth in his words: "The doctor has not died yet . . . their books still live and will never die." For Marcuse's *Ezer Yisrael* is undoubtedly a literary phenomenon of cultural-historical importance, and every historian of culture who attempts to write the history of the new secular literature in Yiddish must dwell on the doctor of Koenigsberg, Moses Marcuse, as one of its first builders and founders.

In very different fashion did another Prussian Jew of that generation inscribe his name in Jewish literature. This man was called Aaron Isaac (Isak). He was an ordinary Jew who

25. *Ibid.*, folio 110.
26. *Ibid.*, folios 128–129.

received a traditional Jewish education, a skilled seal-engraver and energetic merchant who interested himself only slightly in literature all his days.

Aaron Isaac was born in 1729 in a small town of Brandenburg called Treuenbrietzen eight miles from Berlin. When he was fourteen, his father, a shopkeeper and a poor man burdened with many children, died, and the young Aaron henceforth had to be concerned about earning a living. In the first years this did not come at all easily to him. He threw himself from one undertaking to another, and wandered over various German cities. A man with enormous energy, he laid out new paths and opened for Jews a new settlement—Sweden, where, before him, Jews were not permitted to show themselves. Isaac triumphed in his life-battle. He became court jeweler to the king of Sweden, acquired a considerable fortune, and established a whole community in Stockholm. At the end of his restless life of wandering, however, he was greatly tried; he lost his wife and children who died prematurely. Hence, he, like Glückel of Hameln in her time, began in his old age, when he was seventy-two, to write his memoirs. "I wrote this book," Isaac notes in the Hebrew title-page,

for the later generation, for the children of my people, so that my memory may not be lost, that I, Aaron, the son of Rabbi Yitzhak Isaac, may his memory be for a blessing, established myself in the land of Sweden. For, before me, no Jew ever had the right of residence in the entire land of Sweden, until I came here and found grace in the eyes of our lord, the pious and great King Gustav III, may God exalt his majesty and raise him to the heights. I also found grace with all his lords and servants, as your eyes will properly see. And may the redeemer come to Zion. Amen.

As is easily discernible from this title-page, Isaac was not a great expert in Hebrew. He himself notes: "I am not a man of words in the holy language." Hence, he wrote his autobiography in the "vernacular." But the vernacular of this seal-engraver and jeweler, who had much to do with rulers and the high nobility and, moreover, from 1774 on lived in Sweden, was no longer the contemporary ordinary *Yiddish-Deutsch* (Judeo-German) but a strange German which contains, as N. Shtif[27] has noted, a good deal of a popular Yiddish character and is, furthermore, interwoven with numerous Hebrew words and

27. In the introduction to his reworking into contemporary Yiddish of Isaac's *Autobiography*.

expressions. To give the reader some notion of the language of Isaac's memoirs, we present here two extracts:

ז׳ 44: עס קאמען היער אויך אן צווייי בחורים, זיא האטען רעקאמאנדאט־
מאנגען אן מיר. דער איינע הייסט ר׳ משה ליידערסדאָרף, דער אנדערע ר׳ הירש
בר יואל. זיא ווארן ממשפחה הגונה. זיא האטען אויך איינניגע טויזענד רייכס־
טאלער. דיזער ר׳ מוילי וואר דער ערשטע דער זיא וויזיט מאַכטע, אונד
פראגטע זיא אב זיא ניכט עטוואס סחורה מיטגעבראכט העטען פאר אים צו
האנדלען. דיעזע ביידען האטען עטוואס סחורה, אבער זיא ווארען קיינע בעל
משא ומתן ניכט.

(Page 44: There also arrived here two young men who had recommendations to me. One of them was called Moses Lei-dersdorf, the other Hirsch bar Joel. They were from good family. They also had several thousand *Reichsthaler*. Reb Moili was the first who visited them and asked them if they had not brought some merchandise for him to deal in. Both did have some merchandise but they were not businessmen.)

ז׳ 116: עס פינד זיך אן יעטצונד איין שפל ומשופל ושמו משה פייהעס
אָדער משה פאָקעס, איין מוסר דער קעגען ארעמע לייט די היר כמה שנים
געוואוינט האבן, איסט ער מיט מסירות אינגעקומען, דאס זיא היער וועג
זאָלטן, זיא געבן קיינע קאָנטריבוציא, זיא טרייבען האנדל מיט פרעמדע
סחורה דיא פערבאָטן איסט.

(Page 116: There is presently here a very base man whose name is Moses Feihes or Moses Fokes, an informer against poor people who have lived here for many years. He has come with denunciations that they should depart hence, that they do not pay any taxes, that they carry on trade with foreign merchan-dise that is proscribed [i.e., contraband]).

Isaac himself notes, "I am not a historian and scholar," and indicates that he composes his memoirs "only as a memorial of my family."[28] He writes simply, honestly, and earnestly, notes down with fidelity and decency everything that he experienced and witnessed in his restless, wandering life. This is a kind of inventory of the soul, a balance-sheet of an interesting and venturesome human life. And the whole of it is written with such simplicity, such intimate grace, that the reader unwill-ingly begins to like the old court-jeweler with all his claims and sufferings. Isaac's memoirs, however, are interesting not only as a *document humain*. They also have a certain cultural-historical significance, because they provide us with interest-ing features of Jewish existence in Germany in the middle of the eighteenth century and of life in the newly established

28. *Ibid.*, 64.

settlement in the Swedish royal city to which the migrating Jews brought along their old-fashioned way of life, with controversies over a rabbi, over a certain uncle Elie, with arguments over a cemetery, collections of money, etc.

Aaron Isaac's wish that, as a result of his memoirs, his memory not be lost for later generations was, in fact, fulfilled. For not quite a hundred years his manuscript wandered about among his heirs until finally the Jewish Literary Society in Sweden took pity on it and published it in Stockholm in Latin transcription.[29] In 1922 N. Shtif's Yiddish re-working appeared in Berlin and, in this fashion, Isaac's autobiography became accessible to broad circles of Jewish readers. In recent years a scientific edition of Isaac's manuscript[30] was also published, so that his memoirs might be utilized by historians as an important source for the second half of the eighteenth century.

The memoirs of Isaac's contemporary, Dov Ber Birkenthal of the Galician village of Bolechow, have no lesser significance for Jewish history of the eighteenth century than Isaac's. Like Isaac, Ber of Bolechow (1732–1805) was a capable and enterprising merchant. In addition, however, he was also a scholarly Jew, an expert in Hebrew language and literature, who wrote a book on the sectarian movement among Jews entitled *Imrei Binah* which was only discovered fairly recently in the manuscript collection of the Tarnopol library.[31] Ber of Bolechow also wrote in Hebrew his *Zichronot* (Memoirs), which Dr. A. Marmorstein discovered in 1912 in London at the Jewish seminary.[32]

From Ber's memoirs, we know that his grandfather, Rabbi Hirsh ben Jehudah Leib, was born in 1640 and died as a very old man in 1743. The author's father, Jehudah, who also lived to the age of over ninety carried on an extensive wine-trade with Hungary. He had a thorough command of both Polish and Hungarian and was in close relationships with Polish magnates and noblemen, among whom he was highly popular by reason of his pleasant character and the stories and parables of

---

29. *Aron Isaks Sjebtbiografi*, Stockholm, 1897.

30. Unfortunately we have not had the possibility of becoming familiar with this edition.

31. The content of this work, in which many interesting details about the disputation with the Frankists are given, was reported by A. Brawer in his work "Mekor Ivri Hadash Le-Toledot Frank Ve-Siyato," *Ha-Shiloah*, Vols. XXXIII, XXXVIII.

32. Unfortunately the manuscript is not completely preserved. The beginning and the end are lacking, and also in the middle many pages are missing. Bolechow's *Zichronot* were published by M. Wischnitzer in Yiddish translation in 1922.

which he was a great master. Thanks to his knowledge of languages, this wine-merchant had occasion to be a translator between the Hungarian King Franz II Rakoczy and the Polish crown-hetman Shieniavski.[33] Jehudah of Bolechow was also concerned that his son Dov Ber should obtain, in addition to Hebrew studies, a considerable amount of secular education. He engaged a Christian tutor to teach his son Polish and Latin.[34] The knowledge-loving Dov Ber devoted himself diligently to these secular studies. This, however, evoked a certain dissatisfaction among the people of the little village. The fact that Jehudah maintained at his home a Christian tutor who taught a Jewish *bar mitzvah* boy "the language of the priests" stirred suspicion in the pious Jewish circles and apprehension was aroused about Dov Ber's Jewishness. Under the pressure of the environment the young Ber of Bolechow had, for a time, to give up studying foreign languages. When, however, he moved to Tismenitze and settled in the house of his wife's parents, he again betook himself quite eagerly to Polish and Latin and also studied French and German.[35] Moreover, he read books in the languages mentioned—especially German and Polish.

Like the majority of the pioneering *maskilim* of that era, of whom we spoke at length in the sixth volume of our *History,* Dov Ber of Bolechow remained, with all his great thirst for knowledge and culture, firmly attached to the old traditions and faithfully kept all the Jewish customs, just as did the whole mass of orthodox Jews. Especially *le-shem mitzvah* (for the sake of fulfilling a commandment), he was an expert *mohel,* or circumcisor. According to the fashion of that time, he married off his son Joseph when the latter was barely *bar mitzvah* and took for him a girl of eleven as a bride.[36] Of himself, Dov Ber says: "I conducted myself with reverence for God. I used to be careful every day, morning and evening, to worship in the synagogue, as the *Shulḥan Aruch* says that a man's prayer is accepted only in the synagogue."[37] "I also," the author relates, "always looked into the books of Scripture, *Mishnah,* and *Gemara,* and the laws of the *Shulḥan Aruch,* aside from other morality books."

33. Bolechow's *Zichronot,* p. 69.
34. *Ibid.,* 59.
35. *Ibid.,* 134.
36. *Ibid.,* 101.
37. *Ibid.,* 59, 62.

At the same time Ber of Bolechow diligently studied medieval philosophy, the old Christian church writers, Polish history, and Polish religious-polemical literature. "Whatever book came into my hands," he relates in his *Zichronot* (p. 59), "I immediately looked into it and endeavored to grasp the author's purpose."

He also admonishes his children not to be content merely with holy books, but also to read works written in other languages, in which they will "become aware of many worldly things the Jews do not know. And we Jews ought to know everything, as it says in the verse, 'For this is your wisdom and your understanding in the eyes of the nations.' . . . Every wise and understanding Jew ought to know the deeds and acts of other peoples."[38] Like the author of *Sefer Ha-Berit*, Ber of Bolechow in his youth was strongly interested in mysticism, studied the *Zohar* assiduously, and devoted himself much to ascetic, practical Kabbalah. "It seems to me," Ber relates in his old age, "that it is impossible for anyone to endure the kind of self-affliction I endured in my youth."[39]

But the practical merchant in him overcame the ascetic mystic. With great energy he carried on the most varied business affairs, owned a brewery, used to travel for many years to Hungary, there purchase the costliest wines, bring them to Galicia, and sell them to the neighboring landowners. He also used to lend money on pledges,[40] deal in silver and gold,[41] and —at times—also in horses, buy sheep's wool and flax from the landowners in the vicinity, etc. He also devoted himself considerably to communal matters. As one who knew Polish, Latin, and Hungarian well, he had frequent occasion to serve as mediator between the Jewish communities and the landowners and the representatives of the power of the state.

At the time of the historic debate with the Frankists in 1759 in Lemberg,[42] Ber of Bolechow was the official translator on the Jewish side and greatly aided the rabbi of Lemberg, Rabbi Ḥayyim Rapoport, in putting together the response to the theses of the Frankists. Ber was also the actual author of the thorough written statement which the Jewish representatives submitted in regard to the seventh point of the Frankist theses,

38. *Ibid.*, 114.
39. *Ha-Shiloah*, Vol. XXXIII, p. 152.
40. *Zichronot*, 63.
41. *Ibid.*, 96.
42. See our *History*, Part X, Chapter One.

in which the accusation is made against the Jews that there are allusions to ritual murder in the Talmud.

In his old age, when Ber of Bolechow was already in his seventies, he decided to leave for future generations an account of his life and experiences. In the course of several years he wrote his two above-mentioned works, *Zichronot (Memoirs)* and *Imrei Binah.*[43] The latter is one of the most reliable sources for the history of the Frankist movement, and the part of Ber's memoirs that has been preserved gives us a wealth of highly important details about the economic and cultural life of the well-to-do mercantile strata of the Jewish populace in Poland and also about the negotiations of the "heads of the lands" *(roshei ha-medinot)* with the individual communities about payment of the special taxes. As a prosperous merchant and leader of the community, Ber touches very little on the condition of the poor strata of the people but he gives us, in general, a quite clear picture of the economic ruin of Polish Jewry in the eighteenth century, of its civic disabilities, of the discriminations and persecutions that the Jews had to suffer from the secular and spiritual rulers.

With epic calmness he relates how the landowners and nobles used to select from their money the good coins and hide them in their treasure-chambers, while they utilized the rubbed-off and false coins for buying merchandise from Jewish businessmen. In this point—how to rob the Jews—the landowners in general were highly inventive. So, for instance, we read in Ber of Bolechow how the "lord of Tismenitze, Duke Jablonowski wished to rob the property of the inhabitants of Tismenitze . . . So he bade that they bring from his estates in the Ukraine, where he was then mayor and elder, three hundred and fifty barrels of mead and issued an edict to the Jewish leaders to the effect that, as soon as the mead arrives in their town, they [the leaders] are obliged to distribute it among all the inhabitants, and seven days later the entire Jewish community must pay money into the duke's counting-house for all the mead at the rate of eight ducats per barrel. The community was compelled to make estimates of how much each one could give, according to his fortune."[44] Duke Martin Lubomirski made things even simpler; like the medieval knights in their day, he used to attack

43. The works were composed approximately between 1790 and 1800 (see M. Wischnitzer, introduction to Ber of Bolechow's *Zichronot*).
44. *Zichronot*, 65.

travelers, mainly merchants, with his retinue, seize their property "and also killed many people."[45]

Peasant robbers would also compete with the noble robbers, and Ber of Bolechow describes how organized bands of brigands used to attack Jewish communities, plunder and pillage them, and burn their houses.[46] No gentler than the robber bands were the students of the Christian schools. Ber relates how much the community of Lemberg had to suffer from the *Schüler-Geläufe* because of some conflict or quarrel that would arise between a Jew and a student. The students, the children of the nobles and rulers, would assemble, invade the Jewish streets, smite, kill, and plunder Jewish property; and the Jews had to flee from their homes and save themselves. The students robbed and plundered whatever they could take away from the Jews' fortune.[47] The Jewish populace had to suffer no less from the spiritual rulers. Even their right to worship in the synagogues had to be purchased from the bishops with golden ducats.[48] Hence, it is psychologically comprehensible that, after the first partition of Poland, even the aged and sedate Ber of Bolechow exclaims with pain and indignation: "And I will lay my vengeance on Edom."

45. *Ibid.*, 76–77.
46. *Ibid.*, 74–78.
47. *Ibid.*, 137.
48. *Ibid*, 89–108.

CHAPTER SEVEN

Romanelli, Pappenheim, Ben-Ze'ev, Satanow, and Berlin

[The generation of the Meassefim—Philologists and writers—Samuel Aaron Romanelli and his work—Solomon Pappenheim; his part in the controversy over amulets—Pappenheim's *Yeriot Shelomoh* and "Arba Kosot"—Jehudah Leib Ben-Ze'ev and his scholarly activity; his translation of Ben Sira—Isaac Satanow as a personality—His love for imitations and his literary activity—"Half a believer and half a heretic"—Saul Berlin, the heretical rabbi; his satire *Ketav Yosher*—Saul Berlin as a falsifier; his *Mitzpeh Yokte'el* and *Besamim Rosh*; his last will and testament.]

N THE two previous chapters we observed how the logic of life brought it about that the Jewish enlighteners in Prussia, who regarded the language of the Bible with such vast enthusiasm and set as their goal to disclose its beauties to the European world, presented interesting portraits of Jewish life not in their favorite language but in German or in "corrupted German," i.e., the Yiddish vernacular. And precisely those "beauties" which the *Meassefim* attempted to implant in Hebrew literature were, as we noted previously, of very scant value. These sprouts were weak and colorless; they lacked vital juices and life. Yet they did not remain fruitless; they were a promise, a harbinger, of a crisis, of a drive toward a new life, a new world-view.

Among the sea of talentless rhetorical verses and sentimental idylls there would break through—to be sure, in very rare cases—sounds of true inspiration and tones lit up with poetic sparks. Before we proceed to these creations illuminated with sparks of poetry, we must dwell on a very unique phenomenon, the work of an itinerant poet born in Italy who, on his journeys, spent more than three years among the Meassefim, entered into friendship with them, celebrated them and Moses Mendelssohn in poems, and published his most important works, which inscribed his name in the history of neo-Hebrew literature, in Berlin. The name of this poet was Samuel Aaron Romanelli.

Born in the old Jewish cultural center of Mantua in 1757, the young Romanelli obtained a many-sided education. His thorough knowledge of Talmudic literature gave him the possibility of presenting lectures in *battei-midrash*, or studyhouses. In addition, he was a man of extensive European culture; he read and wrote ten languages fluently. Clever, somewhat frivolous, with an ebullient wit, Romanelli reminds one of the medieval poet Jehudah Alḥarizi. Like the latter, he lived off the gifts of patrons whom he used to celebrate in paeans and long poems. But he spent most of his life in poverty and want, for the mocker, the jester, in him would quite frequently overcome the writer of odes. With epigrams and mocking sallies he used to ridicule the "great men," the arrogant plutocrats, and make fun of the old-fashioned, obsolete customs. The enraged "city fathers" would not infrequently drive the impudent jester out of town.

While still quite young, Romanelli made a journey through France, then spent some time in London where he published a textbook of Hebrew grammar.[1] From there he came to Gibralter, whence he was to have returned to Italy; but he was cast away to Morocco, where he spent all of four years[2] in distress and poverty (1786–1789). Through arduous effort, Romanelli finally arrived in Amsterdam and from there went to Berlin, where he found generous patrons in the persons of David Friedländer and his father-in-law, the banker Daniel Itzig. Here he recovered and rested from the toils and troubles he had endured in Morocco. With gratitude, he calls out in the paean which he dedicated to the Meassefim:

O, the skies of Berlin have I seen!
I will no longer remember the toil and trouble,
All that happened to me and the hardships of the road.[3]

1. See *Ben Chanania*, 1862, p. 27.
2. See the introduction to *Massa Ba-Arav*.
3. *Ibid.*

In 1791 Romanelli published, as a wedding gift for the daughter of his patron Daniel Itzig, an allegorical drama *Ha-Kolot Yeḥdalun,* following the pattern of Moses Ḥayyim Luzzatto's *La-Yesharim Tehillah.* Appearing as characters are Venus (*Nogah* or Light), Cupid (*Ḥeshek* or Desire), Fortuna (*Osher* or Wealth) and also Righteousness *(Tzedek),* Beauty *(Tiferet),* Peace *(Shalom),* and Hope *(Tikvah).* Into the dialogues are inserted, in the Italian fashion, arias to be sung. Franz Delitzsch[4] speaks with great enthusiasm about this work and declares that it belongs, along with Luzzatto's *La-Yesharim Tehillah,* to the "most precious jewels of the Jewish nation."[5] Unfortunately the work is extremely rare, and we have not had the opportunity to see it. In 1792 Romanelli published as a gift to the "exalted rich man, the glory of the wise," David Friedländer, a didactic poem entitled "Ruaḥ Nachon" in which he battles from the idealistic standpoint against the materialists who, in the malice of their hearts, have strayed from the right path.

In the same year, Romanelli's *Massa Ba-Arav,* an account of his journey through Morocco, appeared in Berlin. Not without cause did this work go through six editions[6] and also appear in English translation (1886). It is a genuine work of art. In vivid and sharp colors, the author portrays the whole way of life, the horrible economic and cultural situation that prevailed in Morocco a hundred and eighty years ago, and the fearful civic disabilities of the Jews dwelling there. Discernible in the work is not only the educated European, but also the fine eye of the observer and the sure hand of the artist. The reader obtains a colorful picture of the backward Moslem land with its cities and villages. He becomes familiar with the style of the houses, the behavior of the people, their lack of culture, their barbaric superstition, their trade and commerce. This Jew from Mantua observed everything in the wild Moslem country, stored everything away in his memory, and recalled it to life in the pages of his work. From the sultan, the typical Oriental despot with his officials, down to the least porter and beggar—about all these Romanelli knows how to give an account; he witnessed everything with his own eyes.

The author devotes even greater attention to the life of the

---

4. *Zur Geschichte der jüdischen Poesie,* p. 92.

5. J. Klausner, *op. cit.,* pp. 275–276, notes that the style of *Ha-Kolot Yeḥdalun* is overly mellifluous. The work is also not inconsiderably damaged by the "prominent flattery which is proffered in broad measure to the rich patron and his daughter, the bride."

6. See J. Klausner, *op. cit.,* p. 279. We have employed the second edition (Vienna, 1834).

Moroccan Jews and presents a detailed picture of their customs, their cultural backwardness, their way of life, their happy occasions and weddings, and even more of their sufferings and troubles, their servile condition in the barbaric, fanatical land. In vivid, clear images he portrays for us all strata of the Jewish population there, from the rich men, the "Court Jews," to the Jewish prostitutes.[7] Where the poet portrays the civic disabilities of the Moroccan Jews, he becomes emotive, and it is difficult to read nonchalantly such passages as, for instance, the account of how, on a Sabbath, while the Jews were worshipping in the synagogue, soldiers and policemen rushed in and seized all the adults, both men and women, for forced labor.[8]

A particularly powerful impression is made by the last chapter, which describes how, in the time of confusion after the sudden death of the sultan, until one of the deceased king's numerous sons managed by force of arms to occupy his father's throne, the Jewish populace was declared "outlawed." The mob plundered their property, raped the women and murderously beat the men. Furthermore, the victorious pretender to the throne placed upon the Jewish communities enormously large sums of redemption-money to cover the expenses of the war.

Massa Ba-Arav reads like a realistic, moving novel, and it is regrettable that its author wasted his rich powers of creation on "occasional poems," odes, and Italian translations, and in the subsequent twenty years of his life did not write a single work comparable to his traveler's account.[9]

At the beginning of this chapter we noted how weak and colorless were the poetic "beauties" which the Meassefim attempted to plant in Hebrew literature. Hence, the elegiac poem, "Arba Kosot"[10] by Solomon Pappenheim, which was first published in 1790, must be considered a genuine event of great importance in this realm.

7. *Massa Ba-Arav*, Chapter Thirteen, p. 70.

8. *Ibid.*, Chapter Seven, p. 32.

9. The works which he wrote after *Massa Ba-Arav* and which consist of odes and translations of Italian poetic works, are extremely rare and we have not seen them (on these, see W. Zeitlin, *Kirjath Sepher*, pp. 310–311; Klausner, *op. cit.*, pp. 276–278; F. Lachover, *Toledot Ha-Safrut Ha-Ivrit Ha-Hadashah*, I, Chapter Nineteen; and Keller's *Bikkurim*, II, p. 23). Many of Romanelli's poems and translations remained in manuscript after his death. His translation of Maffei's drama *Merope* (1713) was published by a Benedictine monk Weickert in Rome in 1903.

10. The full title (in translation): "The legend of the four cups—let a man read it when he sits down to eat the bread of affliction, and he drinks bitters and forgets his poverty."

Solomon ben Abraham Seligmann (Pappenheim) is an interesting personality in general. In point of fact he belongs to the generation of the Meassefim only chronologically, not according to his philosophy and world view. Born in 1740 in the Silesian village of Zuelz into a rabbinic family, Solomon obtained a traditional education, but while still young was renowned as a "linguist" and writer of *melitzah,* or mellifluous rhetoric. During the amulet controversy between Jacob Emden and Jonathan Eybeschütz, the young Pappenheim came forward as an active adherent of Emden's side[11] and composed a sharp satire against Eybeschütz in which he portrays the great scholar of Prague and his son Benjamin Wolf in the same company with Leibele Prossnitz, Nehemiah Ḥayon, and Shabbetai Tzevi's heir Baruchiah Russo.[12]

Later, apparently in the years when he was "rabbinical assessor" *(dayyan)* in Breslau, he obtained a certain degree of European education and became well versed in medieval Hebrew philosophical works as well as in modern philosophy. A particularly strong influence was exercised on him by Leibniz and Kant. He himself wrote philosophical treatises on the concept of God: *Beiträge zur Berichtigung der Beweise vom Dasein Gottes aus der reinen Vernunft* (1794), and *Abermaliger Versuch über den ontologischen Beweis vom Dasein Gottes* (1800). In complete opposition to Mendelssohn and the Meassefim on the question of "burial of the deceased on the day of death," Pappenheim argued for the traditional Jewish custom and obdurately defended this point of view in his tracts: *Die frühe Beerdigung bei den Juden* (1795); *Die Notwendigkeit der frühen Beerdigung* (1797); and *Deduction einer Apologie für die frühe Beerdigung* (1798).

When David Friedländer, after the publication of the edict concerning the grant of equal civic rights to the Jews, came forth with the demand that Jews worship in the synagogue in the "language of the country" i.e., in German, not in Hebrew,[13] Pappenheim once again issued forth as a decisive naysayer with his brochure *Freimüthige Erklärung über die Kritik des Gottesdienstes der Juden und derem Erziehung der Jugend* (1813). In total opposition to Friedländer and Herz Homberg, Pappenheim endeavors to show that the education of the Jewish youth must remain under the authority of the communities and not be handed over to the government. In regard to ritual and the

11. For Pappenheim's testimony, see *Sefer Hitabkut,* 65–67.
12. This satire, which bears the title *Elonei Mamre Ve-Kiryat Arba,* is published in *Sefer Hitabkut,* 67–71 (Altona, 1761).
13. See above, p. 117.

order of worship, he sets forth purely psychological arguments that a person ought to pray, not in the ordinary, weekday language, but in the language which bears the aura of holiness and godliness.[14] On one *piyyut*, the well-known "Ki Hineh Ka-Ḥomer Be-Yad Ha-Yotzer" (Like Clay are We in the Hands of the Potter), which is recited on the night of Yom Kippur, Pappenheim even wrote a special philosophical commentary (*Ḥomer Be-Yad Ha-Yotzer*, 1803), which Eliezer Zweifel reprinted some sixty years later.

Pappenheim also devoted himself considerably to philological studies. He wrote a major work entitled *Yeriot Shelomoh* on synonyms in Hebrew. In the introduction he makes a, for that time, very interesting attempt to elucidate the development of language through the modern philosophical theory of knowledge. In this connection he dwells especially on the evolution of the human concepts of space and time, and here a certain influence of the then just published *Critique of Pure Reason* by Immanuel Kant is discernible.[15] Unfortunately, very few people at that time understood how properly to appreciate this effort, and because Pappenheim came forward as an opponent of the major principle set forth by the grammarian Jehudah ben David Ḥayyuj[16] which became the foundation of all of Hebrew grammar, namely, that every verb consists of no less than three letters,[17] his *Yeriot Shelomoh* had such limited success that he published only two parts of the work—the first in 1784, the third in 1811. The second part was published after his death[18] by Wolf Heidenheim in 1831, and the fourth remained in manuscript. Also in manuscript is the largest part of another philological work by Pappenheim, a Hebrew lexicon entitled *Ḥeshek Shelomoh*, of which the well known grammarian Heidenheim[19] wrote enthusiastically: "This ingenious work of human

14. See S. Bernfeld, *Toledot Ha-Reformatzyon*, pp. 68–69.

15. *Yeriot Shelomoh*, "Ḥoveret I," "Yeriah III." Pappenheim himself even underscores in the introduction that the ideas he expresses on the essence of time and place are his own and not taken from other men and books.

16. See our *History*, Vol. I.

17. In regard to this question, Pappenheim's contemporary Mordecai Schnaber, in his unpublished work *Sefer Ha-Shorashim* (see his *Tochahat Megullah*, 5–8), took the same view as Pappenheim.

18. Pappenheim died in Breslau in 1814.

19. Wolf bar Shimshon Heidenheim (born in 1757, died in 1832) acquired a great reputation with his classic edition of the *Maḥzor* in the splendid Roedelheim Press. This edition, in which Heidenheim employed numerous ancient manuscripts, is provided with many of his critical explanations and with a German translation. At the end of the edition Heidenheim published a work "Ha-Piyyutim Veha-Paytanim" which is

understanding belongs to the monumental works of our century."[20] Pappenheim managed merely to publish one sample-fascicle (in 1802) and Heidenheim, to whom he transmitted all his manuscripts,[21] reprinted a prospectus of this work (*Kuntres Regel Mevasser*, 1808).

Solomon Pappenheim had little luck with his comprehensive scholarly works. On the other hand, he achieved extraordinary success with his short poetic work, the elegiac poem entitled "Arba Kosot."[22] This poem was so popular that, as early as the 1820's, young *maskilim* used to declaim it by heart,[23] and in 1863 Jonah Willheimer translated it into German and provided it with a special commentary. Pappenheim wrote his poem under tragic circumstances. He had lived through a grievous family catastrophe, losing three children one after the other, and then his beloved wife. The profoundly shattered man poured out his great woe after the fourfold loss in "four cups" (*arba kosot*). In an emotive, elegiac tone he discloses his wrestlings with himself and his doubts concerning the tragic problems of human life, his thoughts on the vanity and ephemeral nature of the earthly, on death and immortality, on man's role and significance in the world.

Pappenheim's poem is far from harmonious integrity. The author's soul was too shaken, and he himself, the *dayyan* and European-educated *maskil*, was still a child of a period of crisis and stood at the crossroads of two different worlds. One need not wonder that in his poem are discernible at the same time the influence of the English poet Edward Young's *Night Thoughts* and that of Jedaiah Ha-Penini's medieval *Behinat Olam*. The same thing is to be noticed in the style and tendencies of the work. Traditional views go hand in hand in it with Kant's philosophical notions. A purely Biblical style is interwoven with expressions from the medieval philosophical books. Genuinely poetic images are woven together with

---

extremely important for the history of Jewish liturgical poetry. Also of scholarly importance is his critical edition of the Pentateuch (1818–1821) with commentaries, explanations, and German translation. Among his philological works the most significant are *Mevo Ha-Lashon* (on Hebrew grammar, 1806), and *Mishpetei Ha-Ta'amim* (on cantillation, 1808). For a discussion of Heidenheim, see L. Levin in *MGWJ*, 1900, pp. 127–138; *ibid.*, 1901, 432–442, 549–558; *ibid.*, 1932, 1–15.

20. *Ha-Meassef*, 5569, p. 53.

21. *Ibid.*, pp. 35, 53, and also in the introduction to the second part of *Yeriot Shelomoh*.

22. First published in Berlin in 1790. On the editions of "Arba Kosot" see *Kohelet Mosheh*, 107; J. Klausner, *Historyah Shel Ha-Safrut Ha-Ivrit Ha-Hadashah*, I, 229.

23. See *Ben Chanania*, 1863, 754.

puffed-up rhetoric, and the honest pathos and tragic echoes of the catastrophe that the poet lived through are watered down by sentimental sighs and cries of woe. In the closing part of the poem, in the fourth *kos*, or cup, the cup of help and consolation (*kos yeshuot*), calmer, more optimistic tones are heard. The motto of that era—"Man is born to enjoy happiness"—finds in Pappenheim a purely national vestment. The poet is filled with a firm belief in the loving providence of God who is, after all, the God of compassion, and his poem concludes harmoniously with cheerful, confident chords.

We noted earlier that Pappenheim's philological works enjoyed very slight success. Much more fortunate in this respect was Pappenheim's younger contemporary, Jehudah Leib Ben-Ze'ev. Born in 1764, in the Polish town of Lelow in the Cracow region, Jehudah Leib was raised on the Talmud and rabbinic codes. At the age of thirteen his father married him off, and the young groom moved to Cracow where he was supported for several years in the home of his father-in-law. From this derives his family name Cracow. Living with his father-in-law, the young Jehudah Leib sat "over Torah and worship." However, he began to be "infected with heresy." In the daytime he used to pore over the Talmud and its commentaries, and at night he would occupy himself secretly, so that the family would not know of it, with such heretical and forbidden subjects as Bible and grammar.[24] After the economic situation of his parents deteriorated, Jehudah Leib had to become concerned about earning a living himself. He betook himself to teaching and set out for other towns seeking pupils.

Thereupon "years of wandering" began for the young Jehudah Leib. Away from home, he became inoculated with the new ideas. He dreamed of Haskalah, or enlightenment, and his ideal was to reach the major center of Haskalah and knowledge where "Moses the son of Menahem, the man of God" dwelt. However, he managed to reach Berlin only in 1787, when Mendelssohn was already dead. He soon became friends with the Meassefim and published in their journal many poems and fables signed J.L.C. (Jehudah Leib Cracow). Like Aaron Wolfsohn and Joel Loewe (Brill), he also wrote "Purim poems" and celebrated in the parodied style of *selihot* and *piyyutim* the joys wherewith the sap of grapes rejoices chess companions.[25] He also wrote, in purely biblical verses, profligate and comic po-

24. See Ben-Ze'ev's introduction to *Otzar Ha-Shorashim.*
25. *Melitzah Le-Furim Al Derech Melitzat Ha-Piyyut Le-Harbot Bah Simhat Purim U-Mishteh Ha-Shikkorim.*

ems which, with their frivolous, cynical content, have no ana-
logue in all of Hebrew literature.[26] Even Immanuel of Rome's
passionate love-songs are, in comparison with Ben-Ze'ev's
wanton poems, quite respectable and veiled in fig leaves.

But this frivolous playboy and witty parodist remained
throughout his life[27] the loyal knight of his "beautiful lady,"
the ardently loved language of the Bible. He served her faithfully and honestly, and bestowed upon her all of his considerable intellectual powers. He himself notes (in his preface to his
Otzar Ha-Shorashim) that he realizes quite well how enormously
difficult it is to renew and extend the fallen Hebrew language.
"I know that it cannot revive after it has fallen so low, unless
'the Lord turn again the captivity of his people.' " However,
it does not even cross his mind to forsake his beloved. On the
contrary, her grievous condition strengthens his desire to be
her defender and devoted servant.

Ben-Ze'ev's productive activity, however, began only when
he left Berlin and settled in Breslau, where he spent approximately ten years. There, in 1796, he published his practical
Hebrew grammar, *Talmud Leshon Ivri*, which went through a
large number of editions, with many later supplements and
notes by various grammarians,[28] and was, for generations, the
true "teacher of the Hebrew language" which, in a popular
form, familiarized the Jewish youth with the principles of *shim-
mush ha-lashon* (syntax) and *darchei ha-shir veha-melitzah* (style
and prosody).

No less popular was his three volume Hebrew-German and
German-Hebrew dictionary *Otzar Ha-Shorashim*, which he
published in Vienna, where he spent the last twelve years of
his life as proof-reader in the well-known Hebrew presses of
Joseph Horshanetzky and Anton von Schmid. His textbooks
Bet Ha-Sefer (Vienna, 1802) and *Yesodei Ha-Dat* (1811) also enjoyed
considerable success. His introductions and critical comments
to various biblical works, for which Johann Gottfried Eich-
horn's three-volume work *Einleitung in das Alte Testament* (1780–
1782)[29] served him as a model, were reprinted in the later edi-

---

26. These poems were never printed. They only circulated in handwritten copies or
were transmitted orally from mouth to mouth.
27. Ben-Ze'ev died at the age of forty-seven in 1811.
28. The most important additions and comments were made by the poet Abraham Dov
(Adam Ha-Kohen) Lebensohn to the oldest edition (Vilna, 1874). On the numerous
editions of Ben-Ze'ev's handbooks, see W. Zeitlin, *Kirjath Sepher*, pp. 22–25, and Joseph
Klausner, *Historyah Shel Ha-Safrut . . .* , I, pp. 159–162.
29. Ben-Ze'ev published his comments in book form (1810) under the same title (in
Hebrew) *Mevo El Mikra'ei Kodesh*.

tions of the Bible that the "Biurists" and their followers published.

Ben-Ze'ev is no longer willing, like Mendelssohn, to remain loyal to the ancient tradition, and endeavors to familiarize the Jewish reader with the achievements of the biblical criticism of the era. He permits himself to speak openly of a second Isaiah who lived in the period of the Babylonian exile, etc. These critical comments, which the author allowed himself in regard to the Holy Writings, created for him a reputation in the orthodox circles as a terrible heretic and "an apostate out of spite." Of significant literary value is Ben-Ze'ev's model translation of Ben Sira, or Ecclesiasticus, which he published (1798) along with a German translation and an extensive introduction. Franz Delitzsch[30] declares with enthusiasm: "His translation is, in its imitation of the gnomic style of the Bible, a masterpiece."

This work of Ben-Ze'ev's is in close affinity with the works of another significant writer of the generation of the Meassefim of whom we must now speak.

We noted earlier the factors that bring the representatives of the Berlin Haskalah into a certain relationship with the Jewish intellegentsia of the eve of the zenith of the Jews in Arabic Spain. There also philological investigations preceded the literary renaissance. Jonah Ibn Jannah and his collaborators, who drew nourishment from Arabic culture, to a certain degree prepared the suitable fertile ground for the upbuilding of Hebrew *belles lettres* with their scholarly works. This was in fact also intended by Ben-Ze'ev, Pappenheim, and their colleagues. However, the distance between the two eras was too great and the social and intellectual forces that dominated them too different. The powerful influence of the related Arabic culture on Ibn Jannah's generation did not lead to assimilation, to self-deprecation. It merely aroused and incited, worked on the somnolent Jewish powers like midwives who evoke the strongest life-processes.[31]

In the era of Samuel Ha-Nagid and Solomon Ibn Gabirol the representatives of Hebrew literature did not know of any "rent in the heart." The cultural abundance surrounding them did not tear them away from their national roots. They were very little concerned about the matter of proving their "usefulness," and were not at all frightened by the question: "What will the

30. *Zur Geschichte der jüdischen Poesie*, p. 110.
31. See our *History*, Vol. I, p. 15.

gentiles say?" Quite different was the situation in the generation of the Meassefim. The transition from the old to the new,
from the narrowly restricted ghetto and the isolated world-
view of the rabbis to the universe of ideas of the enlighteners
and rationalists, was too precipitate. Hence, they lost their
equilibrium, ceased to feel solid ground under their feet, and,
like the hero of Adelbert von Chamisso's well-known romantic
story, lost their own shadow, their independent "I." Education
and custom bound them firmly to the old, narrowly limited
way of life and they rushed toward the wide spaciousness of
European culture. They were dazzled by the wealth suddenly
disclosed before them. But they were unable to absorb the alien
cultural treasures and to merge them harmoniously with their
own culture.

The language of the Bible was certainly deeply loved and
revered by these men. They devoted themselves greatly, as we
have observed, with exploring its ancient treasures and the
uniqueness of its syntax. They also occupied themselves much
with Hebrew meter and verse construction. Ben-Ze'ev speaks
of *darchei ha-shir veha-melitzah* in his *Talmud Leshon Ivri*, David
Friedrichsfeld in his *Zecher Tzaddik*, and Joel Loewe in his
special introduction to *Zemirot Yisrael*. But they were unable
themselves to create new poetic values. In place of independent
creativity, they imitated and copied foreign models; instead of
harmonious artistic forms, they produced artificial and ingenious mosaics, tinselled playthings.

Highly characteristic in this respect is one of the most ver-
satile and gifted writers among the Berlin *maskilim*, Isaac Ha-
Levi Satanow. Born[32] and raised in the small Podolian town of
Satanow, the richly talented young man was attracted to
knowledge and education. After a long period of wandering,
he arrived in 1771 in Berlin, where for many years he gave
Hebrew lessons in wealthy Jewish homes. He devoted himself
intensively to the natural sciences and became familiar with
the philosophic, rationalist tendencies of his time. But the
forty-year-old *maskil* of remote Podolia felt somehow strange
and uncomfortable in the world that was so new to him. He
still sensed too strongly the dominance over himself of the old
patriarchal way of life. He felt drawn by two opposite mag-
netic poles. Hence, his constant wavering, the unexpected con-
trasts in all his behavior. This even let itself become easily
noticeable in his outward appearance. At home he lived the life

32. Isaac Satanow was born in 1732 and died at the end of 1804 in Berlin.

of a completely assimilated Berliner, but he would not part with the beard that he had brought from Podolia. Decked out in modern clothes fitted with artistic taste, he wore over them a long, old-fashioned caftan[33]—"from above spiritual, from below secular," as he himself used to say with a smile.[34] Like his dress, so also was his literary creativity.

This love for masquerade, for falsification, for leading people by the nose through mystifications and pretenses, is the basic feature of all of his literary productivity. Satanow, the marvelous master of language, found no better way to utilize his rich capacities then to copy and imitate all kinds of styles. He pretends that his imitations derive ostensibly from very ancient times and were composed by great Jewish figures; and immediately, in this connection, as a trick, he makes fun of the naive reader who allows himself to be deceived and takes him at his word. Satanow published a work in Berlin and wrote on the title-page: "Printed in Constantinople."[35] He wrote an excellent article "Mi-Darchei Ha-Lashon Veha-Melitzah"[36] in which he presents a scientific over-view of the historical evolution of the Hebrew language and points out with great keenness and a fine feeling for language the bases on which this language must be broadened and extended so that it might be properly adapted to the expression of the new human concepts and modern technical terms. But he published this article not under his own name but under the name of his son, Shema-Solomon (Dr. Schönemann), who could not write even a single line in Hebrew. And when one of the Meassefim expressed his dissatisfaction with his masquerade,[37] Satanow responded with the polemical *Minḥat Bikkurim*, but this time also under the name of his son Schönemann, who knew so little Hebrew.

Satanow published in Berlin his *Sefer Ha-Ḥizzayon*, written in *makama*-style, but he indicates neither the date nor the name of the author. On the other hand, the title-page is surrounded, as in a frame, by a whole series of rhetorical verses in which it is noted through initial letters: "My name is Isaac." Immediately after the introduction is an acrostic which announces: "Isaac Ha-Levi, the author of *Ha-Ḥizzayon*." But if all this is

33. See Franz Delitzsch, *op. cit.*, p. 115: "Under the Polish caftan, over his shaven and trimmed beard, he wore the finest clothing of a German *petit-maitre*.
34. "He is half a heretic and half a believer," his younger contemporary Mendelssohn-Hamburg says of him (*Penei Tevel*, 252).
35. The work, *Divrei Rivot*, is on the dogmas of the Jewish religion.
36. *Ha-Meassef*, 5548, pp. 82–95.
37. *Ha-Meassef*, Vol. VII, pp. 251–266, 396.

still too little, the whole work is interwoven with acrostics such as "Isaac" (folios 12a, 17b, 60a, 68b), "the saying of Isaac" (folio 64a) or "Isaac Ha-Levi" (the closing poem). Some of the acrostics bear the name "Isaac Ha-Levi" both at the beginning and at the end of the lines (folios 13, 14, 15, 16). On two separate pages appear all kinds of stars of David, little rings, and circles, in which the words "Isaac Ha-Levi" are put together out of letters in a very inept way. Also in the last chapter, which discusses grammar and strange combinations of letters, we again obtain through the trick of letter-combination the words: "My name is Isaac."

Isaac Satanow wrote a work entitled *Sefer Imrei Binah* (1784), in which it is demonstrated, in the form of a debate between two colleagues Jedaiah and Noam, that "Kabbalah and philosophy are twins that are firmly bound together, but what philosophy demonstrates openly in a serious tone, Kabbalah does with allusions and hints in which love is hidden." On the title-page, however, Satanow indicates that he found the work in manuscript in a private library with *haskamot* of great scholars of ancient times but the name of the author is unknown. Numerous "great scholars of our time" who saw the work were so enchanted by it that they begged him, Satanow, to publish it "so that many might enjoy its light." Afterwards comes a whole series of *haskamot*—two older ones from the author of *Vavei Ha-Ammudim*, Rabbi Sheftel Horowitz, and of the rabbi of Safed, Naftali Katz, both of whom lived in the seventeenth century. This is followed by quite new ones by numerous rabbis of Satanow's generation. All these *haskamot* are things that never were; Satanow himself fabricated them.

Moreover, Satanow generally did not consider it at all necessary to keep his weakness for mystification secret. He published in Aramaic dialect his *Zohar Ḥibbura Tinyana* (1783), on making peace between Kabbalah and philosophy, and places in front of it, with a mocking smile, two *haskamot*. In one of them it is noted that the publisher Satanow came with the assertion that he copied this document from an old Sephardic parchment manuscript in the Berlin library. In the second *haskamah* the suspicion is expressed that this is merely a mystification, since "I am acquainted with this man and know his manner—that he is of those who deceive."

The same thing is repeated in another work *Mishlei Asaf.*[38] Satanow writes, in the style of the biblical Book of Proverbs,

38. The first part appeared in 1788, the second in 1792.

a collection of maxims and parables, and pretends that this collection ostensibly derives from ancient times and its author is Asaf ben Berachyahu of the sons of the Levites who are mentioned in Chronicles I, Chapter Six. But he also allusively notes his own name, for Asaf consists of the initial letters of Itzik Satanow Polanya.[39] He asserts, indeed, in the preface that "this Sefer Asaf has as yet never existed and no human eye has ever seen it before; lo, the Lord had it come to me by chance." But soon he makes himself appear as someone who did not know this and calls *Mishlei Asaf* "my composition." However, Satanow cannot be content with this. His weakness for mystification is so great that he places before *Mishlei Asaf* a "*haskamah* of great scholars" with the signatures of five rabbis. And the whole *haskamah* is merely pretense; Satanow himself wrote it. In this falsified *haskamah*, which praises the work to the skies and asserts that "this composition is the perfection of beauty for renown and loveliness, its palate is most sweet and its eloquence is more delicious than honey," it is, incidentally, noted that the author of the work is veiled in mystery and his name is unknown. Rabbi Isaac Satanow even asserts "that so he found it, and so it was," but it appears that this is merely pretense, and it is highly possible that Rabbi Isaac himself is the author, "for we know the man and his converse."

All this, however, was still not enough for Satanow. Following this falsified *haskamah* comes a falsified introduction from Satanow's alleged friend, one Joseph Luzzatto of Italy. In this introduction, which the mocking Satanow himself fabricated, the "Italian" Luzzatto deplores the fact that the Hebrew language is forgotten and abandoned, and even some of the "authors of books who style themselves with the title sages and scholars" read and write "with stammering lips, and it is not correct in their mouths." Hence, it is not surprising that these persons are regarded with contempt, and among the peoples of the world Hebrew is considered a dead language. If a chosen few did not preserve Hebrew in its full purity in their mouths, the holy tongue would be lost among our people and would "be forgotten from the heart like one dead."

One of these elite few is, self-evidently, Isaac Satanow. It was he, asserts the "man of Italy," who elevated the Hebrew language to its erstwhile beauty; he disclosed before "the people and the princes" our holy tongue in all its splendor.[40] There-

---

39. *Ha-Meassef,* Vol. VII, p. 252.
40. Also in his introduction to *Sefer Ha-Ḥizzayon,* Satanow repeats several times: "Therefore, we have taken upon ourselves the burden of speaking well in the congre-

upon follows a long paean in which Satanow's wisdom and mastery are lauded in tremendous rhetorical flourishes. With great emotiveness the happy town of Satanow, whose name is praised and revered over all lands and distant islands because it bore to the world its marvelous son Isaac, is greeted.[41]

The truth must be stated: Isaac Satanow was literally a genius in imitation. With marvelous ease he copies the most varied styles. He writes his *Sefer Ha-Ḥizzayon* in the *makama*-style of Alḥarizi's *Taḥkemoni*, the *Zohar Tinyana* in the Aramaic *Zohar* style, *Mishlei Asaf* in the gnomic form of Proverbs and Ben Sira, *Zemirot Asaf* in the emotive style of the Book of Psalms. Shortly afterwards he wrote a Hebrew work in which he teaches the art of piercing more than three hundred pearls at once in one day, and describes with the mien of an expert how to fabricate all kinds of liqueurs and beverages.[42] In all this, great mastery of language is manifested, but in his versatility also lies Satanow's weakness. This man with many masks does not have his own face; this imitator of numerous styles does not, with all his wealth of language, possess his own style. Under all his richly ornamented and variegated textures, his own essence, his own individuality, is not discernible.

Only his *Mishlei Asaf* is a definite exception among his large number of books.[43] This work is not merely an imitation of the biblical Book of Proverbs but an independent work of art in which the author utilized the canonized, classical gnomic style. We have before us not a simple imitation but a related harmoniousness, a new poetic rendering. A man with a profound knowledge of Talmudic literature, the witty and keen-minded Satanow absorbed the folk perspicacity which is collected in

---

gation (on behalf of the language of the Bible) and telling the glory of its praise and majesty, in order to show the peoples and the princes its glory."

41.   Cheer and shout with joy, O dweller in Satanow,
For in your midst has grown up a man of understanding, a master and father.
If the inhabitants of the earth were boasting of their sages,
They would say in the farthest lands: Quite some persons were born in you.
But to *you* they would say: This man was born in your midst,
For through Isaac you will establish a great name among them.

42. See Franz Delitzsch, *op. cit.*, 115–116.

43. It is beyond doubt that, apart from Satanow's published works, several of his works remained in manuscript. On the last page of Naḥman Barash's *Ein Mishpat*, in the list of the manuscripts which the press Ḥinnuch Ne'arim intends to publish, the following works by Doctor Schönemann are found: (1) *Yerushalayim*, "in which are twelve gates designated by the names of the tribes of the Lord; it will inquire about the soul and its powers," and (2) *Har Tziyyon*, "research responsa, and letters, and aphorisms." It is clear that, under this Doctor Schönemann, Isaac Satanow is hidden.

the Talmud and Midrashim, as well as in the mouth of the people, and transmitted it with great mastery in the polished and measured forms of the biblical gnomic sayings and moral lessons.

However, in the third part of this work, in *Zemirot Asaf,* which is written according to the model of the Psalms, this harmonious accord is lacking. It is difficult for the mentally keen author, the wit and imitator, to penetrate into the rich emotional world of the poets of the Psalms. Their religious pathos and lyrical outpouring of the soul are alien to him and unattainable. In forms borrowed from the singers of the Psalms, he transmits the maxims and conclusions of the rationalist-minded Deists of his era. He relates in his psalm-songs the achievements of modern astronomy, indicates that the sun stands in the middle and around it the planets revolve,[44] and even deems it appropriate to insert in one of his "psalms of Asaf" such a tasteless rationalist verse as "Knowledge speaketh unto knowledge and understanding calleth to her friend to make known Thy name to them that seek Thee."[45] It sounds literally like arrogance when, in the song of praise set in front of the book, which was again ostensibly composed by an Italian, a certain Zeraḥyah Ibn Massud, but derives in fact from Satanow's pen, the author of *Zemirot Asaf* is compared to the sun which, with its bright rays, has dispelled the darkness that ruled in the realm of rhetoric and poetry,[46] and his poems are set on an equal plane with the songs of David, the king of Israel.[47]

Only in rare instances, when Satanow in his "psalms" employs metaphors and similes from medieval mysticism, e.g., in the thirty-sixth chapter wherein the divine writings that are eternally inscribed in the universe are marvelled at, are poetic images that have not lost their colors through the arid breath of rationalism obtained. Satanow's rationalist tendency becomes even more prominent in the extensive *biur,* or commentary, which he wrote to *Zemirot Asaf,* following the model of the "Biurists" of his generation. In the same fashion he attempts also to rationalize Kabbalah in the compendium of

44. *Zemirot Asaf,* Chapter Six.
45. *Ibid.,* Chapter Eight, 17.
46.   I will liken you to the sun's coming out in its strength to give light,
    For darkness covered eloquence, and deep darkness covered choice diction.
    God spoke and called Isaac, and there was light.
47.   Because your songs are like the songs of David,
    Which we have ever guarded like the apple of our eye.

Jewish mysticism, the *Zohar*,[48] which he regarded warmly and even defended against the attacks of Jacob Emden.[49]

Isaac Satanow also reprinted works not his own, both old and new, such as Aristotle's *Ethics*, Jehudah Halevi's *Kuzari*, Immanuel of Rome's *Maḥberot*, Ephraim Luzzatto's *Eleh Venei Ha-Ne'urim*, and others. The frivolous Satanow, however, did not have the feeling of responsibility requisite to a serious scholar. The text in his editions is reprinted very negligently, not infrequently erroneously and with omissions, and his important younger contemporary, Mendelssohn-Hamburg, is not entirely unjustified when he calls Satanow "a wise man to do evil and to do good" and characterizes his editions with the angry words, "All the old books which he published are filled with mistakes and errors and defects, and he diminishes from, and adds to, them, and presents in the words of the author his own lying words . . . and of him it is said, 'He who does the work of the Lord with deceit.' "[50]

We observed previously that, for Satanow, his mystifications were merely mocking and trickery. He derived great pleasure from the fact that he deceived the naive reader and led him by the nose. A quite different character, however, is borne by the mystifications and disguises of Satanow's friend and collaborator Saul Berlin. Here it is not a question of play and trickery. We have here to do with an embittered but timorous fighter who employs falsifications as a means of battle in order to attack opponents from a hidden corner, not with a freely uncovered visage but disguised under various masks and with concealed and poisoned weaponry.

Saul Berlin was the son of the president of the rabbinic court of Berlin, Rabbi Tzevi Hirsch ben Aryeh Loeb Levin. Richly endowed by nature, he obtained ordination to the rabbinate at the age of eighteen and some time later became rabbi of Frankfurt-am-Oder. In Berlin and Breslau, where his father-in-law lived, the young Talmudist became acquainted with the local *maskilim* and was soon "infected with heresy." Secretly

---

48. See his *Zohar Tinyana* and also the *Biur* to the fifth chapter of *Zemirot Asaf.*
49. See the closing pages of his *Holech Tamim.* In his *Imrei Binah*, Satanow writes about the *Zohar*: "This Book of Zohar is great and vast. There are in it allusions and uncountable items of divine information built on the foundations of true intellect . . . which were spoken in divine secret with greater force and greater strength than what philosophical speculation spoke, as is known to one who contemplated them with reason and knowledge of their inner intention according to their truth, and the words are ancient" (*ibid.*, folio 12a).
50. *Penei Tevel*, p. 252.

Berlin was in agreement with the *Aufklärer* and, like Wolfsohn-Halle and his collaborators, was persuaded that it was the rabbis who mainly brought it about that the Jewish people remained so barbarized and backward. A bitter enemy of the rabbis, he did not have the courage openly to attack them. Like Leo de Modena in his day, so Berlin, himself sitting on the rabbinic chair, endeavored covertly to undermine the foundations of the camp so despised by him. He, the characterless and vacillating man, believed that in ideological battle one can more easily vanquish the foe not in open battle but through subterfuges and masked attacks.

Berlin's first appearance is associated with the struggle which broke out from the side of the Orthodox rabbis after the appearance of Naftali Herz Wessely's proclamation *Divrei Shalom Ve-Emet*.[51] Berlin wrote a caustic tract *Ketav Yosher*[52] (1784) but did not have the courage to publish it.[53] It merely circulated in handwritten copies, and only after his death did his friends in Berlin print it (1794) but still without the author's name.

The language of *Ketav Yosher* is in places overly mellifluous, following the accepted style of the Meassefim. Nevertheless, one senses in this tract an outspoken literary talent. It is in fact the first satire in neo-Hebrew literature. To be sure, the colors are too thick, and the malicious, hostile hand of the caricaturist

51. See above, Chapter Three.
52. The full title-page: *Sefer Ketav Yosher. Le-Haggid Le-Adam Yishro, Ish Ish Le-Fi Ashuro, Eleh Mi-Poh Be-Harut Appam Be-Ketzef U-Telunah Al Sefer Divrei Shalom Ve-Emet Emunah, Be-Tehilat Hashkafah Al Ha-Kavvanah Ha-Rishonah, Ve-Hacham Be-Ahor Yeshabehenah Le-Va'er Devarav Al Derech Ha-Hochmah Ha-Tzefunah, Ve-Az Gam Hem Yitnu Eideihem Ve-Yatzdikuhu Ve-Aharonah.*
53. Several bibliographers indicate erroneously that Berlin's pamphlet was printed in 1784. Benjacob even asserts that *Ketav Yosher* was published simultaneously both in Frankfurt and in Lemberg. Landshuth, however, has demonstrated (*Toledot Anshei Shem*, 105) that the date indicated in the phrase *Ve-Katuv Yashar* shows merely the year when the pamphlet was composed. However, it was published only after the author's death. This is demonstrated also quite definitely by the review in *Ha-Meassef*, Vol. VII, 271: "The author of this book is hidden from the eyes of the reader, for he did not make known his name on the title-page. But the reviewer knew him and knew that he was one of the greatest men of the generation, and he was a rabbi and *gaon* and president of a rabbinic court and a great sage. He composed this book at the time of the controversies and was not permitted to print it all the days of his life, for he was deathly afraid that they would proceed against him with the ban as they did previously in the case of another book which he composed for the sake of the love of truth . . . Now that the righteous man has perished and has been gathered to his people in the capital city of London, the honor they did him in his death was greater than that in his life."

is discernible. But it cannot be denied that this hand is skilled and competent. The author pretends to be a simpleton. He had heard it said that one of the enlightened, Naftali Wessely, has written a "godless, heretical book," but he has not had occasion to read this book, and so went to discuss it with a teacher from Poland who has a class here and teaches Torah to Jewish children. Later he had a conversation with a "great man in Israel," a rabbi and president of a rabbinic court, and attempted also to learn from him wherewith the author of *Divrei Shalom Ve-Emet* had committed such a great sin.

The author is not content with setting forth these "rebels against the light" and opponents of all reform as ignorant, barbaric, crude, and foolish men. He also incidentally mocks the whole traditional way of life with its awkward old-fashionedness and obsolete world view. When he sharply criticizes the traditional mode of learning in the Jewish elementary schools, he also endeavors to disclose to the reader how harmful for the normal development of the younger generation is rabbinic *pilpul*, with its isolation from the real demands of life. The author also hurls his satiric arrows at the mystics, ridicules the books of Kabbalah with their secrets and "mysteries of mysteries"—and all this in disguised form, with the simple-minded face of "one who does not know how to ask." Only in the closing lines does the author throw off his mask and greet Wessely in exalted, mellifluous phrases and strongly praise his courageous attack in the name of truth and culture.

This tract, however, did not long still the lust for battle of the heretical rabbi. He projected a new achievement which was to have made the enormous impression of a suddenly exploding bomb in the hostile camp. One of the most important rabbis of that time was Raphael Kohen, the chief rabbi of the three communities of Altona, Hamburg, and Wandsbeck. Raphael Kohen acquired renown in the rabbinic world not only with his ritual composition *Torat Yekutiel* (Berlin, 1772) but also with his excellent qualities and noble character. Petty, extraneous motives were alien to him. He knew nothing of giving special respect to influential persons, and in all his dealings his sole purpose was truth and righteousness. However, he was a thoroughly convinced orthodox believer and refused to take account of the demands of the new age. When Moses Mendelssohn's translation of the Pentateuch appeared, he was, as we noted previously (above, p. 42), one of its categorical opponents. Thanks to his great moral authority, this orthodox rabbi who refused to know anything of compromise, was a very serious and dangerous antagonist. Hence, he was especially hated by the *Aufklärer*. Saul Berlin, who celebrated Mendelssohn's translation of the Pentateuch[54] as well as his translation of the Psalms in cumbersome verses, therefore utilized this obdurate opponent as the target of his polemical attacks.

Under a fabricated name, Obadiah ben Baruch Ish Polanya, he wrote a sharp tract entitled *Mitzpeh Yokte'el* against Raphael Kohen's *Torat Yekutiel*, which enjoyed great popularity in rabbinic circles. With bitter sarcasm Berlin criticizes the chief rabbi and great scholar, and especially underscores that what is involved here actually is not a "Torah of Yekutiel." This composition can merely serve as clear proof how ridiculous and removed from life *pilpul*, with all its overly pointed inventions and subtleties, is. The author does not spare any arrows to persuade the reader that Kohen's book, which evoked so much enthusiasm in the rabbinic world with its keenness and great scholarship, is a petty, meaningless work and that it was "a sin to use up the paper which the author of *Torat Yekutiel* wasted with his foolish theories."

But all this was insufficient for Berlin. He apparently had some personal accounts to settle with the author of *Torat Yekutiel*. A man who stood at the crossroads, who had already lost his belief in the old world with its truths and for whom the new world was still an alien one, characterless and without firm moral ground, the heretical Rabbi Saul Berlin was not able to remain in his polemic on the high level of principle in discussing purely social problems and requirements. Hence, he exchanged the reproving lash of satire for the filthy painter's brush of a libeller. The morally clean and righteous Raphael Kohen is charged with the most shameful transgressions—that he is a lover of bribes, and, that out of personal motives, this great figure in Israel and president of a rabbinic court permits such a grievous thing as taking a bribe and manifests "great arrogance and irresponsible frivolity in the matter of ritually improperly slaughtered animals." With rolled-up eyes and a pious mien the author of the tract exclaims: "I swear by God that he [the author of *Torat Yekutiel*] is worthy of having the sages of the generation expose his entire shame for all the deeds which he has committed. He has perpetrated three transgres-

54. For this Moses, the man for the glory of Israel, is like the mitre worn by the
    priest . . .
    Ho, all that thirst, come—Seek out his book and read it—Taste and see—
    Choice honey dripping.

sions: he blinds eyes, he plagiarizes from other authors and decks himself out in the clothing of others, and causes Jews to eat non-kosher food with his decisions." In such a style is all of *Mitzpeh Yokte'el* written.

Saul Berlin's two friends, David Friedländer and Isaac Satanow, helped publish and disseminate this tract. Each of them acted out of special motives—David Friedländer as a bitter enemy of the orthodox rabbis, the frivolous Satanow out of love for mystification, of playing with the reader in disguise and fooling him with masquerades. These two collaborators printed *Mitzpeh Yokte'el* (in 1789) in the printery *Ḥinnuch Ne'a-rim* where Satanow was then working. The publishers attest in a special introduction about the supposedly anonymous author that they know him as "a lover of wisdom" and "connoisseur of insight." As soon as the work came off the press, the publishers immediately circulated copies to many prominent rabbis—among them also, in order to avert the least suspicion, the rabbi of Frankfurt, Saul Berlin, and his father, the rabbi of Berlin. In addition, they sent copies to the Gaon of Vilna and the "man of controversy" himself, Raphael Kohen, the chief rabbi of Hamburg. This they did ostensibly out of love for the truth. They wished the great scholars of the generation to decide which of the two rabbis is right—whether the author of *Torat Yekutiel* or his antagonist with his sharp critique.

The booklet aroused enormous excitement in the rabbinic world. A particularly great sensation was produced in Hamburg. The community was terribly enraged at the anonymous author who had the impudence to shame their chief rabbi, so highly regarded by all, in such an arrogant tone. The rabbinic court of the three neighboring communities immediately issued the verdict that the scurrilous booklet be placed under the ban, that an announcement to this effect be made in the Great Synagogue "after the reading of the Torah," and that his composition be burned and destroyed with "great shame."[55] In Berlin also *Mitzpeh Yokte'el* was committed to fire in the old synagogue courtyard, and many rabbis issued forth sharply against its author, not calling him openly by name but many knowing who was hidden under the mask of Obadiah ben Baruch Ish Polanya. Others, however, debated the question whether the weapon of the ban could be utilized when purely personal motives are intermingled in the case.[56]

55. See Bernfeld, *Dor Tahapuchot*, II, 72.
56. All the details about this controversy, with the relevant documents, were published by Landshuth in *Toledot Anshei Shem*, 87–99.

The man involved, Saul Berlin, also intervened in the controversy. He published a special responsum[57] in which he ostensibly plays the role of the arbitrator on the sidelines and expresses his view as a rabbi in Israel that the rabbis of Hamburg and Altona did not have the right to place the author of *Mitzpeh Yokte'el*, Obadiah ben Baruch, under the ban. He also published in *Ha-Meassef*[58] the response he had received to his inquiry on this subject from the rabbi of Prague, Ezekiel Landau. It is also beyond doubt that Berlin is the author of "Vikkuah Shenei Re'im Zerah U-Feretz," published in *Ha-Meassef*[59]—a conversation between two friends about the "controversy which *Mitzpeh Yokte'el* called forth." There, too, it is noted that the rabbis of Hamburg have no right to excommunicate the author of *Mitzpeh Yokte'el*.[60]

It is further highly probable that Berlin is the author of the very sharp critique, also printed in *Ha-Meassef*,[61] of Raphael Kohen's other work, the morality book *Marpe Lashon*. Testimony to this is provided not only by the extremely cutting and aggressively hostile tone in which this long article is written, but also by the fact that the reviewer always mentions the incident with *Mitzpeh Yokte'el*. He cannot forgive the chief rabbi of Hamburg for refusing to concede that the brilliant author of *Mitzpeh Yokte'el* is right and, moreover, for "having persecuted him with great wrath." The reviewer always mentions the story of the ban and cannot forget

what this reprover did to his opponent, a righteous and upright man, a distinguished man and greater than us in Torah and wisdom and in the fear of God, who was zealous for the Lord of Hosts and who made known the errors and the shame of this author who erred in his previous book called *Torat Yekutiel*, and already every man of Torah has acknowledged the words of the zealous man and said that the truth is with him.[62]

This "just and righteous man who was zealous for the Lord of Hosts," however, refused to be calmed, and while the controversy about his *Mitzpeh Yokte'el* was still raging, Saul Berlin devised a new scandal of much larger scope. In the abovemen-

---

57. We have not seen the brochure but know of it only from the quotations which Bernfeld introduces in his work, *op. cit.*, II, 72–73.
58. The volume for 5550, pp. 222–223.
59. *Ibid.*, 5549, pp. 261–273.
60. Finally Berlin himself admitted that he is, indeed, the author of the pamphlet.
61. The volume for 5550, pp. 362–380. On this article, see above, pp. 99–100.
62. *Ibid.*, 378.

tioned letter which he published in *Ha-Meassef*, he mentions incidentally that he possesses in manuscript a "marvelous book, a collection of responsa of the earlier codifiers, may their memory be for a blessing, and most of these responsa by Rabbi Asher ben Yeḥiel, may his memory be for a blessing." which he intends to publish with his own comments, bearing the title *Kassa De-Harsana*.[63] This work, in fact, was published three years later (1793) at the same *Ḥinnuch Ne'arim* printery under the title *She'elot U-Teshuvot Besamim Rosh.*

The title-page indicates that the responsa were collected by a contemporary of the author of *Bet Yosef,* Joseph Karo—one named Rabbi Isaac di Molina. In the brief introduction the collector di Molina relates that, after being driven from his home, he came to Alexandria and there, in the library of a wealthy patron, found in a thick volume the responsa of Rabbi Asher ben Yeḥiel. Upon becoming thoroughly familiar with this collection, he was convinced that there are in it numerous responsa bearing Rabbi Asher's name and also some without his signature which have remained entirely unknown until now. With the permission of the patron, he, di Molina, copied these responsa in a special collection with the intention of later publishing them in Venice.

The author of the notes and comments i.e., Saul Berlin, indicates, for his part, that he saw the manuscript, which is written in Sephardic script, at the home of a Turkish Jew Ḥayyim bar Jonah Dabi in the Italian city of Casale Monferrato in the region of Piedmont; the Turkish Jew granted him permission to copy the manuscript, only on the condition that he, Berlin, not have the right to publish it for seven years. This period has already long passed; hence, he has now decided to print this collection, which is undoubtedly a genuine treasure of rabbinic literature, and he hopes that even his antagonists will now stretch out to him the hand of peace in gratitude for his precious gift.

Not peace and gratitude, however, awaited Saul Berlin for this volume. Shortly after *Besamim Rosh* appeared, the suspicion was expressed by many persons that the responsa collected in it did not derive from Rabbi Asher ben Yeḥiel and that the collector Isaac di Molina is someone who never existed;[64] all this is pure falsification on the part of the publisher,

---

63. *Ha-Meassef*, 1790, p. 223.

64. We conjecture that Isaac di Molina is not entirely a fabricated person. This name is merely the mask of another Isaac, not of Molina but of Satanow, and it is perhaps not accidental that Molina in *gematria* is equivalent to the same number as *di Satanow* (137). Satanow undoubtedly collaborated with Saul Berlin in fabricating *Besamim Rosh*,

Saul Berlin. Within a few months Rabbi Wolf Landsberg came forth with a composition, *Ze'ev Yitrof*, in which he expresses his firm conviction that *Besamim Rosh* is a fraud. The well known rabbi of Nikolsburg Mordecai Banet also noted in a letter to Saul Berlin's father, the aged Tzevi Hirsch Levin, that the responsa *Besamim Rosh* do not come from Rabbi Asher ben Yehiel. "They are from head to foot only wounds and grievous abscesses from sinful, vile men."[65]

That the work is a fraud—of this no historian of culture no longer has any doubt. The fact is even confirmed documentarily by Saul Berlin's friend and collaborator, David Friedländer.[66] It suffices merely to leaf through *Besamim Rosh* with a certain attentiveness to understand quite clearly what the falsifier really intended with his apocryphal work. In *Mitzpeh Yokte'el* Berlin plays the strictly pious man and accuses the chief rabbi of Hamburg of being one "who causes others to eat ritually unfit food." In *Besamim Rosh*, however, Berlin comes forth as a rationalist Reform preacher of David Friedländer's school.

Rabbi Asher ben Yehiel, who was, as we know,[67] a decisive opponent of secular knowledge and a fellow-battler of the militant fanatic Abba Mari, is suddenly transformed in *She'elot U-Teshuvot Besamim Rosh* into an *Aufklärer* of the end of the eighteenth century. Quite in the spirit of the *maskilim* of Berlin, Rabbi Asher here permits shaving the beard (Responsum No. 18), authorizes riding on the Sabbath (No. 375), and also allows the "wine of idolators" (No. 36). Moreover, he finds it necessary to admonish that one should not be too rigorous in observing the commandments in order not to be compared to

---

and not without reason did he issue forth with a defense-document entitled "Ha-Galui Veha-Hatum" in which he endeavors to show that the responsa in *Besamim Rosh* are not falsified (see Zeitlin, *op. cit.*, p. 334. However, the date there, apparently, is not correctly given; it should be 1794, not 1781).

65. *Literaturblatt des Orients*, 1844, 55: "In conclusion, I looked and, behold, this "head" *(Rosh)* is completely empty and chaotic, and through the slight logic in the rhetoric of his runaway ideas it is recognizable that he did not grasp Rabbi Asher ben Yehiel (Rosh) but rather, from the sole of his foot to his head there is no soundness in him; the woundings of an enemy and the blows of wickedness from men who work evil."

66. In the copy of *Ketav Yosher* that is preserved in Friedländer's library is the inscription in Friedländer's own hand: "This satirical document is from Rabbi Saul of blessed memory, the son of the rabbi, the president of the rabbinic court, our teacher and master, Rabbi Tzevi Hirsch of Berlin, written on the occasion of the persecution of Rabbi Herz Wessely. He is also the author of *Besamim Rosh* which he gave out as the work of an ancient *gaon.*" Of all the historians of culture, only Jost attempted to show that *Besamim Rosh* in fact derives from the Middle Ages (see *Die Geschichte des Judentums und seiner Sekten*, III, pp. 390–400).

67. See our *History*, Vol. III, pp. 84ff.

a *ḥasid shoteh*, or "foolish pietist" (Nos. 115, 118). He also at times expresses ideas that forcibly remind one of the ideational processes of Friedländer and others of his ilk. The strictly orthodox Ashkenazic rabbi who proudly declared to the Sephardic Jews: "Your secular wisdoms are not known to me, and I thank and praise God that He has preserved me from them, for they may—God forbid—lead a person away from the fear of Heaven and from the sacred Torah,"[68] appears in *Besamim Rosh* as a one hundred percent rationalist.

In Responsum No. 251 we read:

If one wishes thoroughly to understand the foundations of the Jewish religion, he must also study Greek philosophy, for it is well known that he who is not conversant with Greek speculative literature is, in general, unable to occupy himself with those problems that are the chief substance of the Torah and the religion. All agree that, to grasp the basic elements of our Torah and its commandments, one cannot be content merely with the literal meaning of the biblical text and the commentaries of our sages, but must also diligently study the philosophical books of the nations of the world.[69]

The principles of the religion, we read further, must be adapted to the requirements of the time. We must at present apply all our thought only for the sake of peace and truth, and promote knowledge of the Creator and His deeds. Man was not created for the law, but the law for man. And if, for instance —*Besamim Rosh* teaches us—we can think that a time may come when the Torah and its commandments will be absolutely harmful for our people and its survival, or that they are no longer in any way capable of bringing happiness, we must cast the yoke of the Torah off ourselves.[70]

68. *Ibid.*, p. 85.

69. *Besamim Rosh*, folio 76a: "For it is a well known thing . . . that no one can obtain knowledge in these matters unless he has filled his belly with the books of the Greeks and has delved deeply into philosophical speculation through their compositions, and even though these matters are the foundation of the Torah and the major element of the faith, nevertheless, it is agreed among all that a man will not arrive at the chief principle of the Torah and the commandments from the understanding that he acquires from the simple writings and from the words of our rabbis of blessed memory, but from the reason that is taught and is customary in the books of the scholars of the nations."

70. *Besamim Rosh*, folio 77a: " 'It is time to work for the Lord; they have nullified Thy Torah.' And if, God forbid, it would be possible to imagine that the time might come when the ordinances and commandments of the Torah would bring evil on our nation, definitely on the generality of the nation, or even if there would be room to suppose that one could not derive happiness from them in any way, then we would throw off the yoke from our neck."

Such thoughts, which even the Aristotelian rationalists, Maimonides and Gersonides, did not permit themselves to express, are placed in the mouth of the fanatically pious Ashkenazic Rabbi Asher ben Yeḥiel. The scandal was enormous. The entire rabbinic world issued forth against the falsifier. His own community turned away from him with disgust; Saul Berlin had to leave his rabbinic post and emigrate from Germany.

Physically and spiritually shattered, he went to London, where he soon (in the fall of 1794) died, lonely and forsaken, in the fifty-fourth year of his life. Meir Jozef, the only person who used to visit the solitary Berlin in London, discovered in the clothes of the deceased a will written not long before his demise. The will is extremely characteristic of this extraordinary man, lost and confused on the paths of life. He requested that he be buried in the clothes in which he was found after his death somewhere in a forest or in another place, only far away from the Jewish cemetery.[71]

71. "No garment in which I am clothed shall be stripped from me, but as they find me so they should lift me up and bury me in one of the forests or in a place which they will find—but far from the graves of the children of my people." This will is published in *Literaturblatt des Orients*, 1844, pp. 712–713; reprinted by Carmoly in *Ha-Orevim U-Venei Yonah*, pp. 40–41.

CHAPTER EIGHT

Wessely's Shirei Tiferet;
MASKILIM IN LITHUANIA AND POLAND

[Wessely's biblical hero epic *Shirei Tiferet*—*Messias* and *Mosaida*—Franco-Mendes and his *Gemul Atalyah*—Joseph Tropplowitz (Ha-Ephrati) and his drama *Meluchat Sha'ul*—"False" and "genuine" enlightenment—Tracts and controversial writings against the "enlightened"—The anonymous *Olam Ḥadash* and Naḥman Barash's *Ein Mishpat*—The author of *Sefer Ha-Berit* against the rationalists—Jehudah Loeb Margolioth and his attack on Mendelssohn's ideas—The circle of Shklov and the Berlin Haskalah—Nevakhovich and his *Kol Shavat Bat Yehudah*—The spiritual crisis—From temporary peace to a new and bitter struggle against the positive sciences—The great mystical wonder.]

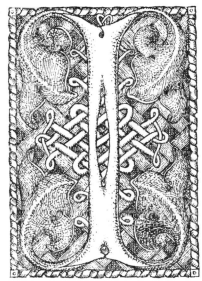

N THE previous chapter we observed how the Meassefim, the enthusiastic admirers of the language of the Bible, devoted a great deal of attention to philological studies and set as their goal to "reveal the beauties of the Hebrew language to all other peoples." But precisely the "beauties" which the Meassefim endeavored to produce in the language of the Bible were, with very rare exceptions, of rather slight value. One of these attempts—and, indeed, one of rather broad scope—must be specially treated, because it had a significant influence on the emergent neo-Hebrew literature. This work belongs to the "lion in the society," Naftali Herz Wessely, the well known author of *Divrei Shalom Ve-Emet*.

When the founders of *Ha-Meassef* applied to Wessely, who was then almost sixty years old, requesting him to adorn the new journal with his poems, the latter modestly noted that in the course of his long literary career he had, in fact, written only a few dozen occasional poems in which he celebrates princes and great men, or persons well known to him. His fields of competence were mainly philology and exegesis. Isaac Euchel relates in his review of *Shirei Tiferet*[1] how Wessely would very frequently repeat that he suffered great pain from the fact that "he had frequently raised his voice to celebrate kings of flesh and blood and not once in honor of the King, the King of kings." One of his disciples once came and informed him that he had had a dream at night in which a heavenly voice chanted for him a paean which he, Wessely, had sung in honor of Moses, "the chief of the prophets." Wessely rejoiced greatly at his disciple's story and promptly decided to compose a hero-poem that would relate Moses' greatness and the miracles God performed with him.

It is beyond doubt, however, that both the disciple's dream and Wessely's decision have a certain relationship to the well known passage that the German scholar Johann Gottfried von Herder wrote in his work *Vom Geiste der hebräischen Poesie*, published in 1782–83. The star of the first national German poet, Friedrich Gottfried Klopstock, the author of the heroic epic *Messias*, in which the founder of Christianity is celebrated, then shone brightly. Herder, the excellent and profound student of ancient Hebrew poetry, dreamed of another hero-epic. "I am surprised," he writes,

that with so many Hebrew heroic poems, our language still does not have an epic on Moses. The redemption of a people from slavery and the education of this people to the purest worship of God and the freest state of ancient times would be, it seems to me, a nobler theme than adventures and battles and journeys . . . Yet, I should like, with this little exposition, to arouse not a German, but a German-Hebrew poet. To him the subject is national; his natural early acquaintance with the poets of his nation must give him an older simplicity than one could demand of a German scholar.[2]

Wessely undertook to become the Jewish national poet of whom Herder dreamed. In the course of the last twenty years of his life he wrote his long hero-epic *Shirei Tiferet*, which embraces the period from Moses' birth to the giving of the Torah. As early as 1789 the first part, in four cantos, was published. The later four parts also appeared while the author was

1. *Ha-Meassef,* 5550, p. 218.
2. *Ha-Meassef,* II, 78.

still alive, and only the sixth part, with the three final cantos (16–18), remained in manuscript and was first published by his son in 1829. Shortly after the first part of *Shirei Tiferet* appeared in print, one of the contributors to *Ha-Meassef* declared emotively that such a magnificent work "has not been produced since the Jewish people went into exile and the Bible was closed."[3] Two German professors, Hufnagel and Spalding, translated into German the first two cantos of *Shirei Tiferet* (1795), to which they gave the title *Die Mosaida*.[4]

There are those who wish to see in Wessely the Jewish Klopstock, and in his *Mosaida* the twin sister of *Messias*. However, the Hebrew epic cannot be compared to its German sister. As a work of art, *Messias* also has enormous defects, for Klopstock was essentially not a writer of epics. On the other hand, he was a profoundly sensitive lyricist, a true poet of broad scope. Naftali Herz Wessely, however, was a rhetorician *(melitz)*, a grammarian, a master of the Hebrew language—but not a poet; and his voluminous poem is, in fact, a stillborn creature.[5] In the prefaces and notes to the individual parts of his epic, Wessely always stresses that his task is "to explicate God's words in easy, poetic form,"[6] "to explain in verse obscure passages of the Torah."[7] And with great smugness and delight he expresses his conviction that the reader will find in his poem quite new ideas and notions of which the earlier commentators did not even dream.

Essentially, Wessely is not unjustified. His *Shirei Tiferet* is, indeed, not a hero-epic but a long commentary "by way of a poem" to the classic biblical narrative which relates with such marvelous epic power the Exodus from Egypt (the biblical pericopes *Shemot* and *Be-Shallaḥ*). The whole rich cycle of Oriental legends and tales with which popular imagination, in the course of centuries, encircled the heroes of this national epic is left entirely untouched by Wessely, in contrast to the Old-

---

3. *Ha-Meassef*, 5550, p. 93: "For there was none like him from the day that Israel went into exile from their land and the books of the Bible were canonized."

4. David Friedrischsfeld notes in his *Zecher Tzaddik* (p. 13) that Wessely's son Menahem published a complete German translation of *Shirei Tiferet*.

5. Even Isaac Euchel, one of Wessely's ardent admirers, must concede in his review of *Shirei Tiferet* (*Ha-Meassef*, 5550, pp. 210–221, 346–352, 357–362) that "the rhetorician Wessely at times forgets that he is a poet" (*ibid.*, p. 361).

6. *Ibid.*, I, VII: "To interpret the words of our God by way of song."

7. *Ibid.*, IX: "To interpret by way of song the unclear figures of speech in the Torah." *Ibid.*, notes to Part Five: "To bring the creatures close to the Torah through the delight of song that tells them in a pleasant voice the depths of the interpretations of the texts in the Torah."

Yiddish paraphrases. He slavishly follows the biblical text and permits himself merely to utilize the medieval commentaries to this text.

On the other hand, however, he is enormously loquacious and wishes to know nothing of the secret of brevity. The shortest phrase in the Bible is watered down and flooded in the paraphrase of *Shirei Tiferet* by a sea of grey, monotonous lines. Naturally, the impression and power of portrayal are not strengthened thereby but, rather, significantly weakened. It suffices, for instance, to compare the powerful scene in the Bible which relates with such marvelous simplicity how before Moses ben Amram, who pastures the flock of his father-in-law, the great miracle suddenly reveals itself in the flame of the burning bush, and *Ehyeh Asher Ehyeh* appoints him as the liberator of his people, with the tedious rhetorical flourishes that are drawn out in *Shirei Tiferet* to dozens of pages (fifth canto).

These hosts of hundreds of glib and colorless lines evoke a truly irksome feeling in the reader. It is difficult to believe that there is any *aficionado* who would be eager to read through to the conclusion in Wessely's *Shirei Tiferet* the endless song of praise that the children of Israel chant immediately after peacefully crossing the Red Sea while Pharoah's army perishes in its stormy waves (thirteenth canto). One line of the biblical "Song of the Sea" *(Shirat Ha-Yam)* is incomparably more valuable than all of Wessely's watery rhetorical flourishes.[8]

The most valuable or, more accurately, the only valuable elements in *Shirei Tiferet* are the rhymed verses in six lines introducing each individual canto. In these didactic lines the author pours out his tender feelings, his enthusiasm before the Creator and for His marvelous deeds. The rhetorician and commentator becomes emotive; in places one feels the honest pathos of the deeply believing man, and Wessely's monotonous, barely alive lines suddenly obtain picturesqueness and expressive power.

In the composition of the cantos, in the technique and construction of the lines, Wessely faithfully follows the older German poets, Klopstock and Wieland. The verses in *Shirei Tiferet* flow smoothly, calmly, set in strict caesura, constructed according to the rigid principles of meter. But what is lacking are the most important of things—poetic feeling and epic power. Wes-

8. Typical is Wessely's indication that the long poem of praise in his *Shirei Tiferet* is a commentary on the biblical poem "Az Yashir" ("Now, take nectar of delightful words from my mouth, for I shall begin to explain the words of our ancestor's song").

sely's lines, written in the style of the Bible, lack the compressed impactedness and pictorial wealth of the biblical sentence. Nevertheless, the cantos of *Shirei Tiferet* evoked, on their publication, no less enthusiasm than Klopstock's epic, which had been published less than twenty years earlier.

For decades, Wessely's epic was regarded as the supreme poetic achievement in neo-Hebrew literature. Even the well known scholar Solomon Jehudah Rapoport concluded that *Shirei Tiferet* has no peer in Hebrew literature "from the day the sacred songs were composed." Several poets wrote epics on biblical themes following the pattern of Wessely's *Mosaida* and, among many young *maskilim, Shirei Tiferet* was so beloved that they used to copy the work diligently from beginning to end and memorize many verses of it.[9] Even in the 1860's, when Abraham Uri Kovner came forth with a sharp critique of Wessely's biblical epic and declared that one line of "the Song of the Sea" is worth more than the whole of *Shirei Tiferet,*[10] the *maskilim* of the older generation saw in his statement extraordinary impudence and a "desecration of sanctities."[11]

Books, like men, have their special fate. In the years when the first cantos of *Shirei Tiferet* appeared and Wessely was preparing the subsequent parts of his epic, a rather young poet lived in a castaway little town in Silesia and wrote his first work, a heroic drama of the biblical era. This work was not greeted with exalted rhetoric and emotive praises; at first, it remained virtually unnoticed. Nevertheless, it is the only work of the generation of the Meassefim which bears quite clearly the stamp of genuine poetic talent.

An attempt to create a historical Bible-drama was made as early as 1770 by a descendant of the exiles from Spain, David

9. Such a complete copy of *Shirei Tiferet* was located in the museum of the Historical-Ethnographic Society in Leningrad.

10. See *Heker Davar*, 41; *Tzeror Perahim*, pp. 48–50.

11. The first person who gave a more or less accurate evaluation of Wessely's *Shirei Tiferet* was the twenty-three year old Franz Delitzsch. In his *Zur Geschichte der jüdischen Poesie* (p. 98) he presents the following description of the Hebrew *Mosaida* which was then so popular: "Die Biblische Bilderwelt war ihm ein heimisches Land, aber er verstand nicht, mit dem Email ihrer Tinten seine Gemälde zu coloriren; das Feenreich des Orientalismus aber war ihm ein verschlossener Hesperidengarten. Darum ist Styl, Bilder, Gedanken—Alles bei ihm mehr germanisch, oft trivial, nicht judenthümlich, orientalisch, überhaupt nicht orientalisch . . . Sein Styl rieselt melodisch dahin, wie ein Bach mit durchsichtigen Wassern—aber der Grund dieses Baches ist nicht der farbige Kies, der flimmernde Goldsand, die bunten orientalischen Perlen der Sage; in semen Wellen spiegeln sich nicht palästinische Alhennen, Alraunen und Saronslilien, sondern echt deutsche Primeln, Schlüssel-und Dotter-Blumen."

Franco-Mendes (David Ḥofshi) of Amsterdam, who later became an active contributor to *Ha-Meassef*, in which he published various poems and a whole series of monographs on "great Jewish figures" (Menasseh ben Israel, D'Aguilar, and others). The young Mendes'[12] interest in poetry was aroused by Moses Ḥayyim Luzzatto, who spent all of eight years in Amsterdam and there wrote his *La-Yesharim Tehillah.*[13] The intellectually curious pupil, however, lacked poetic talent and in his three-act Bible-drama, *Gemul Atalyah,* the influence of his teacher, the wise poet and mystic, is very little discernible. Franco-Mendes himself indicates in the preface that *Gemul Atalyah* was composed following the pattern of two older dramas on the same theme, the Frenchman Jean Racine's and the Italian Pietro Metastasio's. He merely set himself the task of clothing the biblical material in Jewish national forms. These forms, however, are very little distinguished by their poetic beauty in Mendes' work. His verse is wooden, stiff, unpolished, and even frequently not free of grammatical errors. The images are pale and diffuse. Artistic taste was still so little developed at that time, however, that David Mendes' drama evoked no fewer mellifluous odes and sonnets than Joseph Penso de la Vega's *Asirei Ha-Tikvah* had in its day.[14]

David Mendes' drama bears the name of the power-hungry, sinful queen who slaughtered her own grandchildren in order to ascend the throne. Joseph Ha-Ephrati's (Tropplowitz) drama *Meluchat Sha'ul,* written in his youth, tells of the tragic fate of the first Jewish king, the noble but unfortunate Saul, the son of Kish. We have very few biographical details about this poet. It is known only that he was born in 1770 in the small Silesian village of Tropplowitz, spent several years in Ratibor as tutor in the home of a wealthy merchant, and later (after 1791) settled in Prague, where he died in 1804. He made his debut with a successful translation of Kleist in *Ha-Meassef,*[15] and two years later published[16] there a poem of praise "on the peace between Prussia and Austria." This is an ordinary "occasional poem." Nevertheless, one feels in it quite distinctly, especially

12. David Mendes was born in 1713 and died in 1792.
13. See our *History,* Vol. VI, Book Two, Chapter Three.
14. In his old age, a few years before his death, David Mendes completed his second drama *Teshuat Yisrael Be-Yedei Yehudit*—a reworking of Metastasio's *Betulia Liberata.* The work was published by Heidenheim in 1804. A collection of poems by Mendes entitled *Kinnor David* remained in manuscript.
15. *Ha-Meassef,* 5548, pp. 305–312.
16. *Ibid.,* 5550, pp. 353–356.

in the successful portrayals of nature, that he has before him an authentic poet. At the same time Ha-Ephrati began work on his six-act Bible-drama *Meluchat Sha'ul*, which he completed in Prague at the end of 1793 and published in Vienna at the beginning of 1794.

Like the Meassefim, so Joseph Ha-Ephrati of Tropplowitz asserts that he considers his basic task to renew the language of the Bible which has become so forgotten. But how far removed in his entire world-view is this young man of Ratibor from the *Aufklärer* of Berlin. A dreamy romantic, an enthusiastic admirer of Schiller's youthful dramas, Tropplowitz lived in the world of images that his imagination created and, with eyes filled with dread, looked on the tragic face of fate, the visage of the predestined, ruthless decree hanging over man's destiny.

Joseph Tropplowitz's youthful work still suffers greatly from insufficient maturity. Numerous scenes are absolutely superfluous. Others are carried through very naively, for instance, the scene in the third act where Jonathan and David enter into battle against the Philistines and Jonathan's youngest brother promptly returns and announces the tidings that David has vanquished the mighty giant Goliath. A literally irksome impression is also made by the closing scene. In this scene, set on Mount Gilboa, King Saul and his older son perish tragically. David appears, sees the dead body of his friend Jonathan and the dying Saul, and laments in tender verses the tragic death of the two noblest of heroes. Immediately afterwards, however, he begins, out of a clear blue sky, to declaim a long didactic poem, consisting of scores of six-line verses, about the "illusory honor" that men pursue with such avidity and passion throughout their lives.[17]

Nevertheless, even with all these defects, *Meluchat Sha'ul* by the twenty-three-year-old Tropplowitz is a significant phenomenon in Hebrew literature. The attempt of the aged

17. This poem, which Tropplowitz wrote following the pattern of a poem by Albrecht von Haller suffered much in the later editions of *Meluchat Sha'ul* at the hands of the Jewish censors in Russia. All of thirteen verses were thrown out by the censor because in them "rulers" who carry on wars, "corrupt the land with murders and robberies and destroy entire cities," are spoken of. Also in other verses the censor's red pencil made various "corrections." While in the first Vienna edition is printed "there was a cruel king," we read in the later Russian editions "there was a cruel man." The word "king" was thrown out; a king cannot be cruel. In the first edition we read "Woe to the rulers of the land, who increase robbery and murder." In the Russian editions the "rulers of the land" are exchanged for the "provokers of the land." Also in these editions the term "the heart of the princes and the heart of the governors" is exchanged for "the heart of the wealthy and the heart of the rich," etc.

Wessely to produce a hero-epic in the language of the Bible remained unsuccessful, despite all the enthusiasm that it evoked in its day. But at the same time as Wessely, the young, romantically-minded poet of Ratibor undertook to create a hero-drama and successfully achieved his goal.

In the previous volume[18] we considered the factors which brought about the grievous "birth pangs" of dramatic art among the Jews, and led to the fact that the kernels of drama, which were sown in Jewish cultural life from ancient times, had no opportunity for so long a time to ripen and produce mature fruits. There we noted the significant factor that the ethical-monotheistic world view established by the Hebrew prophets lacked the most important life-motive of Greek tragedy: belief in blind faith, in the predetermined decree which man is unable to avoid, and in the idea that the more stubbornly one fights against his fate predestined by alien and merciless powers, all the more inevitable, all the deeper, becomes his downfall. The entire world view of the monotheistic Jew, with his assured belief in the God full of compassion under whose loving Providence every creature exists, could not allow the classical tragedy of ancient Greek fashion to develop on Jewish soil.

But the hero of Joseph Ha-Ephrati's drama lived in the pre-prophetic era. The God of Israel is still the stern God Yahweh, the God of the burning deserts and wild, sharply peaked mountains, a jealous, vengeful God who is a rigorous judge only and refuses to know of compassion. This God of war, the national God of the militant Hebrew tribes, demands that the vanquished foe be ruthlessly annihilated, even if he already lies powerless and weaponless at the feet of his conqueror. The slightest memory of the fearful national enemy, Amalek, must be wiped out with fire and sword. But the better among the people, the noble, heroic spirits, could no longer be satisfied with this primitive, bloodthirsty morality. And the proud, heroic king Saul, the man who "from his shoulders and upward was taller than any of the people" (I Samuel 9:2), of whom one of the characters in *Meluchat Sha'ul* declares that "already in your mother's womb were you appointed a king, and since your birth have you been irradiated with royal glory," has the courage to set himself against the old morality and not obey the cruel command of the stern God Yahweh.

18. *Ibid.*, p. 270ff. See also our work "Tsu Der Geshikhte Fun Der Yidisher Folks-Dramatik," *Bikher-Velt*, 1929, I, pp. 32–41.

Meluchat Sha'ul

With the exquisite sensitivity of a true artist, Joseph Trop-plowitz understands how to create out of this motif the starting-point of the whole drama. From this moment on Saul becomes a tragic personality. His grievous fate is already deter-mined. Fate, the merciless decree, hangs over him. As early as the first scene Saul declares bitterly: "I am still king, but I no longer rule." And he sees before himself the stretched-out hand that wrests the crown from his head. But he, the courageous battler, will not surrender. He fights with wild stubbornness, without rest and without cease, but he is already mentally ill and broken. The fatal, inevitable circle closes around him ever more straitly. In order to drive away the hypochondria of the melancholy king and the terrifying images that press down upon him, the red-haired youth, the shepherd with his magical harp in hand, appears. Saul is enchanted by the wondrous tones which the young David calls forth with his magical fingers, but apprehends, with his keen instinct, that this youth, endowed with radiance and joy, is destined to become his heir on the throne. Saul appreciates David's greatness, but he can-not forget that the latter will become the robber of his throne. So he sees in David the most dangerous foe and lurks for him to take his life.

However, it is not merely the thirst for power that moves Saul to stubborn battle for the crown that is already tottering on his head. His heart is filled to overflowing with great love for his people, which he united out of the separated tribes. He sees in it the only and chosen people, and to reign over such a nation is the greatest privilege. To fight for such a throne is a matter of honor, a question of glory and self-respect. Uncon-sciously the miserable king senses that the battle is lost. Never-theless, he carries the struggle further and obdurately devotes his last mental powers to it.

Increasingly he loses his psychic equilibrium in this hopeless struggle. He, who had compassion on the weaponless, captured foe, makes a blood bath among the innocent priests of Nob. All his life he had fought against the witches and sorcerers who mislead the people. And now he himself turns, in the last night before his tragic end, to the witch of En-Dor in order to hear the final decree from the dead lips of the "seer," strong as iron, whom the witch had summoned out of the valley of shades. The tragic battle is soon finished. Immediately, at the begin-ning, Saul, surrounded by the enemy warriors, meets his death —his true redeemer and liberator. The proud, heroic battler, however, falls by his own hand. His bleeding heart is stabbed through by his own sword. "Tell my people," he says to his weapon-bearer "that its king has fallen by his own sword, not at the hands of the Philistines."

Besides the central figure, several female figures in *Meluchat Sha'ul* are portrayed with special success—above all, Saul's wife Ahinoam. In gentle, tender tones the poet portrays not the queen, but the suffering woman who shares the pain of her unfortunate husband. And later appears in the background the silhouette of another suffering woman, the young Michal, whose heart bleeds in the struggle between two great loves—love for her mentally ill father and for her beloved David, the handsome, noble hero of Bethlehem.

Much attention is also merited by Joseph Ha-Ephrati's language and verse construction. Several of Saul's monologues, with their powerful speech and mighty lines polished like steel, sustain comparison with Moses Ḥayyim Luzzatto's masterful verses. The colorful and unique scene at night[19] with the witch of En-Dor is a totally new phenomenon in Hebrew literature. It is certainly a great loss for this literature that Joseph Ha-Ephrati's first drama was also his swan song. In the premature grave of the poet who died so young the rising neo-Hebrew poetry buried one of its loveliest hopes.[20]

We already know that at the same time that Tropplowitz's hero-drama of the biblical era appeared, successful attempts were also made to create "family portraits" and comedies of modern life. These attempts must be credited to the editors of *Ha-Meassef*, Isaac Euchel and Aaron Wolfsohn-Halle. However, these "family portraits" were written not in Hebrew but in Yiddish. We have seen how Euchel and Wolfsohn fight in their comedies not only against the orthodox Jews and the old way of life but also against the "false" and "spurious" enlighteners who consider "frivolity as enlightenment and luxury as freedom." However, in Hebrew literature also attacks were made from various sides on the tendencies discernible in the Berlin Haskalah after Mendelssohn's death. The most characteristic thing in this connection is that these attacks were made not only by the orthodox camp but also by men who declared themselves Mendelssohn's ardent admirers and preached enlightenment and education.

19. On this theme, see the previous volume, p. 339.
20. While the author was still alive (in 1801) a certain Naftali Hirsch bar David translated *Meluchat Sha'ul* into Yiddish under the title *Gedulat David U-Meluchat Sha'ul*. The translation is talentless and distorted. Nevertheless, it enjoyed a certain success and went through several editions.

In the tracts and battle documents with which the orthodox issued forth against the "enlighteners," one major motif is naturally dominant: fear of anything new, of everything not hallowed by tradition, by the custom of the fathers. However, at times they set forth other motifs which have a cultural-historical interest. Typical in this respect, for instance, is the anonymous brochure *Olam Ḥadash*,[21] published in London in 1789. The unknown author deplores the fact that in recent times heretics and deniers who call themselves "of the present, or new, world" *(olam ḥadash)* have increased. They wish to nullify our sacred Torah, and there are among them those who declare that our teacher Moses was a lawgiver just like other lawgivers and kings who used to issue statutes according to the custom of their lands. They argue that God's will is only that a person should do no evil to another, but the matter of food that is not permitted, the prohibition against eating meat with milk, fasting, the matter of unleavened bread on Passover, and the like—all these are of no concern to Him.

These "men of the present day," the author further complains, cast off the yoke of Heaven. The behavior of our fathers is repugnant to them; they say it is a matter of foolish custom. And so they change their clothing, their whole mode of conduct, their language. They speak and read only "the language of priests" *(galaḥut)*. They are ashamed of everything that reminds them of Jewishness, for they are terribly afraid that— God forbid—it will be recognized that they are Jews, and this, after all, may hurt their livelihood. They literally crawl out of their skins only to be like the peoples of the world. To speak Yiddish is, among them, the supreme disgrace. They speak only the language of the gentiles, sometimes French—this is the most honored language among them—sometimes, High German. Even the little children, as soon as they can say "mama" and "papa," are already taught the language of the gentiles and are raised "according to the way of the gentiles."

The author adds in this connection with a certain sarcasm that their entire intent is not to be recognized as Jews; however, this is of no avail. People know very well whence they derive. They wish to forget that we are in bitter exile and great degradation; they bedeck themselves and make themselves

21. Because *Olam Ḥadash* is rare and difficult to find, we quote here the title-page (in full): "This booklet is called *New World (Olam Ḥadash)* and is called *Upside-Down World (Olam Hafuch)*, because of the new and changed things, as is explained within, that were found and seen in our time. May the Lord turn and correct our heart for good. Printed in London in the year 1789."

great. They always hope that they will be granted honorable positions. But these are empty dreams; they will not even be permitted to be cowherds. In any case, we will not be granted any other position that can provide a bit of a livelihood, even if we are stuffed with science and knowledge. This chasing after the newest fashions, this self-adornment of their women with great luxury, these high-towered, powdered perukes on their heads—all such things merely enrage the peoples of the world powerfully against us. The latter say with annoyance that it is now literally impossible to distinguish between a Jew and the greatest lord. Do you still complain—they argue—that you are in exile? Would that our children were in such exile!

We noted earlier that not only the orthodox issued forth against the "men of the present world" *(olam ḥadash)*, against the Berlin *Aufklärer*, but also those who themselves struggled for education and knowledge. At the same time that Euchel's and Wolfsohn's satires against "false" and "spurious" enlightenment appeared, the young Naḥman bar Simḥah Barash published (Berlin, 1796) his pamphlet *Ein Mishpat*. He speaks very enthusiastically of Mendelssohn and the latter's translation of the Pentateuch. Mendelssohn, Barash declares, "translated the Torah for us into a noble, fine language, while before him we spoke in a confused, corrupt language that made us a shame and a mockery. The Bible was, among us, like a sealed book, because the Hebrew language and its rules were very little understood in our midst." "God," Barash exclaims emotively, "said: 'Let there be light!', and Moses [Mendelssohn] was born. He is the father of all Bible translators. He pointed out to us the right way in the wilderness of life." But a misfortune occurred: Moses the godly man died, and after his death the chief spokesmen became petty, worthless little souls. They speak from all pulpits, preach overthrow of the Torah, blaspheme Holy Scripture and the words of the great prophets. They even assert: This is the Torah which Moses [Mendelssohn] has commanded us.

After Moses' death, the author continues, many began to grope about. They assembled around Aaron;[22] the latter produced for them the golden calf, and everyone dances around the new idol. These "assembled ones" (a reference to the Meassefim) stormed the wall which our sages built throughout the generations. Like the pernicious little foxes, they break in through all the splits and fissures. They speak mockingly of the ordinances of our sages, declare everything superstition. They

22. An allusion to Aaron Wolfsohn, who then published his *Siḥah Be-Eretz Ha-Ḥayyim*.

assert that it was not God who commanded Moses the precepts of the Torah; Moses himself fabricated them, and the whole Torah is merely a collection of Jewish customs. They publicly desecrate the Sabbath, cast off all the commandments of the Torah, gorge themselves and guzzle drink, follow all the desires of their heart—and all this is called among them "a generation of knowledge and a wise and understanding people." They are always establishing societies, societies of friendship and love;[23] but the friendship and fraternity consist only in spending the nights merrily with full beakers of wine and doing what their heart desires without hindrance. The author exclaims bitterly: "See, O God, how we have become a shame! Fallen is the crown from our head. There is no more ben Menahem [Mendelssohn] who renewed and refreshed the spirit of our people."

The harbingers of the Haskalah period in Lithuania and Poland, of whom we spoke at length in the last chapters of the sixth volume, also issued forth against the tendencies which the Berlin enlightenment assumed after Mendelssohn's death.

We observed earlier[24] the reasons why a controversy between Mendelssohn and the grammarian Solomon Dubno broke out. In the letter quoted above, Dubno notes explicitly that several collaborators whom Mendelssohn involved in the Torah commentary *(Biur)* are highly suspicious persons, for they have entirely cast off the yoke of the Torah and of them it has truly been said, "Turn away from the tents of these wicked men."

The incident with Solomon Dubno was merely a harbinger of the conflict that had to become ever sharper as time went on, for the tendencies which Dubno already noted—free thinking and the public rejection of the ritual laws of the Torah and the customs hallowed by tradition—assumed considerably more prominent forms after Mendelssohn's death. This had to evoke an emphatic protest on the part of the pioneers of enlightenment who appeared in Lithuania and Poland in the second half of the eighteenth century. These men grew up in a social and cultural environment different from that of the *maskilim* of Berlin. Among them the roots binding them to the ancient culture of their people and to the heritage of their fathers still remained in full strength.

They, too, were "truth seekers," but moderate and irenically

23. An allusion to *Die Gesellschaft der Freunde* that Isaac Euchel, Aaron Wolfsohn, and others founded in the winter of 1791–1792.
24. See above, pp. 43ff.

minded. They were certain that the real truth can in no way contradict the cultural heritage of their people, the Torah of their ancestors. They merely sought new means of finding the truth hidden in the sacred Jewish books, of bringing it closer and making it comprehensible to the whole people. And they were sure that to achieve this goal—and in this consisted their enlightening role—one must utilize knowledge and education. Not to wrest themselves out of their own familiar environment was their desire, but to widen it, to ventilate it, to open the closed shutters so that more light might penetrate and dispel the dark shadows.

We noted with what annoyance and disgust one of these representatives of culture, the author of *Sefer Ha-Berit*,[25] regarded the materialist-rationalist views of his time.

Phineḥas Hurwitz, who lived for some time in Berlin, had opportunity to become closely acquainted with the radically rationalist tendencies that appeared ever more clearly in the enlightening circles, and he attacked them in a sharp polemic in his *Sefer Ha-Berit*, published in 1797. We have already noted[26] the anger with which Hurwitz protested against the attempt to explain "the giving of the Torah" in purely "rationalist fashion" and to represent Moses, the "father of the prophets," as an overly subtle politician, versed in the natural sciences, who, in an extremely ingenious way, "deceived the whole generation of the wilderness." Such indignant pages against the heretical "breakers forth among the people" are found in very considerable measure in *Sefer Ha-Berit*. "Superficial philosophical ideas," Phineḥas Hurwitz laments,

now dominate many minds. Basing themselves on these ideas, they transgress all the laws of the Torah. But they are not content with themselves sinning; they also wish to make many others sin. They publicly preach their heretical ideas. They print and distribute their writings to the Jewish youth, constantly praise philosophical speculation and the greatness of human reason. Their whole intent is to hunt for souls, to lure young hearts into the nets of heresy . . . And ever greater among the people grows the number of those bitten by the deceiving serpent, and the plague becomes increasingly widespread . . . I cannot look on at how they turn the youth away from faith and bow down only before reason. I do not address the heretics, for I know very well that "all who come to her will not return." They are already dried-out pages, living corpses. I do not speak to the dead but

25. See our *History*, Vol. VI, pp. 260ff.
26. *Ibid.*

to the children of Israel who have not yet let themselves be seduced by the wicked. It is them whom I warn that they should not be persuaded by the seducers and not follow their ways.[27]

With no less indignation did Jehudah Loeb Margolioth, the author of *Or Olam* and *Tal Orot*, issue forth against the radically rationalist tendencies of the *Aufklärer*. We have already noted[28] that Margolioth declared that the complaint that philosophy and speculation lead man away from the right path and bring him to heresy is "a disgusting lie." However, he deplores the "corruption of the generations" and indicates that the "breakers forth" who throw off religious commandments out of profligacy and licentiousness have increased among us. They assert that they do so because "we are wise in the study of philosophy." Philosophical ideas presumably have enlightened them and opened their eyes.[29]

Especially interesting in this respect is Marglioth's polemic work *Atzei Eden*, published in 1802. Margolioth here attacks the acknowledged founders and guides of the Berlin Haskalah— Moses Mendelssohn and his important work *Jerusalem*.[30] Margolioth can in no way concur with Mendelssohn's basic thesis that the Torah of Moses does not command Jews to *believe* in certain dogmas, but merely commands them to *fulfill* the precepts and statutes that elevate human life and bring man temporal and eternal happiness. In this connection, he adduces arguments intended to show that in the Jewish religion there are also precepts which demand not merely *doing* but *believing* as well. With special sharpness he attacks Mendelssohn's thesis that the Jewish people possesses a divinely revealed *legislation* but not a *religious revelation*, and that the "eternal truths" do not, in fact, require confirmation through miracles and wonders, since they are "laws of reason" based on the human mind.

Margolioth can in no way agree with Mendelssohn's endeavor to set forth man's critical intellect as the supreme tribunal in matters of belief and to establish in purely rationalist fashion the necessity and "rationality" of Jewish ritual. "How, for instance," he asks, "is it possible to explain in a rationalist way that, through the priest's sprinkling of himself and the altar with the blood of the sacrifice, the abundance of holiness

27. *Sefer Ha-Berit,* 1797, folio 117a.
28. See our *History,* Vol. VI, p. 258.
29. *Tal Orot,* 1843, 61.
30. An interesting feature: Margolioth indicates, incidentally, that he also gave a special sermon in which he polemicized against the theses of Mendelssohn's *Jerusalem.*

is aroused?" He is firmly persuaded that in the Torah are interwoven laws and commandments that regulate both man's deeds and his beliefs. The religious ritual and cultic ceremonial is closely bound up not only with directing man's dealings and conduct but also with his dogmas of faith.

Like Solomon Maimon in his *Lebensgeschichte*,[31] Margolioth also criticizes Mendelssohn's proposition about the competence and authority of a religious community. To be sure, he explains, the state ought to maintain the principle of complete freedom of conscience. But just as the state has the right to demand that its citizens fulfill everything necessary for the general good, so also the religious community must be given the right to demand of its members that they not publicly violate the laws of the religion and reject the firmly established religious cult. If a Jew is a member of a religious community, Margolioth asserts, he does not have the right openly to transgress its religious laws and dogmas.

It is interesting to note that our author deems it necessary to stress that he distinguishes Mendelssohn as a *person* from the tendencies so prominently carried through in his *Jerusalem*. Margolioth knows very well of Mendelssohn's "rent in the heart." He knows that Mendelssohn the rationalist nevertheless remains the *Stockjude*, or complete Jew, who concludes that the "laws, prescriptions, commandments and rules of life" of the Torah of Moses must remain unalterable and are eternally obligatory on every member of the Jewish people. Indeed, Margolioth notes in this connection that though he was not personally acquainted with Mendelssohn, he knows that the latter did not cast off the yoke of the commandments.[32] But the rationalist ideas that Mendelssohn expressed—these, he asserts, undermined faith among his followers.

Margolioth wrote his *Atzei Eden* when he already lived in Frankfurt-Am-Oder and had opportunity to become intimately familiar with the new tendencies that manifested themselves at the end of the eighteenth century in the progressive Jewish circles of Prussia. He could see with his own eyes how the enlightenment movement and the battle for reform and equal civic rights were interwoven with the epidemic of conversions which then grew with frightening rapidity in the larger Prussian communities. "The number of those who

31. See above, pp. 129ff.
32. *Atzei Eden*, 7: "Even though I did not know him in life myself, I suspected of him that the foundation of the faith was weakened by his hand."

thirstily drink the philosophical ideas drawn from the peoples of the earth keeps growing," Margolioth laments.

> They spend all their time with these and cast off the yoke of the Torah entirely. And if you try to reprove one of them, asking why he abandons the Torah, he replies proudly: I occupy myself with the most important thing that can be, with seeking out God *(ḥakirot elohut).* After all, I thereby fulfill the great commandment: "Know thou the God of thy father and serve him" (I Chronicles 28:9).[33]

In this connection, Margolioth provides a picture, interesting from the cultural-historical point of view, of how the enlightenment process took place in his milieu among many of the young Jewish students.

Those who wished to tear themselves out of the constricted four cubits of the law and strove for European education, Margolioth relates, at first came with arguments such as the following: Our Torah is very precious to us, but Torah with a worldly occupation is very good *(tov Torah im derech eretz).* After all, it is written: "It is a wise and understanding people." But we and our generation are void of all knowledge whatsoever. We speak stammeringly in a corrupted language. The people around us regard us with contempt as wild men. And precisely in our generation we see how many of our neighbors wish to live with us in peace and endeavor to regard us with love and friendship. Why, then, should we, through our ignorance, destroy the bond and make ourselves despised by the nations of the world?

But, Margolioth further relates, as soon as they obtained a taste of contemporary philosophic ideas, the bond with the religion of their fathers was immediately weakened. They cast off all the commandments and precepts, and refuse to know of the customs of the fathers. More than anything else they fear being considered backward and insufficiently enlightened. So they do everything to demonstrate that the tree of knowledge has opened their eyes, that they have penetrated into the gates of wisdom; and, thanks to the light of knowledge, they have persuaded themselves that the teaching we have obtained as a legacy from our ancestors is false and the heavy yoke of tradition must be cast off. Moreover, they publicly preach their sinful ideas. They desire to catch as many people as possible in their nets. They wish to mislead the whole people into follow-

---

33. *Atzei Eden,* 15–16.

ing in their ways.[34] "Bitterly my heart laments," Margolioth exclaims, "when I recall how many of my people have been lost."

Margolioth dwells especially on a foreign writer who, in his view, had a particularly noxious effect on the Jewish youth of his generation. The author of *Atzei Eden*, to be sure, does not name this writer, but it is not difficult that he means none other than Voltaire.

"With special rapidity," Margolioth emphasizes,

do those who have absorbed the poison of the well-known heretic who lived in the land of France remove themselves from the faith. He was the chief spokesman who spread his pernicious ideas over the whole world. Arrogantly he came forward and mocked all religions. Everywhere he sowed his poisonous seeds. Enormous is the number of those whom he seduced with his works when he was still alive, and also after his death ... He made all the religions of Europe the target of his hatred, bespattered them with his bitter mockery, wished to shatter and destroy them ... .[35]

While Phineḥas Hurwitz, Jehudah Loeb Margolioth, and their collaborators were carrying on a battle against the "heretical" tendencies, the ideas of the Berlin Haskalah began gradually, in lines so thin that they were barely discernible, to penetrate into the Lithuanian-Polish provinces[36] which had just come, following the partition of Poland, under the rule of czarist Russia. Typical in this respect is the physician Jacob Elijah Frank, a practitioner in the White Russian town of Kreslavka (Kraslava), who obtained his medical education in Germany. In his memorandum[37] "Can a Jew Become a Loyal and Useful Citizen," which he submitted in 1800 to Gavril Romanovich Derzhavin, this doctor raised on the Berlin Haskalah explains the developmental history of the Jewish faith in the following naively "rationalist" fashion: Judaism in its pristine form based itself on simple Deism and on the demands of pure morality. The later teachers of the Jewish people, some of whom were dreamers, i.e., *misled deceivers*, and some *common*

34. *Ibid.*
35. *Ibid.*, 16.
36. The first year's issues of *Ha-Meassef*, 1785–1788 had the following subscribers in Poland and Lithuania. In Vilna, Joseph Elyehs (two copies), the doctor Jacob Lubschitz, Michael Gordon, Shemaiah Berlin; in Shklov, Yoshea bar Roizes; in Lublin, Jacob ben Naftali; in Warsaw, Simeon Hollender.
37. Published by J. Hessen in his "Jews in Russia" (Russian), pp. 446–448.

deceivers, crippled and disfigured the true spirit of Jewish doctrine through mystical Talmudic commentaries to the Biblical text. They obscured the concepts of truth and falsehood. Instead of practical virtues, useful for life, they introduced crude, foolish prayers and spiritless and senseless ordinances. For egotistic motives and petty personal profit they led the blinded people through the hallowed darkness of superstition wherever they wished.

But this Doctor Frank was not alone. He found like-minded colleagues among the members of the Shklov circle which played such an important role among the pioneers of Haskalah in Lithuania and White Russia.[38] We noted in the sixth volume what an important center of commerce Shklov became after the last quarter of the eighteenth century, following the accession of the whole region to Russia with the first partition of Poland. Wealthy Jewish merchants of Shklov carried on business with Moscow, St. Petersburg, and other important Russian centers. Some of these merchants had social relationships with high Russian officials, for instance, the previously mentioned Joshua Zeitlin and Nathan Note Notkin who were respected by the well known Prince Grigori Aleksandrovich Potemkin and consequently became large-scale purveyors and military contractors for the Russian army. These relationships brought it about that, as early as the end of the eighteenth century, a small colony of Jews migrating from Shklov was formed in St. Petersburg.

The following point is highly significant. Out of nine persons who, in 1800, made an agreement in St. Petersburg with the church administration of the local German colony about obtaining a definite place for a Jewish cemetery, five explicitly note that they came from Shklov.[39] Already in the last years of Catherine II's reign Joshua Zeitlin's son-in-law, Abraham Peretz, a rich government purveyor and tax-farmer *(otkupshtshik)* who had a close relationship with Speranski, Kankrin, and other Russian officials, settled in St. Petersburg. Peretz invited to Petersburg the well known pioneer of Haskalah, Mendel Levin (Lefin), as a tutor for his son. With Peretz from Shklov to Petersburg came his good friend Jehudah Leib Nevakhovich[40] and the above-mentioned wealthy military contractor

38. See our *History*, Vol. VI, p. 281.
39. L. Gordon, "Toward a History of the Jewish Settlement in Petersburg" (Russian; in *Voskhod*, 1881, II).
40. He was born in Letichev in the Ukraine in 1776. Hence, he used to sign himself Jehudah Leib ben Noah of Letichev.

Nathan Note of Shklov. Also living in Petersburg at that time was the medical doctor Zaleman and the European-educated Ettinger.[41]

Thus, a small Jewish colony which, in a certain respect, may be considered a "miniature" *(ze'er anpin)* of the Berlin community was formed in St. Petersburg. The role of the Berlin financiers and bankers was played in Petersburg by such wealthy tax-farmers and purveyors as Peretz and Notkin. Rich and enterprising, they had acquaintanceship with the most prominent strata of Christian society. Raised on the literature of the Berlin enlighteners and coming into daily contact with the Russian nobility and prominent officials, the European-educated merchants also felt as painfully as their brethren in Berlin not only the social-legal oppression of the Jewish people but also the contempt and cold hostility with which Christian society regarded the very name Jew. This feeling of bitterness soon obtained its literary redress and found its full expression, thanks to the above-mentioned Jehudah Leib Nevakhovich.

In 1803 when, by order of the czar, a committee was formed for the purpose of considering the question of regulating the legal-economic condition of the Jews, special deputies from various Jewish communities were invited to the capital for this purpose. This made a strong impression on the small Jewish colony of Petersburg. As the *Toleranzpatent* of Joseph II in his day evoked enormous enthusiasm among the *Aufklärer* of Berlin, so the *maskilim* of Petersburg praised Alexander I's decree to the skies and greeted him as the liberator and redeemer of the Jewish people. When the Jewish deputies traveled to Petersburg and the committee began its sessions, Nevakhovich published (in 1803) his Russian pamphlet dedicated to Kotshubey, the Minister of the Interior, and entitled *Vopl' dscheri yudeyskoy*, the first Russian document written by the hand of a Jew. A year later (1804) Nevakhovich reprinted his work in Shklov in Hebrew translation under the title *Kol Shavat Bat Yehudah, Ve-Hi Melitzah Yesharah Avur Am Yehudah, Le-Hasir Mi-Menu Telunot Ha-Ammim.*[42]

Despite the fact that the Russian text appeared before the Hebrew, it is beyond doubt that several parts, for instance, "Ma'amar Sinat Ha-Datot Ve-Emet Ve-Shalom," were originally written in Hebrew. In the Hebrew style of *Kol Shavat Bat*

41. Zaleman and Ettinger are noted among the subscribers to *Ha-Meassef* for the year 1809.
42. The work is reprinted in *He-Avar*, II, 1918.

Jehudah Leib Nevakhovich

Yehudah, as well as in the author's entire world-view, the influence of the Meassefim is strongly discernible. In the preface to the Hebrew translation, as well as in the work itself, the author speaks with great enthusiasm of the eighteenth *saeculum* (century) as of "a generation of knowledge, the like of which has not been seen among the people from the day that man appeared on the earth," a "generation of science, of love for mankind, of democratic modesty, when powerful and mighty lords listen to the truth from the mouths of small and petty people, a generation whose like is not to be found in history, a generation in which the star of Russia which has accepted me, the daughter of Judah, as its daughter has risen high."[43]

In the above-mentioned "Ma'amar Sinat Ha-Datot" the view is set forth that religious hatred *(sinat ha-dat)* is driven out of Europe with mockery. There peace and justice now reign, and all the peoples live fraternally and happily under their protection. Nevakhovich sees as one of the most glorious harbingers of the commencement of this bright era Alexander's order to establish the abovementioned "Committee," which, according to the author's firm conviction, will occupy itself "with improving the condition of the unfortunate Jews and raising them to the high levels of happiness and well-being." Emotively he exclaims: Who can tell, who can describe, all the benefits which this empire (Russia) has given us, or its great kindness to the homeless Jews? All these gracious acts are deeply inscribed in my heart; I will never forget them and will always praise the children of Russia and raise my voice to tell all other peoples of their righteousness.[44]

Proudly the author addresses the "foreigners" *(chuzhez-'emtsi);*

And you, proud and jealous foreigners, who exult in your culture and did, indeed, enter into the gates of knowledge considerably earlier than the Russians; nevertheless, the latter have overtaken you in tolerance and love for mankind . . . You who glory in your freedoms and your republics—come here to these snow-covered plains and first learn to know true love for mankind.[45]

The author of *Kol Shavat Bat Yehudah* attempts to dream while awake; what he desires, he considers as having already happened and been accomplished. He portrays how the Jew

43. *Kol Shavat Bat Yehudah,* 4, 11.
44. *Ibid.,* 34.
45. *Ibid.,* 7, 32–33, 35; Russian text, 60, 63.

who is everywhere a mockery and a laughter and has been hurled like a piece of chaff through a stream from land to land finally found rest on the Russian borders. There the sun of compassion rose shining before him. The two-headed eagle spreads its wings lovingly over him. Forgotten is the contemptuous name *Zhid,* and he is respectfully called "Hebrew." He is permitted to settle freely in the land and placed in a position of equality with all other peoples.[46]

Nevakhovich, however, was not at all a "dreamer of the ghetto" but a practical businessman who had lived in recent years exclusively in the milieu of the "loving Russians;" he knew very well how far removed these still were from "tolerant" and "friendly" relationships with Jews. And so, in fact, he addressed the "beloved sons of Russia" with a humble petition that they accept the "bitter cry" of the miserable "daughter of Jehudah:" To you, you sons of Russia who love mankind, who love peace and strive for tolerance, to you I call. Before you I pour out my embittered heart. Why are the Jews so shamed and despised? Why does the name Jew arouse wrath and hatred? I have become a shame and a mockery among the nations. They frighten their little children with me . . . O Christians, you are renowned for your virtues of compassion and graciousness. Have mercy upon us. Turn your noble hearts to us. Why are we so despised by you? What will you gain if we were to abandon the religion of our fathers in order to enjoy life? Have you not heard of the words that Moses Mendelssohn, our famous writer, addressed in his *Jerusalem* to his Christian fellow-citizens: "We cannot, after all, abandon our faith sincerely and wholeheartedly. What, then, would you gain by increasing non-believing brethren among yourselves?"[47] Why do you so shame the house of Israel? Why do you drive it out of your hearts?

How proud I would be if you would call me "brother" and "fellow-citizen." Dear children of the northland, see how our justice-loving kings teach you to live in peace with all the peoples that dwell together with you. Fulfill their will . . . In this time, when all the nations of Europe have entered into bonds of peace and fraternity, the house of Israel remains a mockery and derision. Who can describe this anguish? Who can recount the pain of the man who is despised by everyone? If all the thunders of the colossal storm and the angry, roaring

46. *Ibid.,* 34.
47. *Vopl' dscheri yudeyskoy,* 10, 12, 16.

sea were poured together with the cries of woe of this miserable, shamed person, then perhaps men would first have some notion of the pain of his soul . . . Greatly embittered is my heart and I beg mercy.[48]

It is characteristic that Nevakhovich writes almost as if he did not notice the catastrophic distress and economic disabilities of the Jewish populace in the Pale of Settlement. He, the cultivated intellectual, complains mainly of the fact that he "is removed from the hearts of his fellow-citizens" when he is, after all, so proud that he can call the Russians "fellow citizens." Hence, he humbly pours out his bitter heart before the "beloved Russians" and the "philanthropic Russians." He begs "graciousness from the cultured men." With tears he pleads for their good will.

In this fashion *Kol Shavat Bat Yehudah* is in fact transformed into a *cri de coeur* of an intelligent "son of Judah" who humbly begs the "noble Russians" to cast off the old prejudices, to turn their "gentle hearts" to the cultured fellow-citizens of Jewish faith and generously accept them into their society.

The "beloved Russians," however, remained deaf to the "cry of woe" of *Bat Yehudah*. The "Statute Concerning the Jews," published in 1804 with the confirmation of the "gracious king" and "redeemer"[49] Alexander I, manifested itself not as a charter of freedom but as a code of punishment, as a charter of disabilities which magnified the distress and poverty of the Jewish populace. Then the author of *Kol Shavat Bat Yehudah* forgot Mendelssohn's words that he himself had quoted, and from Jehudah Leib ben Noah he was transformed into Lev Nikolaevich Nevakhovich and, together with his friend Peretz, found the fraternity that he desired with his "fellow-citizens" in the bosom of the Orthodox Church.[50]

Thus, the logic of life led in the small colony of St. Petersburg to the same results as in the Prussian capital, Berlin: apostasy and assimilation.

This was a harbinger of the crisis, the turning point in the spiritual and intellectual tendencies of Lithuanian-White Russian Jewry. The peaceful bond between Torah and knowledge, between piety and enlightenment, fell apart. The motto of the

48. *Ibid.*, 19, 27.

49. *Kol Shavat Bat Yehudah*, 36, where Alexander I is greeted: "This is our king and this is our redeemer."

50. Nevakhovich later participated in Russian literature and attained renown with his play *Suliota* which was played in St. Petersburg with great success (on this see the *Memoirs* of the artist Karatigin, Vol. I, 15–16).

Vilna Gaon that every defect of knowledge in the secular sciences produces a hundredfold defect in studying the Torah was decisively rejected. Every branch of knowledge, all the secular sciences, were declared pure heresy. The pioneer of Haskalah and knowledge-hungry Rabbi Solomon Chelm,[51] who was greatly respected in his generation by everyone, was declared a heretic and denier in the subsequent generation because of his love for science and his self-deprecation before the author of *A Guide for the Perplexed*. And it was at this time that the legend to the effect that Chelm wrote his commentary to Maimonides precisely on the Sabbath was created.

On the foreground of Jewish life appeared a powerful new movement that won many thousands of hearts. The motto of this movement was not science but pure wonderment, not reason but emotion and exalted enthusiasm. And the creator and leader of this movement, who lived in the middle of the eighteenth century, was himself transformed into a miracle, a legendary hero and half-mythical personality who bore the name Israel Baal Shem Tov. Of him we shall speak in the subsequent part of this *History*.

51. See our *History*, Vol. VI, pp. 241ff.

BIBLIOGRAPHICAL NOTES

The Berlin Haskalah

CHAPTER ONE

THE JEWS OF BERLIN AND MOSES MENDELS-SOHN

On the rise of the Jewish community in Berlin in the eighteenth and nineteenth centuries see Ludwig Geiger, *Berlin 1688–1840*, 2 vols. (1895); idem, *Geschichte der Juden in Berlin*, 2 vols. (1871); R. Lewin, "Die Judengesetzgebung Friedrich Wilhelms II," *MGWJ*, LVII (1913), 74–98, 211–34, 363–72, 461–81, 567–90; Raphael Mahler, *Divrei Yemei Yisrael: Dorot Aharonim*, Vol. II (1954); J. Meisl (ed.), *Pinkas Kehillat Berlin 1723–1854—Protokollbuch der jüdischen Gemeinde Berlin* (Hebrew and German, 1962); idem, in *Arim Ve-Immahot Be-Yisrael*, Vol. I (1946), 80–140; H.G. Sellenthin, *Geschichte der Juden in Berlin* (1959); E.L. Landshuth, *Toledot Anshei Shem* (1884); L. Davidsohn, *Beiträge zur Sozial- und Wirtschaftsgeschichte der Berliner Juden vor der Emanzipation* (1920); M. Stern, *Beiträge zur Geschichte der jüdischen Gemeinde zu Berlin*, 6 vols. (1926–34); S. Stern, *Der preussische Staat und die Juden*, 2 vols. (1925, reprinted 1962); S. Stern-Täubler, "The Jews in the Economic Policy of Frederick the Great," *Jewish Social Studies*, XI (1949), 129–52; D. Friedländer, *Akten-Stücke die Reform der jüdischen Kolonien in den Preussischen Staaten betreffend* (1793); I. Freund, *Die Emanzipation der Juden in Preussen*, 2 vols. (1912); H. Rachel, *Das Berliner Wirtschaftsleben im Zeitalter des Frühkapitalismus* (1931); H. Rachel et. al., *Berliner Grosskaufleute und Kapitalisten*, 3 vols. (1934–39); J. Jacobson (ed.), *Die Judenbürger-bücher der Stadt Berlin, 1809–1851* (1962); M. Sinasohn (ed.), *Adas Jisroel, Berlin* (1966); I. Eisenstein-Barzillay, "The Ideology of the Berlin Haskalah," *PAAJR*, XXV (1956), 1–37, XXIX (1960–61), 17–54; and E. Hurwicz, in *Yearbook of the Leo Baeck Institute*, XII (1967), 85–102.

On the German Enlightenment and the beginning of Haskalah in German Jewry, see Isaiah Berlin, *The Age of Enlightenment* (1956); Ernst Cassirer, *The Philosophy of the Enlightenment*, trans. Fritz C.A. Koelln and James P. Pettegrove (1955); Wilhelm Dilthey, *Friedrich der Grosse und die deutsche Aufklärung*, Vol. III of *Gesammelte Schriften* (1927); Jacob Katz, *Tradition and Crisis: Jewish Society at the End of the Middle Ages* (1961); idem, *Die Entstehung der Judenassimilation in Deutschland und deren Ideologie* (1935); M. Wiener, *Jüdische Religion im Zeitalter der Emanzipation* (1933); S. Stern-Täubler, "The Jew in the Transition from Ghetto to Emancipation," *Historia Judaica*, II (1940), 102–19; idem, "Die Judenfrage in der Ideologie der Aufklärung und Romantik," *Der Morgen*, XI (1935), 339–48; A. Shohet, "Beginnings of the Haskalah Among German Jewry" [Hebrew], *Molad*, XXIII (1965), 328–34; idem, *Im Ḥilufei Tekufot: Reshit Ha-Haskalah Be-Yahadut Germania* (1960); Isaac Eisenstein-Barzillay, "The Jew in the Literature of the Enlightenment," *Jewish Social Studies*, (1956), 243–61; idem, "The Background of the Berlin Haskalah," pp. 183–97 in *Essays on Jewish Life and Thought Presented in Honor of Salo Wittmayer Baron* (1959); idem, "The Ideology of the Berlin Haskalah," *PAAJR*, XXV (1956), 1–37; idem, "The Treatment of the Jewish Religion in the Literature of the Berlin Haskalah," *PAAJR*, XXIV (1955), 39–68; idem, "National and Anti-National Trends in the Berlin Haskalah," *Jewish Social Studies*, XXI (1959), 165–92; and M. Eliav, *Ha-Ḥinnuch Ha-Yehudi Be-Germania Be-Yemei Ha-Haskalah Veha-Imantsipatsia* (1960).

Moses Mendelssohn's collected works were first printed in *Gesammelte Schriften*, ed. G.B. Mendelssohn, 7 vols., Leipzig (1843–45). A splendid, but incomplete, new edition of Mendelssohn's collected works was published in *Gesammelte Schriften*, *Jubiläumsausgabe*, ed. I. Elbogen, J. Guttmann, and K. Mittwoch, 7 vols., Berlin, Breslau (1929–38).

The most recent and best biography of Mendelssohn is Alexander Altmann, *Moses Mendelssohn: A Biographical Study* (1973).

On the life and thought of Moses Mendelssohn, see also H.M.Z. Meyer, *Moses Mendelssohn Bibliographie* (1965); S. Shunami, *Bibliography of Jewish Bibliographies*, 2nd ed. (1965), No. 5, 3953–57; B. Badt-Strauss: *Moses Mendelssohn, der Mensch und das Werk* (1929); B. Berwin, *Moses Mendelssohn im Urteil seiner Zeitgenossen* (1919); I.A. Euchel; *Toledot Rabbenu Ha-Ḥacham Mosheh Ben Menaḥem* (1788); M. Kayserling, *Moses Mendelssohn, sein Leben und seine Werke*, 2nd ed. (1888); H. Walter, *Moses Mendelssohn,*

Critic and Philosopher (1930); M.A. Meyer, *The Origins of the Modern Jew* (1967), 11–56; D. Friedländer, "Moses Mendelssohn," *Biographie Universelle* (1821), 274–82; F.W. Schütz, *Leben und Meinungen Moses Mendelssohn nebst dem Geiste seiner Shcriften in einem kurzen Abrisse dargestellet*, Hamburg, 1787; J. Guttmann, in *Bericht der Hochschule für die Wissenschaft des Judentums*, XLVIII (1931), 31–67; S. Hensel, *Die Familie Mendelssohn 1729–1847*, 18th ed., 2 vols. (1924); A. Kohut, *Moses Mendelssohn und seine Familie*, (1886); N. Rotenstreich, *Jewish Philosophy in Modern Times* (1968), 6–29; idem, in *Yearbook of the Leo Baeck Institute*, XI (1966), 28–41; F. Bamberger, in *MGWJ*, LXXII (1929), 81–92; idem, in K. Wilhelm (ed.), *Wissenschaft des Judentums im deutschen Sprachbereich* (1967), 521–36; *Gedenkbuch für Moses Mendelssohn* (1929); S. Rawidowicz, in: *Sefer Bialik* (1934), 99–140; idem, "Moses Mendelssohn," (Hebrew), *Ha-Tekufah*, XXII (1929), 498–520; J. Katz, in *Zion*, XXIX (1964), 112–32; "Briefe von, an und über Mendelssohn," ed. Ludwig Geiger and R.M. Werner, *Zeitschrift für die Geschichte der Juden in Deutschland*, I (1887), 109–35; "Briefe von, an und über Mendelssohn," ed. Ludwig Geiger, *Jahrbuch für jüdische Geschichte und Literatur*, XX (1917), 85–137; Ludwig Geiger, "Mendelssohniana," *MGWJ*, IL (1905), 349–57; Isaac Eisenstein-Barzillay, "Moses Mendelssohn," *JQR*, LII (1961), 69–93, 175–86; and O. Zarek, *Moses Mendelssohn: Ein jüdisches Schicksal in Deutschland* (1936).

CHAPTER TWO

MENDELSSOHN'S TRANSLATION OF THE TORAH AND HIS PHAEDON

For Mendelssohn's correspondence with Johann Caspar Lavater, see Otto Justus Basilius Hesse, *Schreiben des Herrn Moses Mendelssohn in Berlin an den Herrn Diaconus Lavater zu Zürich, nebst Anmerkungen über dasselbe* (1770).

Many of the items listed above on Mendelssohn's life and thought contain material on the Lavater "affair," as well as on the other topics discussed in this chapter. On the controversy with Lavater, see also Michael Guttmann, "Die Stellung Mendelssohns zur christlichen Umwelt," *MGWJ*, LXXIV (1930), 401–13, and Walter Jacob, "Moses Mendelssohn and the Jewish Christian Dialogue," *Journal of the Central Conference of American Rabbis*, XIII (October, 1965), 45–51.

Mendelssohn's early attempt at producing a Hebrew journal, *Kohelet Musar*, was reprinted, with a Hebrew introduction, by I. Edelstein in *Festschrift zum 50-Jahrigen Bestehen der Franz Josef-Landesrabbinerschule in Budapest*, edited by L. Blau (1927), Hebrew section, pp. 55–76.

On Mordecai Gumpel Schnaber (Levisohn) see article "Levisohn, Georg," in *Encyclopedia Judaica*, Berlin (1934); E. Carmoly, *Histoire des médicins juifs, anciens et modernes* (1844); and M. Steinschneider, *Catalogus Librorum Hebraeorum in Bibliotheca Bodleiana* (1852–60), col. 1618, No. 6146.

Mendelssohn's translation of, and commentary to, the Pentateuch and other books of the Bible are discussed in many of the works on his life and thought noted above. Specific discussions include P. Sandler, *Ha-Biur La-Torah Shel Mosheh Mendelssohn Ve-Si'ato* (1940); H. Englander, "Mendelssohn as Translator and Exegete," *Hebrew Union College Annual*, VI (1929), 327–48; and S. Rawidowicz, "Mendelssohn's Translation of Psalms" [Hebrew], in *Sefer Klausner* (1938), 283–301.

On Solomon Dubno, see Franz Delitzsch, *Zur Geschichte der jüdischen Poesie* (1836), 118; "Correspondence between Joseph Elias of Vilna and David Friedländer of Berlin regarding the Complaints of Solomon Dubno against Moses Mendelssohn" [Hebrew], *Ha-Sharon*, Supplement to *Ha-Karmel*, VII, No. 5 (1866), 36–38; P. Sandler, *Ha-Biur La-Torah Shel Mosheh Mendelssohn Ve-Si'ato* (1940), 16–30; R. Mahler, *Divrei Yemei Yisrael*, IV (1956), 30–33; Beit-Arié, in *Kiryat Sefer*, XL (1964–65), 124–32; A. Marx, *Studies in Jewish History and Booklore* (1944), 219–21; and Zobel, in *Kiryat Sefer*, XVIII (1941–42), 126–32.

Jerusalem and Other Writings by Mendelssohn, edited and translated by Alfred Jospe, appeared in English in 1969. This work includes not only *Jerusalem* but Mendelssohn's most important letter to Lavater and selections from other of his writings dealing with Jewish and general religious matters.

On Mendelssohn's religious views, and especially his understanding of Judaism, see S. Holdheim, *Moses Mendelssohn und die Denk-und Glaubensfreiheit im Judentume* (1859); M. Kayserling, *Moses Mendelssohns philosophische und religiöse Grundsätze mit Hinblick auf Lessing* (1856); E. Cassirer, "Die Idee Religion bei Lessing und Mendelssohn," in *Festgabe zum zehnjährigen Bestehen der Akademie für die Wissenschaft des Judentums* (1929), 22–41; S. Rawidowicz, "The Philosophy of *Jerusalem*" [Hebrew] in *Sefer Bialik*, ed. Jacob Fichmann (1934), 99–140; A. Lewkowitz, "Mendelssohns Anschauung vom Wesen des Judentums," *MGWJ*, LXXIII (1929), 257–63; F. Levy, "Moses Mendelssohn's Ideals of Religion and their Relation to Reform Judaism, *Yearbook* of the

Central Conference of American Rabbis, XXXIX (1929), 351–69; W. Rothman, "Mendelssohn's Character and Philosophy of Religion," *Yearbook* of the Central Conference of American Rabbis, XXXIX (1929), 305–50; M. Lazarus, "Moses Mendelssohn in seinem Verhältnis zu Juden und Judentum," *Deutsche Revue*, XI (1886), 215–28; J. Guttmann, "Mendelssohns Jerusalem und Spinozas Theologisch-Politisches Trakat," *Achtundvierzigster Bericht der Hochschule für die Wissenschaft des Judentums in Berlin*, pp. 33–67; J. Katz, "Le-Mi Anah Mendelssohn Be-Yerushalayim Shelo?," *Zion*, XXIX (1964), 116–132; F. Bamberger, "Mendelssohns Begriff vom Judentum," *Korrespondenzblatt des Vereins zur Gründung und Erhaltung einer Akademie für die Wissenschaft des Judentums*, X (1929), 4–19; idem, "Die geistige Gestalt Moses Mendelssohns," *MGWJ*, LXXIII (1929), 81–92; J. Auerbach, "Moses Mendelssohn und das Judentum," *Zeitschrift für die Geschichte der Juden in Deutschland*, I (1886), 1–44; D. Patterson, "Moses Mendelssohn's Concept of Tolerance," in *Between East and West: Essays Dedicated to the Memory of Bela Horovitz* (1958), 149–63; and A. Altmann, "Moses Mendelssohn, Leibniz, and Spinoza," in *Studies in Rationalism, Judaism, and Universalism in Memory of Leon Roth*, ed. Raphael Loewe (1966).

CHAPTER THREE

NAFTALI HERZ WESSELY AND THE MEASSEFIM

On Naftali Herz Wessely, see W. Zeitlin, *Bibliotheca Hebraica Post-Mendelssohniana* (1891–95), 413–18; E. Carmoly, *Wessely et ses écrits* (1829); W.A. Meisel, *Leben Und Wirken Naphtali Hartwig Wesselys* (1841); S. Mandelkern, "Toledot Naftali Hertz Weisel," *Ha-Asif*, II (1887); J.L. Landau, *Short Lectures on Modern Hebrew Literature*, 2nd ed. (1938), 62–74; J. Klausner, *Historyah Shel Ha-Safrut Ha-Ivrit Ha-Ḥadashah*, 2nd ed., Vol. I (1952), 103–50 (includes bibliography); D. Sadan, *Be-Tzetecha Uve-Oholecha* (1966), 51–54; P. Sandler, *Ha-Biur La-Torah shel Mosheh Mendelssohn Ve-Si'ato* (1940), 136–45; J.S. Raisin, *The Haskalah Movement in Russia* (1913), Index; Z. Fishman, in *Ma'anit* (1926), 17–20 (includes bibliography); and M.S. Samet, in *Meḥkarim . . . Le-Zecher Tzevi Avneri* (1970), 233–57.

On the important Hebrew Haskalah journal *Ha-Meassef*, see S. Bernfeld, *Dor Tahapuchot* (1914); M. Eliav, *Ha-Ḥinnuch Ha-Yehudi Be-Germania* (1960); B.Z. Katz, *Rabbanut, Ḥasidut, Haskalah* (1956), 248–66; J. Klausner, *Historyah Shel Ha-Safrut Ha-*

Ivrit Ha-Ḥadashah, 2nd ed., Vol. I (1952); R. Mahler, *Divrei Yemei Yisrael, Dorot Aḥaronim*, IV (1954), passim; H. Sheli, *Meḥkar Ha-Mikra Be-Safrut Ha-Haskalah* (1942); and B. Wachstein, in *YIVO-Bleter*, XIII (1938).

The first edition of Ephraim Luzzatto's *Eleh Venei Ha-Ne'urim*, limited to one hundred copies, was published in London in 1768. A second edition, with an introduction by M. Letteris, appeared in Vienna in 1839. A more recent edition, with an introduction by J. Fichmann, was published in 1942.

On Ephraim Luzzatto, see J. Fichmann, in *Shirei Ephraim Luzzatto* (1942), V–XX (introduction); J. Klausner, *Historyah Shel Ha-Safrut Ha-Ivrit Ha-Ḥadashah*, 2nd ed., Vol. I (1952), 295–306; R.N. Salomon, in *Transactions* of the Jewish Historical Society of England, IX (1922), 85–102; and C. Roth, in *Sefer Ḥayyim Schirmann* (1970), 367–70.

CHAPTER FOUR

MENDELSSOHN'S DISCIPLES; THE PERIOD AFTER HIS DEATH

Aaron Wolfsohn-Halle's *Jeschurun, oder unparteyische Beleuchtung der dem Judentume neuerdings gemachten Vorwürfe* was published in Breslau in 1804.

On Wolfsohn-Halle, see Z. Rejzen, *Leksikon Fun Der Yidisher Literatur*, Vol. I (1928), 904–10; idem, *Fun Mendelssohn biz Mendele* (1923), 25–68; J. Cohn, "Einige Schriftstücke aus dem Nachlasse Aron Wolfssohns," *MGWJ*, XLI (1897), 369–76; Z. Zylbercweig, *Leksikon Fun Yidishn Teater*, Vol. I (1931), 652–4; and B.D. Weinryb, "Aaron Wolfsohn's Dramatic Writings in their Historical Setting," *JQR*, XLVIII (1957–58), 35–50.

Joel (Brill) Loewe's chief work is his introduction and commentary to Moses Mendelssohn's German translation of the Book of Psalms (1785–1788). He also wrote commentaries to Ecclesiastes and Jonah and, with Aaron Wolfsohn-Halle, to the Song of Songs in Mendelssohn's Bible translation project. Only the first part of his *Ammudei Lashon*, an attempt at a scientific grammar of Biblical Hebrew, was published (1794). He was the first to translate the Passover *Haggadah* into German.

On Loewe, see P. Sandler, *Ha-Biur La-Torah shel Mosheh Mendelssohn Ve-Si'ato* (1940), Index; S.J. Fuenn, *Keneset Yisrael* (1887–90), 433f.; F. Lachower, *Toledot Ha-Safrut Ha-Ivrit Ha-Ḥadashah*,

Vol. I (1963), 79f., 146; and W. Zeitlin, *Bibliotheca Hebraica Post-Mendelssohniana* (1891–95), 215.

Herz Homberg's published works include *Ben Yakir: Über Glaubenswahrheiten und Sittenlehren für die israelitische Jugend in Fragen und Antworten eingerichtet*, 2nd ed. (1826); *Bnei-Zion: Ein religiös-moralisches Lehrbuch für die Jugend israelitischer Nation* (1815); and *Rede bei Eröffnung der religiös-moralischen Vorlesungen für Israeliten in Prag* (1818); and *Imrei Shefer*, 2nd ed. (1816).

On Homberg, see P. Sandler, *Ha-Biur La-Torah* . . . (1940), Index; J. Klausner, *Historyah Shel Ha-Safrut* . . . , 2nd ed., Vol. I (1952), 211–23; R. Mahler, *Divrei Yemei Yisrael, Dorot Aharonim*, Vol. I, Book 2 (1954), Index; idem, *Ha-Hasidut Veha-Haskalah* (1961), Index; R. Kestenberg-Gladstein, *Die neuere Geschichte der Juden in Böhmen*, Vol. I (1969), Index; A.F. Pribram, *Urkunden und Akten zur Geschichte der Juden in Wien*, Vol. II (1918), Index; B. Wachstein, *Die Inschriften des alten Judenfriedhofes in Wien*, Vol. II (1917), Index; M. Grünwald, *Vienna* (1936), Index; M. Eliav, *Ha-Hinnuch Ha-Yehudi Be-Germania* (1960), Index; Roubik, in *Jahrbuch der Gesellschaft für Geschichte der Juden in Čechoslovakishen Republik*, V (1933), 319–37; and Singer, in *Jahrbuch . . . Čechoslovakischen Republik*, VII (1935), 209–28.

David Friedländer's published works include: *Gebete der Juden auf das ganze Jahr* (in Hebrew characters, with notes; 1786); ed. and trans., *Sefer Ha-Nefesh Leha-Hacham Rabbi Mosheh Mi-Dessau [Mendelssohn's Book of the Soul]*, 2nd ed. (1789); *Aktenstücke die Reform der judischen Kolonien in den Preussischen Staaten betreffend* (1793); *Sendschreiben an Seine Hochwürden, Herrn Oberconsistorialrath und Probst Teller zu Berlin von einigen Hausvätern jüdischer Religion*, 3rd ed. (1799); *Über die Verbesserung der Israeliten im Königreich Pohlen: Ein von der Regierung daselbst im Jahr 1816 abgefördertes Gutachten* (1819); "Briefe über die Moral des Handels, geschrieben im Jahr 1785," *Jedidja*, I, 1 (1817), 178–213; *Beitrag zur Geschichte der Verfolgung der Juden im 19. Jahrhundert durch Schriftsteller* (1820); *Für Liebhaber morgenländischer Dichtkunst* (1821); "Briefe über das Lesen der heiligen Schriften nebst einer Übersetzung des sechsten und siebenten Capitels des Mica, als Beilage," *Zeitschrift für die Wissenschaft des Judentums*, I (1822–23), 68–94; and *An die Verehrer, Freunde und Schüler Jerusalems, Spaldings, Tellers, Herders und Löfflers* (1823).

On Friedländer, see H.D. Hermes, *Über das Sendschreiben einiger Hausväter jüdischer Religion an den Herrn Oberconsistorialrath Teller und die von demselben darauf erthielte Antwort* (1799); V. Eichstädt, *Bibliographie zur Judenfrage* (1938); M.A. Meyer, *The Origins of the Modern Jew* (1967); M. Eliav, *Ha-Hinnuch Ha-Yehudi*

Be-Germania (1960); *Gesamtregister zur MGWJ, 1851–1939* (1966); H. Fischer, *Judentum, Staat und Heer in Preussen* (1968); Ludwig Geiger, in *Allgemeine Zeitung des Judentums*, LXXVII (1913), 474ff.; idem, "David Friedländer," *Allgemeine Deutsche Biographie*, VII, 393–97; J. Jacobson, "Aus David Friedländers Mussestunden," *Zeitschrift für die Geschichte der Juden in Deutschland*, VI (1935), 134–40; J. Meisl, "Letters of David Friedländer" [Yiddish], *Historishe Shriftn*, II (1937), 390–412; M. Stern, "Gutachen und Briefe David Friedländers," *Zeitschrift für die Geschichte der Juden in Deutschland*, VI (1935), 113–30; E. Täubler, "Zur Geschichte des Projekts einer Reform des Judenwesens unter Friedrich Wilhelm II," *Mitteilungen des Gesamtarchivs der deutschen Juden*, I (1909), 23–29; I. Elbogen, "David Friedländers Übersetzung des Gebetbuchs," *Zeitschrift für die Geschichte der Juden in Deutschland*, VI (1935), 130–33; E. Fränkel, "David Friedländer und seine Zeit," *Zeitschrift fur die Geschichte der Juden in Deutschland*, VI (1935), 65–77; I. Freund, "David Friedländer und die politische Emanzipation der Juden in Preussen," *Zeitschrift für die Geschichte der Juden in Deutschland*, VI (1935), 77–92; E. Littmann, "David Friedländers Senschreiben an Probst Teller und sein Echo," *Zeitschrift für die Geschichte der Juden in Deutschland*, VI (1935), 92–112; B. Rippner, "David Friedländer un Probst Teller," in *Jubelschrift zum siebzigsten Geburtstage des Prof. Dr. H. Graetz* (1887), 162–71; and R.O. Spazier, "David Friedländer," in *Gallerie der ausgezeichnetsten Israeliten aller Jahrhunderte, ihre Portraits und Biographien* (1834), 101–07.

On Henriette Herz, see H. Landsberg (ed.), *Henriette Herz: ihr Leben und ihre Zeit* (1913); J. Fürst, *Henriette Herz: Ihr Leben und ihre Erinnerungen*, 2nd ed. (1858); A. Kohut, *Des Ewig-Weibliche in der Welt-Kultur- und Literaturgeschichte* (1898), 7–14; L. Geiger (ed.), *Briefwechsel des jungen Börne und der Henriette Herz* (1905); H. Herz, *Schleiermacher und seine Lieben: Nach Originalbriefen der Henriette Herz* (1910); Reinicke, in *Der Monat*, XIII, No. 4 (1961), 46–54; M. Hargrave, *Some German Women and their Salons* (1912); B. Meyer, *Salon Sketches: Biographical Studies of Berlin Salons of the Emancipation* (1938).

There are a number of collections of letters of Dorothea Schlegel, Mendelssohn's daughter: *Briefe von Dorothea Schlegel an Friedrich Schleiermacher*, Vol. VII, N.S., of *Mitteilungen aus dem Literaturarchiv in Berlin* (1913); *Briefe von Dorothea und Friedrich Schlegel an die Familie Paulus*, ed. Rudolf Unger (1913); *Briefe von und an Friedrich und Dorothea Schlegel*, ed. Joseph Körner (1926); *Der Briefwechsel Friedrich und Dorothea Schlegels 1818–1820*, ed. Heinrich Finke (1923); and *Dorothea v. Schlegel geb. Mendelssohn und deren Söhne Johannes und Philipp Veit: Briefwechsel*, ed. J.M. Raich, 2 vols. (1881).

On Dorothea Schlegel, see F. Deibel, *Dorothea Schlegel als Schriftstellerin im Zusammenhang mit der romantischen Schule* (1905); M. Hiemenz, *Dorothea von Schlegel* (1911); L. Geiger, "Dorothea Veit-Schlegel," *Deutsche Rundschau*, CLX (1914), 119–34; M. Kayserling, *Die jüdischen Frauen in der Geschichte, Literatur und Kunst* (1879); J. Körner, "Mendelssohns Töchter," *Preussische Jahrbücher*, CCXIV (1928), 167–82; E. Mayer-Montfort, "Dorothea Schlegel im Ideenkreis ihrer Zeit und in ihrer religiösen, philosophischen und ethischen Entwicklung," *Gelbe Hefte: Historische und politische Zeitschrift für das katholische Deutschland*, II, 1 (1925–26), 414–33, 489–517; B. Meyer, *Salon Sketches: Biographical Studies of Berlin Salons of the Emancipation* (1938), 21–47; F. Muncker, "Dorothea Friederike Schlegel," *Allgemeine Deutsche Biographie*, XXXI, 372–76; S. Stern, "Der Frauentypus der Romantik," *Der Morgen*, I (1925), 496–516; and M. Susman, *Frauen der Romantik*, 3rd ed. (1960), 40–76.

CHAPTER FIVE

SOLOMON MAIMON, ISAAC EUCHEL, AND AARON WOLFSOHN-HALLE

The literature on Jean Jacques Rousseau is vast and will be found in any standard bibliography. On the great French enlightener's influence on Jewish life and thought, see especially P.M. Masson, *La Religion de Rousseau* (1916), and L. Poliakov, *Histoire de l'antisémitisme*, Vol. III (1968), 118–26.

The correspondence between Rahel Levin and August Varnhagen von Ense was published in *Briefwechsel zwischen Varnhagen und Rahel*, ed. Ludmilla Assing, 6 vols, (1874–75).

On Rahel, see *Rahel: Ein Buch des Andenkens für ihre Freunde*, 3 vols. (1834); H. Arendt, *Rahel Varnhagen: The Life of a Jewess* (1957; German ed., 1959); B. Badt-Strauss, *Rahel und ihre Zeit* (1912); F. Behrend, "Rahel Varnhagen an Schleiermacher," *Zeitschrift für Bücherfreunde*, N.S., IX, I (1917–18), 87–90; O. Berdrow, *Rahel Varnhagen: Ein Lebens- und Zeitbild* (1900); E. Graf, *Rahel Varnhagen und die Romantik* (1903); E. Key, *Rahel Varnhagen* (1913); S. Liptzin, *Germany's Stepchildren* (1944); M.A. Meyer, *The Origins of the Modern Jew* (1967), Index; and J.E. Spenlé, *Rahel* (French, 1910).

Solomon Maimon's *Gesammelte Werke*, edited by Valeris

Verra, have recently been published in six volumes (1965–71). A new edition of his Hebrew work *Givat Ha-Moreh*, edited by S. H. Bergmann and N. Rotenstreich, was published in 1966.

Maimon's *Autobiography (Lebensgeschichte)* was translated from the German by J.C. Murray and published in 1888; the work was reprinted in 1954 with an essay on Maimon's philosophy by S.H. Bergmann. Another translation into English of the *Autobiography* was published by Moses Hadas in 1947. N.J. Jacobs provided a valuable bibliography of writings on Solomon Maimon in *Kiryat Sefer*, XLI (1965–66), 245–62.

An extensive literature has been produced on Maimon's writings. Among the most important works are: S. Atlas, *From Critical to Speculative Idealism* (1964); idem, "Solomon Maimon's Treatment of the Problem of Antinomies and Its Relation to Maimonides," *Hebrew Union College Annual*, XXI (1948), 105–53; idem, "Maimon and Maimonides," in *Hebrew Union College Annual*, XXIII, Part One (1950–51), 517–47; idem, "Solomon Maimon's Conception of the Copernican Revolution in Philosophy," in *Harry A. Wolfson Jubilee Volume* (1965); idem., in *Journal of the History of Ideas*, XIII (1952), 168–87; S.H. Bergman, *The Philosophy of Solomon Maimon* (1967); I. Boeck, *Die ethischen Anschauungen von S. Maimon in ihren Verhältniss zu Kants Morallehre* (1897); S. Daiches, "Solomon Maimon and His Relation to Judaism," in *Aspects of Judaism* (1928); L. Gottselig, *Die Logik Salomon Maimons* (1908); M. Gueroult, *La philosophie transcendentale de Salomon Maimon* (1929); F. Kuntze, *Die Philosophie Salomon Maimons* (1912); F. Lachower, *Al Gevul Ha-Yashan Veha-Ḥadash* (1951); C. Rosenbaum, *Die Philosophie Solomon Maimons in seinem hebräischen Kommentar gibath-hammoreh zum moreh-nebuchim des Maimonides* (1928); N. Rotenstreich, *Sugyot Be-Filosofiyah* (1962); and A. Zubersky, *Solomon Maimon und der kritische Idealismus* (1925).

Isaac Euchel's *Reb Chenech, Oder Vos Tut Men Damit* was published in *Arkhiv Far Der Geshikhte Fun Yidishen Teater Un Drame*, I (1930), 94–146.

On Euchel, see M. Erik, *Di Komedies Fun Der Berliner Oyfklerung* (1933), 42–61; J.L. Landau, *Short Lectures on Modern Hebrew Literature*, 2nd ed. (1938), Index; J. Klausner, *Historyah Shel Ha-Safrut Ha-Ivrit Ha-Hadashah*, 2nd ed., Vol. I (1952), 131–43; and N. Slouschz, *The Renascence of Hebrew Literature* (1909), 41.

On Aaron Wolfsohn-Halle, see above, bibliographical notes for Chapter Four.

CHAPTER SIX

MOSES MARCUSE; DOV BER OF BOLECHOW

Only three copies of Moses Marcuse's *Sefer Refuot* (1790) have survived. Substantial extracts from it were published by N. Prylucki in his *Zamlbikher Far Yidisher Folklor*, Vol. II (1917), 1–55.

On Marcuse, see Zalman Rejzen, *Leksikon Fun Der Yidisher Literatur*, Vol. II (1927), 345–47; idem, *Fun Mendelssohn biz Mendele* (1923), 83–104; and *Leksikon Fun Der Nayer Yidisher Literatur*, Vol. V (1963), 519ff.

The memoirs of Aaron Isaac (Isak) in Yiddish, completed in 1804 with an introduction in Hebrew, were published under the title *Sjelfbiografi* in Stockholm in 1897. A new Yiddish edition, edited by N. Shtif and Z. Rejzen, *Aaron Isaacs Autobiografia*, appeared in 1922. A German version, edited by Z. Holm, *Denkwürdigkeiten des Aaron Isak*, appeared in 1930, and an annotated critical version in Swedish, edited by A. Brody and H. Valentin, *Aaron Issacs Minnen*, was published in 1932.

On Isaac, see H. Valentin, *Judarnas historia i Sverige* (1924), Index, and idem, *Judarna i Sverige* (1964), Index.

The chief literary work of Dov Ber Birkenthal of Bolechow, *Imrei Binah*, a study of false-Messiah movements in Judaism and an account of the celebrated debate between the rabbis and the Frankists at Lemberg in 1759, was discovered in 1910 and published by A.J. Brawer in *Ha-Shiloah*, XXXIII and XXXVIII. A manuscript of his memoirs was found in Jews' College, London, in 1912 and published by M. Wischnitzer, with an introduction, in 1922. The memoirs were published in Yiddish translation, under the title *Ber Bolekhover's Zikhroynes*, and in English, under the title *The Memoirs of Ber of Bolechow* in the same year.

On Dov Ber, see M. Wischnitzer, in *JQR*, XII (1921–22), 1–24, and M. Balaban, in *Festschrift . . . S. Poznanski* (1927), 25ff.

CHAPTER SEVEN

ROMANELLI, PAPPENHEIM, BEN-ZE'EV, SATANOW, AND BERLIN

Samuel Aaron Romanellis' *Massa Ba-Arav*, originally published in Berlin in 1792, was reprinted, with an introduction, by H. Schirmann in Romanelli: *Ketavim Nivharim* (1958). It was translated into English by S. Schiller-Szinessy under the title *Romanelli's Travels in Morocco* (1887).

In his late twenties Romanelli lived for a time in London, where he wrote a Hebrew translation of Alexander Pope's *Essay on Man* under the title *Massah Al Ha-Adam* and an elegy on the death of Moses Mendelssohn (1786).

In 1807 Romanelli published *Zimrat Aritzim, Raccolta di inni ed odi*, Italian translations of poems and prayers composed by members of the Napoleonic "Sanhedrin" in honor of the French emperor. In 1808 he published in Turin *Maḥazeh Shaddai . . . Illusione felice ossia visione sentimentale*, a metaphysical poem with an Italian translation.

Romanelli's Hebrew translation of the drama *Temistocle* by the Italian playwright Metastasio under the title *Talmon* is still in manuscript.

On Romanelli, see his *Ketavim Nivḥarim*, edited by H. Schirmann (1968), 7–12 (includes bibliography); A.B. Rhine, in *JQR*, II (1911), 49–52; S. Schiller-Szinessy, *Romanelli's Travels in Morocco* (1887), introduction; and R. Fahn, in *Mizraḥ U-Ma'arav*, V (1932), 345–6.

On Solomon Pappenheim, see F. Delitzsch, *Zur Geschichte der jüdsichen Poesie* (1836), 110; J. Klausner, *Historyah Shel Ha-Safrut Ha-Ivrit Ha-Ḥadashah*, 2nd ed., Vol. I (1952), 254–60; F. Lachower, *Toledot Ha-Safrut Ha-Ivrit Ha-Ḥadashah*, Vol. I (1963 ed.), 96–99; H.G. Shapira, *Toledot Ha-Safrut Ha-Ivrit Ha-Ḥadashah* (1939), 346–54; H.A. Wolfson, in *Jewish Studies in Memory of Israel Abrahams* (1927), 427–40; and W. Zeitlin, *Bibliotheca Hebraica Post-Mendelssohniana* (1891–95), Index.

Jehudah Leib Ben-Ze'ev's logical grammar, *Talmud Leshon Ivri* (1796) was utilized as the chief source for the study of Hebrew in Eastern Europe for more than a century. It was reprinted a considerable number of times and exercised a good deal of influence on later grammarians. His major achievement is *Otzar Ha-Shorashim* (1807–08), a Hebrew-German and German-Hebrew dictionary inspired by the linguistic studies of Rabbi David Kimḥi. Ben-Ze'ev's *Melitzah Le-Furim*, an anthology of ironic prayers for Purim (1800), also contains numerous parodies on familiar Jewish texts and poems, chiefly in the genre of the fable. His work on the principles of Judaism, *Yesodei Ha-Torah*, was published in Vienna in 1811.

On Ben-Ze'ev, see R. Fahn, *Tekufat Ha-Haskalah Be-Vinah* (1919), 38–46; G. Bader, *Medinah Va-Ḥachameha* (1934), 44–46; and J. Klausner, *Historyah Shel Ha-Safrut . . .* , 2nd ed., Vol. I (1952), 178–90.

On Isaac Satanow, see J. Klausner, *Historyah Shel Ha-Safrut...*, 2nd ed., Vol. I (1952), 165–77; G. Kressel, *Leksikon Ha-Safrut Ha-Ivrit Ba-Dorot Ha-Aharonim*, Vol. II (1967), 490–3; and Werses, in *Tarbiz*, XXXII (1963), 370–92.

On Saul Berlin, see C. Roth, *The Great Synagogue of London 1690–1940* (1950), 108–24, 180–201; Samet, in *Kiryat Sefer*, XLIII (1967–68), 429–41; and M. Wunder, in *Kiryat Sefer*, XLIV (1968–69), 307–8.

CHAPTER EIGHT

WESSELY'S *SHIREI TIFERET*; MASKILIM IN LITHUANIA AND POLAND

On Naftali Herz Wessely, see above, bibliographical notes under Chapter Three.

One of David Franco-Mendes' most important contributions is "Ahavat David," an article outlining a project for an encyclopedia in Hebrew, published in *Ha-Meassef* (1785). A number of his biographies of renowned Sephardic Jews were published in the same journal (1785ff.) and, long after his death, in *Ha-Maggid* (1860–66). His *Sefer Tikkunim* is a critical work on some of Maimonides' writings.

On Franco-Mendes, see J. Melkman, *David Franco-Mendes* (1951; includes bibliography); H. Schirmann, in *Behinot*, VI (1954), 44–52; M. Gorali, in *Tatzlil*, VI (1966), 32–46; and J. Klausner, *Historyah Shel Ha-Safrut Ha-Ivrit Ha-Hadashah*, 2nd ed., Vol. I (1952), 200–03.

Parts of a newly discovered book of Hebrew poems by Joseph Tropplowitz (Ha-Ephrati), were published by A.Z. Ben-Yishai, in *Behinot*, XI (Fall, 1957), 59–71. His popular Hebrew drama *Meluchat Sha'ul* was published in a new edition, with an introduction, by G. Shaked (1968).

On Tropplowitz, see J. Klausner, *Historyah Shel Ha-Safrut...*, 2nd ed., Vol. I (1952), 193–99; J.L. Landau, *Short Lectures on Modern Hebrew Literature*, 2nd ed. (1938), 86–95; A. Yaari, in *Kiryat Sefer*, XII (1935–36), 384–88; and G. Kressel, *Leksikon Ha-Safrut Ha-Ivrit Ba-Dorot Ha-Aharonim*, Vol. II (1967), 32–33.

On Jehudah Loeb Margolioth, see G. Kressel, *Leksikon ...*, Vol. II (1967), 419; J. Klausner, *Historyah Shel Ha-Safrut ...*, 2nd ed., Vol. I (1952), 85–86; B. Dinur, *Be-Mifneh Ha-Dorot* (1955), 264–65; and R. Mahler, *Divrei Yemei Yisrael: Dorot Aharonim*, Part One, Vol. IV (1956), 40–44.

Jehudah Leib Nevakhovich's *Vopl' dscheri yudeyskoy*, first published in St. Petersburg in 1803, was reprinted in *Budushchnost*, Vol. III (1902). The Hebrew version of the pamphlet, with some changes and additions, was published under the title *Kol Shavat Bat Yehudah* in Shklov in 1804 (reprinted in *He-Avar*, II, 1918).

On Nevakhovich, see B. Katz, in *Ha-Zeman*, III (1904), 11–15; idem, in *He-Avar*, II (1918), 197–201; J. Klausner, *Historyah Shel Ha-Safrut* . . . , 2nd ed., Vol. III (1953), 20–24; and J. Hessen (Gessen), *Yevrei v Rossii* (1906), 78–98, 136–39.

Glossary of Hebrew and Other Terms

Glossary of Hebrew
and Other Terms

Aggadah (or Haggadah): The non-legal part of the post-Biblical Oral Torah, consisting of narratives, legends, parables, allegories, poems, prayers, theological and philosophical reflections, etc. Much of the Talmud is aggadic, and the Midrash (see below) literature, developed over a period of more than a millennium, consists almost entirely of Aggadah. The term *aggadah*, in a singular and restricted sense, refers to a Talmudic story or legend.

Baal Shem (in Hebrew, "master of the Name"): A title given to persons believed capable of working miracles through employing the divine Name. The title was not uncommon in Eastern Europe in the seventeenth and eighteenth centuries, where it frequently implied a quack or impostor who produced magical amulets, pronounced incantations, etc.

Bar Mitzvah: The Hebrew words mean "one obliged to fulfill the commandment," but the term is generally employed to denote the ceremony marking the induction of a boy, when he has reached the age of thirteen, into the Jewish community and into adult observance of the commandments of the Torah.

Bet Ha-Midrash: In the Talmudic age, a school for higher rabbinic learning where students assembled for study and discussion, as well as prayer. In the post-Talmudic age most synagogues had a Bet Ha-Midrash or were themselves called by the term, insofar as they were places of study.

Derush: Homiletical interpretation of Scripture.

Gabbai: Originally, in Talmudic times, the term meant a "collector or tax-gatherer." The *gabbai tzedakah* was the charity collector or overseer of the poor. The use of the term was later extended to designate the treasurer of the synagogue or other community institutions and sometimes its general officers, even those without financial functions.

Gemara: The second basic strand of the *Talmud* (see below), consisting of a commentary on, and supplement to, the Mishnah (see Mishnah).

Haskalah: The movement for disseminating modern European culture among Jews from about 1750 to 1880. It advocated the modernization of Judaism, the westernization of traditional Jewish education, and the revival of the Hebrew language.

Haskamah (Plural, Haskamot): Approbations or authorizations by respected rabbinic authorities, sometimes inserted in Hebrew books. The practice of inserting *haskamot* became particularly widespread after the synod of rabbis in Ferrara in 1554 decided that Hebrew books should obtain prior approval by Jewish authorities in order to prevent suppression or censorship by the officials of the Church. Later a *haskamah* was frequently solicited by the author of a book as testimony of his work's scholarly value and its orthodoxy.

Ḥeder: The Hebrew term means "room" and refers to a school for teaching children the fundamentals of Judaism. The ḥeder figured prominently in traditional Jewish education in Eastern Europe.

Ḥochmat Yisrael: The Hebrew term means "wisdom of Israel" and was used by those scholars who wrote their contributions to the Science of Judaism (or *die Wissenschaft des Judentums*) in Hebrew. The term is generally identical with the Science of Judaism.

Kabbalah: The mystical religious movement in Judaism and/or its literature. The term Kabbalah, which means "tradition," came to be used by the mystics beginning in the twelfth century to signify the alleged continuity of their doctrine from ancient times.

Kapparah (plural, Kapparot): A custom, not mentioned before Geonic times, consisting in having a fowl killed on the morning preceding the Day of Atonement as a kind of vicarious redemption for an individual's sins. It was opposed by many eminent rabbinic authorities because of its superstitious character.

Maḥzor (In Hebrew, "cycle"): A term commonly used to designate the Festival Prayer Book. At first the Maḥzor contained prayers for the whole year, including the daily and Sabbath services, but most Ashkenazic Maḥzorim now contain only the festival prayers.

Maskil (plural, Maskilim): An adherent of Haskalah (see above).

Meassefim: The contributors to the Hebrew journal *Ha-Meassef*, the major organ in Hebrew published by the proponents of Haskalah (see above) in Germany in the last decades of the eighteenth century and the first of the nineteenth.

Midrash (plural, Midrashim): The discovery of new meanings besides literal ones in the Bible. The term is also used to designate collections of such Scriptural exposition. The best-known of the Midrashim are the *Midrash Rabbah*, *Tanḥuma*, *Pesikta De-Rav Kahana*, *Pesikta Rabbati*, and *Yalkut Shimeoni*. In a singular and restricted sense, *Midrash* refers to an item of rabbinic exegesis.

Mishnah: The legal codification containing the core of the post-Biblical Oral Torah, compiled and edited by Rabbi Judah Ha-Nasi at the beginning of the third century C.E.

Mitzvah (plural, Mitzvot): A Hebrew term meaning "commandment," and referring to any precept of the Torah, positive or negative. According to the Talmud, there are 613 mitzvot in the Pentateuch, apart from other commandments ordained by the rabbis.

Parnass (from the Hebrew term *parnes,* meaning "to foster" or "to support"): A term used to designate the chief synagogue functionary. The *parnass* at first exercised both religious and administrative authority, but since the sixteenth century religious leadership has been the province of the rabbis. The office of *parnass* has generally been an elective one.

Peshat: One of the major types of biblical exegesis developed in the Talmudic age. Peshat is an attempt to grasp the literal meaning of the scriptural text.

Pilpul: In Talmudic and rabbinic literature, a clarification of a difficult point. Later the term came to denote a sharp dialectical distinction or, more generally, a certain type of Talmudic study emphasizing dialectical distinctions.

Remez: The Hebrew term means "veiled allusion" and refers to a type of biblical exegesis developed in the rabbinic age which attempted to grasp the hidden allusions in the scriptural text.

Sidra [h] (plural, Sidrot): A Hebrew word meaning "order" or "arrangement," and signifying a section of the Pentateuch prescribed for reading in the synagogue on a particular Sabbath.

Sod: The term means secret or mystery, and is used to designate that type of biblical exegesis, developed in the rabbinic age, which sought to grasp the esoteric or mystical significance of the scriptural text.

Talmud: The title applied to the two great compilations, distinguished as the Babylonian Talmud and the Palestinian Talmud, in which the records of academic discussion and of judicial administration of post-Biblical Jewish law are assembled. Both Talmuds also contain Aggadah (see above), or non-legal material.

Torah: In its narrowest meaning, the Pentateuch. Torah is also known in Judaism as the Written Law. In its broader meaning, Torah comprises as well the Oral Law, the traditional exposition of the Pentateuch and its commandments developed in the late Biblical and post-Biblical ages. In its widest meaning Torah signifies every exposition of both the Written and the Oral Law, including all of Talmudic literature and its commentaries. The term is sometimes used also to designate the scroll of the Pentateuch read in the synagogue service.

Wissenschaft des Judentums, die (German for "the science of Judaism): The modern type of scientific and critical exploration of Jewish history, literature, and religion, initially developed in Germany in the first half of the nineteenth century.

Yayin Nesech: The term literally means "wine of libation" and refers to the wine offered by heathens as libations to their idols. Later, the term came to refer to any wine touched by heathen hands and, hence, forbidden to Jews.

Yeshivah (plural, Yeshivot): A traditional Jewish school devoted primarily to the study of the Talmud (see above) and rabbinic literature.

Zohar: The chief work of the Spanish Kabbalah (see above) traditionally ascribed to the *Tanna* Simeon ben Yohai (second century) but probably written by the Spanish Kabbalist Moses de Leon at the end of the thirteenth century.

Index

Index

Index